THE CHRISTIAN WAY

THE
CHRISTIAN WAY

A STUDY OF NEW TESTAMENT ETHICS
IN RELATION TO PRESENT PROBLEMS

by

SYDNEY CAVE
D.D.
PRINCIPAL, NEW COLLEGE, LONDON

PHILOSOPHICAL LIBRARY, INC.
New York

Published in the United States by

PHILOSOPHICAL LIBRARY, INC.

15 East 40th Street, New York, N. Y.

PREFACE

THE days have gone when it could be assumed that, although the doctrines of Christianity might occasion difficulty, its ethical teaching was simple and necessary, and could be so formulated as readily to gain the acceptance of those who professed the Christian faith and the admiration of those who rejected it. Outside the Roman Church, there is now no consensus of opinion in regard either to the method or the content of Christian Ethics. New Testament scholars differ much in their descriptions of the Teaching of Jesus, and Christians, whether scholars or not, are divided, and sometimes even passionately divided, in regard to the application of that teaching to the social and political problems of our age. If a Christian teacher be a lover of peace, he is tempted to write only of Christian doctrines and leave undiscussed the ethical implicates of Christianity. In that way he can avoid giving offence to some whose judgment he prizes, and also save himself the embarrassment of discussing problems in regard to which he has no expert knowledge. But if, like the writer of this book, he is responsible for the preparation of men for the ministry, he may not, through academic scruples or dislike of controversy, refuse to discuss those moral problems which will confront them in their work.

For many years the writer has conducted a Seminar on Christian Ethics with his senior students. In no part of his teaching has he been so conscious of the limitations of his knowledge and the inadequacy of his conclusions. Yet his students have spoken with a gratitude which surprised him of what they had gained from this course. Till recently we used as the basis for discussion Professor Brunner's massive and suggestive book, *The Divine Imperative*. Our students have gained much from its wise judgments and sober realism but they have complained that it does not deal explicitly with the question to which they most desired an answer : What is the significance of the Teaching of Jesus, and how is it to be related to our modern situation ? This book is an attempt to give some answer to this question.

The writer has sought to learn from those who are expert, as he is not, in social and political science, but, much as he has learnt from books, he has learnt more from personal contacts. It was his privilege to be the pupil of Dr. P. T. Forsyth who helped him to find in the Cross the centre of his thinking. His student days were followed by eight years in India, where for three of these years as Principal of a College he had day by day to speak on the Gospels to a great class of students two-thirds of whom were Hindus. He thus learnt to explore the Teaching of Jesus from the standpoint of Eastern as of Western needs, whilst in other years, in administrative work in a great mass movement area, he met, and had to try to solve, problems of missionary casuistry much like those with which St. Paul had to deal. In his thirteen years later at Cambridge, as a member of Professor Burkitt's Seminar, he had the opportunity of studying the Gospels anew in the company of distinguished scholars. He has also gained much from those who, as he went about among the Churches, have shared with him their perplexities both in regard to their business responsibilities and to their guidance of sons and daughters who were facing the difficulties of modern marriage with assumptions very different from those of their parents. In these discussions many a layman has expressed his regret that he did not know where to turn for guidance.

The writer is very grateful to all who have helped him by sharing with him their problems. He would like to feel that what he has written may be of use not only to theological students by providing material for lectures or seminars, and to those in the Christian ministry who cannot, if they would, evade the perplexing issues of our time, but also to others who, in business or the professions, are seeking to express their Christian faith in Christian practice.

It has not been easy for the writer to decide on the selection and arrangement of his material. As there is no general agreement among Protestant scholars in regard to the proper approach to Christian Ethics, it may be well to indicate the method and order of this book.

The Introduction deals with the Modern Dilemma, the erosion of ancient sanctions by " the acids of modernity ", and the inadequacy of that Mutilated Message, which, ignoring the stern social teaching of the Old Testament and the teaching of the Epistles, has identified the Christian message with an interpretation of the Teaching of Jesus which, by separating it from His life and death, makes it seem not a Gospel but merely good advice.

Part I deals with the Ethics of the New Testament. It speaks first of that Mission of Jesus through which alone His teaching can be understood. The attempt is then made to explore the meaning of those words of His which perplex us modern men, unused as we are to Eastern modes of speech. There follows a summary of some New Testament Interpretations in which special emphasis is laid on the significance of St. Paul's attempt to relate the Christian faith to the moral problems of converts living in a pagan world.

The Second Part deals with Method and Motives. The first of its two sections on the Method and Scope of Christian Ethics has inevitably to be somewhat technical, and to those who are not students of theology may seem of little interest. The second section, Motives and Sanctions, deals with the characteristic Evangelical affirmations on Law and Grace, and Faith and Works, and also with Evangelical Asceticism and The Relevance of the Eternal.

The Third Part speaks of Life in Community. In the chapter on Marriage the writer has thought it best to speak on the problems of modern marriage with entire frankness, and as one who recognizes that much teaching which claims to be Christian has been perverted by a false asceticism. In the chapter dealing with The Community of Industry, the Indictment of the Churches is examined, and an attempt is made to explore the social implicates of Christianity. In the chapter dealing with The Community of the State, after an exposition of the relevant teaching of the New Testament, a brief summary is given of those theories on Church and State which still influence and divide modern Christians. A discussion on The Justice of the State leads to a statement of the Four Freedoms, the last of which, Freedom from fear of war, necessitates a discussion of the gravest problem of Christian Ethics—the Christian attitude to war. The writer is well aware that these chapters on Industry and the State will seem to some disappointing because inconclusive. But it is New Testament Ethics that he is seeking to expound and, where the New Testament gives no direct guidance, he dare not claim the authority of Christ for the partial solutions of party programmes, or for his own, or others', private prejudices.

A brief Epilogue speaks of The Church's Task, for we are not called to live the Christian life in isolation. In spite of its failures and its divided witness, the Church is still used by Christ in His ministry to men, and it is as members of His Church that we may discover and reveal the relevance of New Testament Ethics to the problems of our age.

In the preparation of this book for the Press, the writer owes much to friends at New College, London. The Rev. J. B. Binns, M.A. read the typescript and has helped in the revision of the proofs ; the typescript was read also by Dr. G. F. Nuttall and the proofs by Dr. J. Trevor Davies. To all he is deeply grateful.

CONTENTS

INTRODUCTION

PART I

NEW TESTAMENT ETHICS

PART II

METHODS AND MOTIVES

PART III

LIFE IN COMMUNITY

EPILOGUE

INTRODUCTION

THE CHRISTIAN WAY

CHAPTER I

THE MODERN DILEMMA

(1) " AN AGE WITHOUT STANDARDS "

THE Christian Gospel is Good News of God, not news of man, and it has for its first concern not what men must do but what God has done. It speaks of the God who in Christ has drawn near to men in forgiving love, enabling them to enter into that communion with God which is eternal life. In this mission of the Son, God's revelation of Himself to men found full and personal expression. In Christ's words and deeds, in His Cross and Resurrection, there is disclosed the nature of God's character and rule, and so the secret of this mysterious universe. It is the task of Christian Theology to explore these great redemptive facts. Christian Ethics is derivative ; it asks, Since God has so acted, what ought we men to do ?

The very success of Christianity has made it hard for some to realize this dependence of Christian Ethics on the Christian facts. Christianity has been so potent an influence in our civilization that its moral values have come to be accepted as part of the natural heritage of Western man. Christian beliefs may be abandoned, but Christian sentiments remain. In our country a political leader would have had few followers had he echoed Hitler's words : " Providence has ordained that I should be the greatest liberator of humanity. I am freeing men from the restraints of an intelligence that has taken charge ; from the dirty and degrading self-mortifications of a chimaera called conscience and morality and from the demands of a freedom and personal independence which very few could bear ".[1] Everyone knew that in the past there had been monstrous cruelties, but these, it was thought, belonged to the past alone. Education and enlightenment had made impossible their repetition. Who could believe that our age would witness the deliberate repudiation of all morality, and the awful and cold-blooded cruelties of Belsen and of Buchenwald ?

No one who lived in London during the time of the great air-raids could fail to notice not only the courage of ordinary men and women but their faith that righteousness was a reality, and that forces so evil as those to which we were opposed would not be allowed in the end to triumph. Like Ernst Renan, many " lived by a faith they had abandoned ", and showed in the time of danger that they prized more than they had realized those conceptions of justice, duty and self-discipline which, in times of peace, they had regarded as outmoded survivals of the " Victorianism " it had become fashionable to deride. But a society cannot live for ever by a faith it has abandoned. A time comes when the capital of the past is used up, and an abandoned Christian faith ceases to provide the impulse to Christian character.

There are those who warn us that that time is near, and that the distinctive feature of our age is its rejection of Christian moral standards. In every age all have found it hard to do right, and some have thought it more pleasant to do wrong. And yet the distinction between right and wrong was not regarded merely as an expression of a personal preference. So long as men and women believed themselves to be responsible beings, called to choose, and accountable to God for their choices, life might be tragic, but it was not trivial. With George Eliot they might regard God as " inconceivable ", and Immortality as " unbelievable ", and yet hold that Duty was " peremptory and absolute ".[2] Less well known than her views is Nietzsche's shrewd comment on them," They have got rid of the Christian

---

[1] Erich Meissner, *Confusion of Faces*, p. 118.
[2] From her conversation with F. W. H. Myers in the Fellows' Garden of Trinity College, Cambridge.

God, and now think themselves obliged to cling firmer than
ever to Christian morality ; that is *English* consistency ". " In
England, for every little emancipation from divinity, people
have to re-acquire respectability by becoming moral fanatics
in an awe-inspiring manner. That is the *penalty* they have to
pay there. With us it is different. When we give up Christian
belief, we thereby deprive ourselves of the *right* to maintain a
stand on Christian morality. We have again and again to
make this point clear in defiance of English shallow-pates.
Christianity is a system, a view of things, consistently thought
out and *complete*. If we break out of it a fundamental idea,
the belief in God, we thereby break the whole into pieces ; we
have no longer anything determined in our grasp." It is
because in England this has not been realized that " Morality
is not as yet a problem for the English ".[1]

We have reason to be grateful that in our country more have
agreed with George Eliot than with Nietzsche. Yet for us
English, too, morality has now become a problem, for an age
without faith becomes, at last, an " Age without Standards ",
and, in the opinion of so competent an observer as Sir Richard
Livingstone, our age may already be so described.[2] Right and
wrong are, for many, words which have ceased to have any
intelligible content, and the sense of liberation from the restrictions of traditional morality has brought not the joy of freedom
but the *malaise* which comes from lives lived without aim or
meaning. We are all aware of the psychic injury suffered by
a child if he finds that the one he has trusted as his father is
not his father. That is the plight of many in the modern world.
They have lost their heavenly Father and feel not liberated
but merely insecure. Poor Heine's boast, " We are of age ; we
do not need a father's care ", no longer expresses the modern
mood. Many have lost the sense of a father's care but not

---

[1] *The Twilight of the Idols. The Works of Friedrich Nietzsche*,
Vol. III. E.T. by Thomas Common, pp. 167 f.

[2] " If we are looking for a catchword to describe our age, various
phrases would occur to the mind : we might call it the Age of Science,
or the Age of Social Revolution, or the Age without Standards. None
would be exhaustive, none quite just ; but the last would have some
claim to consideration ". *Education for a World Adrift*, p. 10.

their sense of need.   They have ceased to give glory to God, but can no longer echo Swinburne's words :

Glory to Man in the Highest! for Man is the master of things.[1]

It is " things ", not Man, which seem to be master.   The ever-increasing control of the resources of nature has been accompanied by an increasing " Devaluation of man ",[2] and secular optimism has given way to secular pessimism.

(2) THE DEVALUATION OF MAN

The factors in the modern devaluation of man are too well known to need more than a brief reference.   Biology and the New Psychology have seemed to bring man nearer to the brutes ; the substitution of machinery for tools has deprived man of the dignity of creative work, and two world wars have destroyed his sense of security and his confidence to mould his future. And this devaluation of man has been accompanied by a growing uncertainty about moral values.

Charles Darwin's *Origin of Species*, published in 1859, was written as a contribution to biology, and Darwin himself described his theory as " The Origin of Species by Means of Natural Selection or the Preservation of Favoured Races in the Struggle for Life ".   But his theory came to be described, in Herbert Spencer's phrase, as that of " The Survival of the Fittest ".   Biologically the " survival of the fittest " meant merely the survival of those that have survived, but by many the " fittest " were identified with the most successful.   Thus understood, the theory accorded well with the economic individualism of the mid-Victorian era, with its naïve superstition that the self-interest of the individual would somehow secure the good of all, and with that strange belief in inevitable progress which had already found fantastic expression in Herbert Spencer's *Social Statics*.   The ethical implicates of this conception were at first but little realized.   Thus T. H. Huxley rejected with scorn the suggestion that " when Christian dogmas

[1] *Hymn of Man.*
[2] The title of a suggestive book by Victor Monod, " *Devalorisation de l'homme* ".

vanish, virtue will vanish too, and the ancestral ape and tiger will have full play ". " The safety of morality lies . . . in a real and living belief in that fixed order of nature which sends social disintegration upon the track of immorality, as surely as it sends physical disease after physical trespasses ".[1] Seven years later that vigorous but muddled writer, in his famous Romanes Lecture on *Evolution and Ethics*, admitted that our ethics could not be based on the evolutionary process. " For his successful progress, throughout the savage state, man has been largely indebted to those qualities which he shares with the ape and the tiger ". " But in proportion as men have passed from anarchy to social organization, and in proportion as civilization has grown in worth, these deeply ingrained serviceable qualities have become defects ". " The practice of that which is ethically best—what we call goodness or virtue—involves a course of conduct which, in all respects, is opposed to that which leads to success in the cosmic struggle for existence ". " The ethical progress of society depends, not on imitating the cosmic progress, still less in running away from it, but in combating it ".[2] Some more recent biologists deny that successful survival has depended only on what Huxley called " ruthless self-assertion ". That view ignores the " mutual aid and mutual support " which as Prince Kropotkin showed, " is a feature of the greatest importance for the maintenance of life, the preservation of each species, and its further evolution ".[3]

The hypothesis that man's bodily constitution has an animal ancestry is the concern not of religion nor of ethics, but of biology. Darwin himself " had no intention of writing atheistically ".[4] T. H. Huxley, as we have seen, came to realize that the doctrine of " the Survival of the Fittest " does not provide sanctions for man's ethical ideals. It was in Germany that the " Ethics of Evolution " gained immense influence ; the doctrine of " the Survival of the Fittest " went only too well with

[1] " Science and Morals ", 1886. *Evolution and Ethics and Other Essays*, Eversley Edition, p. 145 f.

[2] *Op. cit.* pp. 51 f. ; 81 ff.

[3] F. W. Jones, *Design and Purpose*, p. 46.

[4] From a letter to the great American botanist, Asa Gray, quoted in J. Langdon Davies, *Man and His Universe*, p. 233.

Bismarck's doctrine of " blood and iron ", and with the Lutheran tradition of the world as the " devil's sphere ". This doctrine was used by militarist writers to justify their preparation for the First World War, and later by Hitler to support his teaching on " the right of the victory of the best and strongest in the world "—in other words, the domination of the world by Nazi Germany. This conception of " the Survival of the Fittest " has thus been used to degrade man to the level of " the ape and tiger ", and was a contributory cause of those world wars which have, for the time, destroyed the favourite dogma of the modern man—the belief in inevitable progress.

A second factor in the devaluation of man has been the dominance in the inter-war years of Freudian Psychology. The disillusionment which marked the end of the First World War had led to a revolt against anything which could be called " Victorian ", and the work of Freud, begun before the outbreak of the war, now came into great prominence. His discovery of the significance of the Unconscious was of the greatest importance for psychotherapy. But his popular influence was due less to his genius as a psychologist than to the fame of his " anthropology ", his interpretation of man as a creature dominated by sex. Some of the technical terms of his psychology became part of the working vocabulary of many who had read none of his books. Whereas Freud recognized that civilized life was impossible without inhibitions, some believed that all inhibitions were to be abandoned. Freud later spoke not only of the *libido* but of the death-instinct, and for him, as M. Maritain put it, " man is but the place of intersection and of conflict of a primarily sexual *libido* and a desire for death ".[1] For Freud, religion was an " illusion " due to the Oedipus complex. If a man believes in God, it is due to " the emotional strength " of his " memory-image of the overrated father of his childhood ", and to " the lasting nature of his need for protection ".[2] For Jung, the founder of the School of Analytical Psychology, God was " a function of the unconscious,

---

[1] *True Humanism*, p. 21.
[2] *New Introductory Lectures on Psycho-Analysis*, E.T. by W. J. H. Sprott, p. 209.

namely, the manifestation of a split-off sum of *libido* which has activated the God-*imago* ".[1]

Man then was free, free from belief in God, from bondage to morals and convention, but somehow this freedom brought neither confidence nor joy. Those for whom life seemed meaningless could not believe that for others it had dignity and meaning. The world had become " a place of fallen idols and vanished ideals ", and this, as Mr. Sampson has pointed out, accounts for the eagerness with which many turned to Mr. Lytton Strachey's *Eminent Victorians* which " exposed with careful malice the defects of idols and the fallibility of ideals ". " Seriousness in any form of art was outmoded; and so the shallow ideas and mocking tones of *Eminent Victorians* were taken as the utterance of an oracle ".[2]

The deterioration in the estimate of life's dignity and meaning was accentuated for the many by the mass slaughter of the First World War, the disillusionment of the troubled peace, and the mass unemployment due to causes over which the workers had no control. The machine, which should be man's servant, seemed to have become his master. It is not surprising, as Dr. Fromm points out, that Mickey Mouse became so popular a film. " There the one theme—in so many variations—is always this : something little is persecuted and endangered by something overwhelmingly strong, which threatens to kill or swallow the little thing. The little thing runs away and eventually succeeds in escaping or even harming its enemy. People would not be ready to look continually at the many variations of this one theme unless it touched upon something very close to their own emotional life. Apparently the little thing, threatened by a powerful, hostile enemy is the spectator himself; that is how he feels and that is the situation with which he can identify himself ".[3]

No age has more proudly asserted man's supremacy over nature, and yet the " humanism " which proclaimed man's self-sufficiency was accompanied by a sense of powerlessness and

---

[1] *Psychological Types*, E.T. by H. G. Baynes, p. 301.
[2] *The Concise Cambridge History of English Literature*, p. 1041 f.
[3] *The Fear of Freedom*, p. 114.

frustration.   Life for many ceased to have dignity because it
seemed devoid of meaning.   As Mr. Noel Coward put it, in his
Twentieth Century Blues,

> In this strange illusion
> Chaos or confusion,
> People seem to lose their way.
> Nothing left to strive for,
> Love or keep alive for.

In Germany there was a still greater collapse of faith, and
a more general abandonment of any view of God or the world
which could give life meaning.   When the Nazis came into
power, all was changed.   Instead of indifference and uncertainty, there was passionate devotion to the dictates of the
Führer.   For irreligion, there was a new religion—the religion
of blood and soil which for long menaced the security of the
world.   Those of our land who had thought they had " nothing
left to strive for ", discovered that there were values which they
prized more than life itself.   For the time uncertainty vanished
and many, in spite of the hardships and dangers of war, found
an inner peace which before they lacked.

Now that the stress of war has passed, is our age once more
to be an " Age without standards " ?   If so, the victory won
may prove illusive.   If morality be regarded as a mere convention, and God as the projection of men's hopes or fears,
then the way is open for the false religions which relieve the
maimed will of the many from the burden of decision, and the
nihilism, which robs the individual life of meaning and responsibility, may in our land, too, be followed by the totalitarianism
in which the individual is nothing ; the state or class is all.

Observers of our Western scene comment on the dangers
which come from lack of faith in life.   Thus Dr. Fromm writes,
Democracy " will triumph over the forces of nihilism only if
it can inspire people with a faith that is the strongest the human
mind is capable of, the faith in life and in truth and in freedom
as the active and spontaneous realization of the individual
self ".[1]   Professor Laski writes in a similar strain.   " Without

[1] *Op. cit.* p. 238.

a renovation of faith there can be no restoration of confidence in the values we seek to establish ". But how is that faith to be created if, as he says, " The faith we have to build is a faith in the values of this world, not in the values of another ", and if it be true, as he holds, that " the secularization of society is a final achievement in the evolution of mankind " ?[1]

Dr. Julian Huxley who, in his *Religion without Revelation*, sought to provide modern men with an *Ersatz* religion, a religion without God, would have us turn to psychology for our ethics. Unlike Dr. Waddington, who claims to find the nature of the good in " the revelation of the nature, the character and direction of the evolutionary process as a whole, and in the elucidation of the consequences in relation to that direction, of various courses of human action ",[2] Dr. Huxley admits that, although " we can discern direction ", " we cannot discover a purpose in evolution ". " Progress is a major factor of past evolution, but it is limited to a few selected stocks. It may continue in the future, but it is not inevitable ; man, by now become the trustee of evolution, must work and plan if he is to achieve further progress for himself and so for life ".[3] Modern psychology, he claims, can make up for the loss of " ethical absolutes ". " For a justification of our moral code, we need no longer have recourse to theological revelation or to a metaphysical Absolute. Freud in combination with Darwin suffice to give us our philosophic vision ".[4] It is not easy to believe that this *Ersatz* ethics, based on Freudian psychology, will be any more effective than was his *Ersatz* religion.

The recognition of the need of religion to meet the ethical needs of our time provides no proof of its reality. It is an indication of the vacuum which has to be filled. It is significant that Mr. H. G. Wells who, as a simple believer in the sufficiency of science, had earlier prepared blue-prints for Utopia, entitled his last book *Mind at the End of its Tether*. " *Homo sapiens*, as he has been pleased to call himself, is played out ". " The

---

[1] *Reflections on the Revolution of our Time*, pp. 176 f.
[2] *Science and Ethics*, p. 19, and cp. his *The Scientific Attitude*, p. 27.
[3] *Evolution the Modern Synthesis*, pp. 576 ff.
[4] *Man the Trustee of Ethical Progress*, Hibbert Journal, April 1943.

writer sees the world as a jaded world without recuperative power. In the past he has liked to think that Man could pull himself out of his entanglements and start a new creative phase of human living. In the face of our universal inadequacy that optimism has given place to a stoical cynicism . . . Ordinary man is at the end of his tether. Only a small, highly adaptable minority of the species can possibly survive ".[1]

Our Western world desperately requires what Christianity provides. The Christian Gospel meets our need for forgiveness, and enables us to enter into a life of communion with the God made known to us in Christ. In meeting this deepest need which many do not feel, it meets also needs which are more generally realized ; it delivers from frustration, saves from neuroses, and provides sanctions for individual and social ethics. But the Christian message is not to be commended because it meets these patent needs of modern men. Were it merely useful, it would soon cease to be of use. It demands attention not because it may be helpful but because it is true, and it speaks not of comfort only but of judgment. It may be accepted or rejected ; it ought not to be possible to think of it merely as a pretty fancy, well suited to young children, but not to those who face the tasks of adult life. Yet that is how many think of the Christian message, and, in consequence, it seems to them to be in clear contradiction to their own experience of the hard realities of life. For this grave misunderstanding of Christianity some modern preaching of it is in part responsible. The Christian message has been so conformed to secular optimism that it seems irrelevant to an age which has experienced too much of the power of evil to believe that evil can be eliminated by a few gracious words.

(3) A MUTILATED MESSAGE

At the close of the nineteenth and the beginning of the present century, no religious books had more popularity than those which praised the personality of Jesus and presented Him

---

[1] pp. 18 and 30. The book was published in 1945, the year of victory.

as the great Teacher, the supreme " Hero " of religion. The
critical study of the Bible had shown how varied were its
teachings, whilst many were repelled by what they regarded
as the needless complications of traditional theology. The
modern man, it was said, was tired of dogma ; all that he needed
was " the simple teaching of Jesus ". This concentration on
the Teaching of Jesus was, at the time, a necessary corrective
to the kind of churchmanship which seemed more concerned
with orthodoxy than with obedience, and which sometimes used
its sombre estimate of the sin of man as a pretext for evading
the demands of social justice. This new emphasis on the Words
of Jesus did much to Christianize the ideals of a democracy
which thought it had discovered the way to peace and social
justice. The stern teaching of the Old Testament could be
forgotten ; the theology of the Epistles ignored. All that was
needed was the teaching of Jesus on love to men based upon
His proclamation of the love of God. If love had been given
the depth of meaning which it has in the New Testament, that
simplification of the Gospel would have been less inadequate.
But by many the love of God was interpreted not by its perfect
manifestation in Christ's Cross, but from the analogy of human
love, and love to men was preached as if love would always
melt the hardest heart. Karl Heim tells us that after the First
World War the deepest cause of estrangement from Christianity
was this superficial belief in a kindly Father-God, and quotes
the bitter words of a German who had suffered much in a
Russian camp. " The dear, kind old God is dead. He fell in
the war like many others ". " The God of our good parson lies
in the snow with the typhus-corpses among the rats ". Heim
goes on to say that if the God of Christian faith had been such
a God, He would have fallen not first in the World War but
when Christians were burned as torches in Nero's gardens, and
Christian maidens handed over to the Pretorian guards for
outrage.[1] Instead, faith in a God of love survived, because
God's love was not conceived as that of an indulgent father,
careful only for his children's comfort, but as the God whose
love and holiness and power were made manifest in Christ's

[1] *Jesus der Herr*, pp. 211 f.

Cross and Resurrection and in the presence of His Spirit in the Church.

In our country, which had experienced the sorrow of bereavement but not the bitterness of defeat, this mutilation of the Christian message survived the shock of the First World War. The sternness of our Lord's teaching and the incidents of His rejection and crucifixion, were ignored, and some preachers so spoke of the invincibility of love as to suggest that they had never heard of Annas and of Caiaphas, or of Judas Iscariot who had lived with Jesus and yet betrayed Him.[1] The failure of the policy of appeasement, and the sufferings of the Second World War, are in clear contradiction to that version of the Teaching of Jesus which implied that goodwill was a sufficient guide to conduct, and that, if God loved men, He was bound to secure their comfort. There was a time when men rejected Christianity because they disbelieved in miracles or in the Divinity of Christ. In our age a commoner cause is this : what they understand by Christianity has been disproved by their experience of life.

This misunderstanding could not have arisen had the Teaching of Jesus been presented in its completeness—in its sternness as well as its graciousness, in its proclamation of judgment as well as its offer of comfort, and with its warning that for His disciples, as for Himself, fidelity to God would bring no immunity from suffering. Yet even if the Teaching of Jesus be presented in its completeness, it still cannot be understood in isolation. His Teaching has for its background that of the Old Testament, and the Teaching of Jesus (the *didache*) needs to be studied in the context of the Preaching (the *kerugma*)—the Proclamation

---

[1] A tragic comment on such teaching, almost too painful to quote, is provided by what Mr. R. Ellis Roberts reports in his life of H. R. L. Sheppard, the most popular Broadcast preacher of the inter-war period. Shortly before his death, Dr. Sheppard's wife left him for another man. When Mr. Roberts went to see him in his despondency, Dr. Sheppard told him, " I can never preach again. I have never preached anything but Love. I cannot preach that any longer. I cannot preach anything else. I shall not preach again ". To this Mr. Roberts replied : " You will preach truth, Dick," and received the answer, " I wonder. You don't think they mean the same, Ellis ? I suppose it depends on what one means by Love ". *R. L. Sheppard*, pp. 328 f.

of His Life and Death and Resurrection as the great redemptive acts of God.

What a man teaches depends not only on what he knows and believes but on the beliefs and knowledge of his hearers, for a teacher has to relate his teaching to the needs of those whom he addresses. Thus St. Paul, when writing to converts from paganism, had to give many a warning against idolatry. Our Lord had no such necessity for He spoke to Jews, and the Jews had already learnt that there was but one God, the God who was both just and holy. It was this just and holy God whom He worshipped and proclaimed. He, too, held God in awe and, when He spoke of this just and holy God as a God of love, did so not as one who is repeating a truism, but as one who reports a strange and amazing discovery. We miss the import of His words if we forget that the Father, whose love He bade men trust, was the God who had at all costs to be obeyed, and whom His hearers had already learnt to fear. We may learn, not only from His speech but from His silences—from what He did not need to say because His hearers had already gained from the Old Testament the realization of God's holiness and power.

The Old Testament differs from the Scriptures of other religions in that it proclaims a God whose righteous will is the norm of history and of individual lives. For its writers the world is not, as for the Hindu sage, the field of *maya*, illusion, from whose activities the wise man seeks to flee by asceticism or by mysticism. Instead, the world is the sphere in which God works and in which His will must be obeyed. God had made Himself known to men not by abstract teaching but by His redemptive acts. He had chosen Abraham and his seed to serve Him ; He had made with Abraham a covenant, and this covenant He confirmed when He delivered the Israelites from Egypt. This deliverance was associated with the giving of the Law at Sinai. The Ten Commandments reveal the distinctive strength and glory of Old Testament piety ; in them religion and ethics, reverence to God and moral obligation, are inextricably combined. Ancient as they are, they are still relevant to modern needs, for they provide the sanctions of a stable society.[1]

This association of religion and ethics was made still more intimate by the great teaching prophets who related religion both to individual and to social justice. For these prophets, God was not an oriental despot desiring compliments and flattery, nor was He the otiose spectator of the events of history. Instead, He was the living God who ruled with undeviating justice.

Our Lord thus addressed those who had already learned from the Old Testament that God was just and holy. Unless this be remembered, His words of grace may easily be sentimentalized. The Old Testament speaks more than does the New of social righteousness, and the warnings of the prophets are as relevant to our age as to theirs, reminding us that we have to seek to do God's will not merely in home and Church but in every sphere of life. Much of the *malaise* of modern Christianity has come from the loss of the sense of paradox, tension, surprise and wonder. The Old Testament reminds us that God our Redeemer is God the Creator, that it is the Ruler of this immeasurable universe and the Judge of nations whom we dare through Christ to call our Father, and that His love is the love of the just and holy God—the God whom we must fear as well as trust.

Not only was the teaching of Jesus inseparably connected with that of the Old Testament. His whole conception of His vocation was related to that great drama of history of which the Old Testament is the record. He was not merely the supreme teacher continuing and completing the teaching of the prophets. He was the Messiah, the Son of Man, whose mission was the climax of those redemptive acts by which God had sought to make for Himself a people who should be the agent

---

[1] It is interesting to remember that it was on the recapitulation of these Ten Commandments that the anti-Nazi Church leaders based their message on the Day of Repentance in November 1943 when, as yet, Germany seemed undefeated. Stewart Herman, *The Rebirth of the German Church*, p. 71.

of His self-manifestation. A study of the ethical teaching of Jesus has to be based on the exploration of the nature of His mission. Nor are the Gospels our only source for the understanding of the teaching of Jesus. Much may be learnt from the other New Testament books, and especially from the Epistles of St. Paul, for in these Epistles the ethical demands of Christianity are related to the needs of converts living in a pagan environment and lacking the moral discipline of Jewish morality.

PART I

NEW TESTAMENT ETHICS

CHAPTER II

THE MISSION OF JESUS

THE modern view that the importance of Jesus lies primarily in His teaching is not that of the New Testament and the many attempts which have been made to compile an Ethic of Jesus without regard to His place and mission are based on a radical misunderstanding of His significance. Were He primarily a teacher, then we might well complain that most of the problems which perplex us find no answer in His teaching and that what are taken to be His commands are self-contradictory and incapable of fulfilment. A teacher has to ensure that his words are understood and make provision for their accurate preservation. His teaching, and, in particular, the Sermon on the Mount, has been presented as a new Law, but laws should be precise and the record of His words lacks such precision. And if the novelty of His teaching is assigned to the greater inwardness of His demands, then it is strange, indeed, that His teaching should from the first have been called a Gospel. What Good News is there in being told that, whereas Moses prohibited murder and adultery, Jesus forbad any revengeful or impure thought ? There is no Good News here, but only the condemnation of us all.

Those who acclaim Jesus primarily as an ethical teacher, speak much of the originality and relevance of His teaching. But, were He a teacher of ethics only, it would be hard to prove either the originality or the relevance. The commands in which He summed up what God requires from men, " Thou shalt love the Lord thy God with all thy heart, and with all thy soul, and with all thy mind and with all thy strength ", " thou shalt love thy neighbour as thyself ",[1] are derived from the Old Testament. Nor can we claim that He was the first to make clear the

[1] Mark xii. 30 f.

requirement of forgiving love. Before His time a Jewish teacher
had written, " Love ye one another from the heart ; and, if a
man sin against thee, speak peaceably to him, and in thy soul
hold not guile : and if he repent and confess, forgive him ".
" And if he be shameless and persist in his wrongdoing, even
so forgive him from the heart ; and leave to God the avenging ".[1]
Nor is it easy to show that our Lord's teaching, if He was a
teacher only, is relevant to our modern needs. He addressed
Jews who had no responsibility for the government of their land
and who lived in an agrarian society quite unlike the complex
industrial order in which we live. Many of the problems which
perplex us most find in His words no direct answer. If, with
the writers of the New Testament, we believe that He was not
a teacher only but the Son of God who, for us men and for
our salvation, so lived and died that in Him was fulfilled the
prophets' vision of the coming of God's Kingdom, then these
questions of the originality and the immediate relevance of His
teaching are without significance. Truth is no less true because
it has been taught by others, and the relevance of His teaching
is differently conceived if we believe that He left behind Him
a Church which had the guidance of the divine Spirit, the
Comforter, who would interpret His words and relate their
meaning to the needs of future ages.

The other great Asiatic who has been acclaimed as the great
teacher, Gautama the Buddha, had, if tradition may be believed,
forty-five years from the time of his enlightenment in which to
teach. The mission of Jesus lasted certainly not more than three
years and possibly less than half that time.[2] The earliest Gospel
speaks little of His teaching, and its longest section deals with
the events of His last days on earth. It was not as a teacher
that St. Peter depicted Him. Instead, he spoke of " the good
tidings of peace by Jesus Christ ", how that God " anointed him

---

[1] *The Testament of the Twelve Patriarchs, The Testament of Gad,*
vi. 3, 7. (*Apochrypha and Pseudepigrapha,* edited by R. H. Charles,
II. p. 341 f.)

[2] Professor A. T. Olmstead of Chicago in his *Jesus in the Light of
History,* published in 1942, p. 281, gives what seem to be convincing
arguments that the first Easter Sunday was April 9th, A.D. 30, and
that Jesus preached his Nazareth Sermon on December 18th, A.D. 28.

with the Holy Ghost and with power : who went about doing
good and healing all that were oppressed by the devil ".   Him
the Jews had slain but God had raised Him up.[1]   It is St. Luke
who records these words—St. Luke who wrote the Gospel which
makes the most immediate appeal to modern men.   Yet the
description he records of the earthly life of Jesus is not that of
the supreme teacher but that of One in whom God's power had
been active for men's deliverance.   We shall have later to
explore the meaning of our Lord's ethical teaching but it would
be futile even to attempt to do so without considering first the
import of His mission.

It is significant that the mission of Jesus was preceded by
that of John the Baptist who, like another Amos, had denounced
the sins of his contemporaries.   Let them not rely on being
God's chosen people.   It was not enough to have Abraham for
their father, for God could make from stones children of
Abraham.   God's judgment was near, and by their works would
they be judged.   Many Jews were looking forward with eagerness to the coming of the Messiah ; John foretold that His
advent was near, but spoke of it as a ground not of comfort but
of apprehension.[2]   And Jesus was among those whom this
austere prophet baptized.

How could Jesus have come to be baptized with John's
baptism of repentance unless he, too, had sins of which to
repent ?   Thus Mr. Middleton Murry writes, " He would have
sought no baptism for the remission of sins, had he not been
conscious of sin.   He came out also to see and to hear a prophet ;
he would have seen him and heard him, but he would not have
sought his baptism for no cause, and become one with the outward ritualists whom he so passionately condemned ".[3]   Mr.
Murry's words show a misunderstanding of the baptism of Jesus
and of those words used by both John and Jesus which in our
version are translated " repent " and " repentance ".   These

---

[1] Acts x. 36–9.   [2] Matt. iii. 7–10.   Cp. Mark. i. 4 ff. ; Luke iii. 7 ff.
[3] In a book representing his earlier views, *The Life of Jesus*, 1926,
p. 31.

English words suggest " penitence ", sorrow over sin, but that is not the meaning of the Greek words employed (μετανοεῖτε, μετανοία). The Gospel word, " Repent ye " (μετανοεῖτε), represents " the prophetic imperative " of a Hebrew word which our English version of the Old Testament translates most often by " turn ye ", sometimes by " return ", and in two passages only by " repent ".[1]

Yet Mr. Murry was right in saying that " Jesus would not have sought his baptism for no cause ". His baptism was not an empty rite. It had a cause, but that cause was not a need He felt to repent of sin but His self-dedication to His mission. And that self-dedication was confirmed by the heavenly voice He heard, " Thou art my son ; the Beloved in whom I am well-pleased ". " Thou art my Son "—these words go back to Psalm ii. 7, and have a Messianic meaning ; " the Beloved in whom I am well-pleased "—these words, as Dr. Armitage Robinson has shown,[2] represent an independent translation of Isa. xlii, 1. " The significance of the quotation consists in the fact that this passage in Isaiah represents the *ordination formula* of the Suffering Servant of the Lord. By combining the two passages, accordingly, the voice succeeds in at once anointing the unique Son as the Messiah and ordaining him as the Suffering Servant. Or, to express the same thought in slightly different terms, it not alone confirms to Jesus' consciousness the fact of his Messiahship, but it serves at the same time to define the nature of that Messiahship as one issuing in suffering, trial, death—the cross ".[3]

The story of the Baptism of Jesus is followed by that of His temptations. These temptations Jesus faced in solitude. The record of them must thus have come from Him ; it seems probable that He spoke of them to His disciples when, after

---

[1] See J. W. Bowman, *The Intention of Jesus*, pp. 29 f., 231. The Hebrew word used in these passages is *shūb*, " a relatively colourless word, denoting merely to *turn back* or to *return* ", not *nāḥam* which conveys the sense of sorrow over sin.

[2] The same independent translation from the Hebrew as is found in the quotation from Isa. xlii given in Matt. xii. 18. *St. Paul's Epistle to the Ephesians*, p. 231.

[3] J. W. Bowman, *op. cit.*, p. 39.

Peter's confession of Him as the Messiah, He sought to free them from false conceptions of His Messianic task. " The devil can cite scripture for his purpose "—Shakespeare might have added that he can do so with accuracy. The Old Testament speaks with two voices of God's deliverance. Which of them was the Word of God ? Jesus was hungry. Why not so use His power as to meet His own needs, and later to make impressive proof of His Messianic dignity ? What chance was there that one walking the common ways of life would win a hearing for His message ? Why not, instead, so act that God would be forced to save Him in so spectacular a way that all would recognize Him for what He was ? The Jewish people were restless under the yoke of Rome. Why not compromise, be a politician, and win the kingdoms of the world in the world's way, by which alone success would be attained ?[1] All these temptations were temptations connected with His Messianic vocation. He would not seek those easier ways which might have brought Him recognition and what men call success. Instead, He would live in entire obedience to God, even although that obedience might mean the apparent failure of His mission. He rejected those conceptions of the Messiah which looked forward to earthly greatness and temporal power, and accepted His Messiahship as a Messiahship of service, even although that should mean that He became the Suffering Servant of the Lord.

John the Baptist was put in prison and Jesus came " proclaiming the Gospel, the Good News of God ; the time was fulfilled and the kingdom of God was near ; repent, change your minds ($\mu\epsilon\tau\alpha\nu o\epsilon\tilde{\iota}\tau\epsilon$) and believe in the Gospel ".[2] John's teaching had been one of doom, and even his prophecy of the coming of the Messiah was minatory. Jesus, whom John foretold, spoke of His message as a Gospel, Good News of God, which men could receive by a change of mind, an act of faith. St. Luke explains this Good News by referring at once to our Lord's Sermon in the synagogue at Nazareth. The scripture which was fulfilled in Him was the reading from Isa. lxi. The Spirit of the Lord was upon Him because He was anointed to preach Good News to the poor, to proclaim release to the captives, recovery of

[1] Matt. iv. 1-11.   [2] Mark i. 14 f.

sight to the blind, to set at liberty them that are oppressed and to proclaim the acceptable year of the Lord.[1] The passage in Isaiah goes on, " and the day of vengeance of our God ", but these words Jesus did not quote. His coming would mean crisis, judgment, for men would judge themselves by their attitude to Him, but His work was primarily redemptive, and His message the Good News of God.

That Gospel, that Good News of God, was inseparably connected with the imminence of God's Kingdom.   " The time is fulfilled, the kingdom of God is at hand ".[2] The words introduce us at once to modern perplexities about our Lord's teaching.   Was that kingdom immanent or transcendent, present or merely future ?   Did its coming depend on man's response, or would it come solely by God's catastrophic act ?   In more technical language : which interpretation of the Kingdom is correct, the " liberal " or the " eschatological " ?   That is a question to which for long there was no consentient answer. Ritschl had brought the phrase " Kingdom of God " back into current Christian speech.   Christianity, he argued, was not, as Lutheran theologians had tended to teach, a circle with one centre, Justification by Faith, but an ellipse with two *foci*, Justification by Faith and the Kingdom of God.   In this way he sought to redress the " injustice " which had been " done to the ethical interpretation of Christianity " by the exclusive emphasis on its redemptive aspect.[3] The phrase " Kingdom of God ", so common in the Synoptic Gospels, had been little emphasized, and to many the words came as a new discovery.   Ritschl himself was a strong State-Churchman, contemptuous of Pietism, and showing little interest in social reform, but in our country, and in the United States, the phrase " Kingdom of God " became a rallying cry for those in the Church who were deeply conscious of social wrongs, and who found in the phrase the apt expression of what was called the " Social Gospel ".   Such phrases as " build ", " extend " or " spread " the Kingdom became current coin, and by many the coming of the Kingdom of God was identified with that belief in progress which in that period of

[1] Luke iv. 18 f.   [2] Mark i. 15.
[3] *Justification and Reconciliation*, III. p. 11.

peace and increasing prosperity was characteristic of the Western world.

The " eschatological " interpretation of the Kingdom of God was the exact antithesis to all this. Its first and most poignant exposition was the little book of Johannes Weiss, first published in 1892, entitled *The Preaching of Jesus on the Kingdom of God* (*Die Predigt Jesu vom Reiche Gottes*). Weiss admitted the attractiveness to modern men of the " liberal " interpretation of the Kingdom of God, but denied that that interpretation had anything to do with the teaching of Jesus. The Kingdom for Jesus lay entirely in the future. It is true that Jesus spoke of the Kingdom as being " in men's midst " but that was only " a bluffing answer ".[1] The Kingdom of God was purely " supernatural and in exclusive opposition to this world ".[2] At first Jesus had hoped that the Kingdom would come in His own lifetime, and this explains the haste with which the disciples were bidden to pass from town to town ; there was no time for any delay, so near was the coming of the Kingdom.[3] When the Kingdom did not then come, Jesus believed that it was God's will that first He should die that so He might, within the lifetime of His followers, return on the clouds. " God will then destroy this ruined world over which the devil ruled and create a new world ". The judgment will take place not of the living only but of the dead. " The land of Palestine will exist in transfigured splendour and become the centre of the new Kingdom. The Gentiles will cease to have dominion over it, but, instead, will acknowledge God : sorrow and sin will cease to be ; and those in the Kingdom will see the living God and serve Him in eternal righteousness, innocence and blessedness. Jesus and those faithful to Him will rule over the new-born twelve tribes in which the Gentiles also will be included ".[4]

In the second, and much longer, edition of his book, published eight years later, Weiss admitted that in his first edition he had " put the ethical teaching of Jesus into too narrow association with His eschatological teaching and that, by placing the world-view of Jesus and His estimate of earthly life in the dazzling

[1] p. 20 on Luke xvii. 21.   [2] p. 49.
[3] Matt. x. 23.   [4] pp. 62 f.

light of the speedy end of the world, he had made the Ethics
of Jesus too negative, ascetic and world-fleeing ".   There were
times when " the strain relaxed and the pressure was lessened
of the violent message which was laid upon His soul ".   " The
thought of the downfall of the world receded . . . and He gave
Himself to the things of this life, rejoiced with the glad, mourned
with those that wept.   This was no longer the gloomy and stern
prophet but a man among men, a child of God among the
children of men.   From such a mood there came those words
and parables, whose freshness will never grow old, in which
there is little trace of world-weariness, asceticism or of the end
of the world or of judgment.   In such times He uttered those
moral aphorisms which . . . in their inner beauty have an eternal
validity for men of every age ".[1]

Johannes Weiss's book was not translated into English
and the extreme " eschatological " interpretation aroused little
interest here until the publication in 1910 of Schweitzer's *The
Quest of the Historical Jesus*, an admirable translation of the
German book published four years earlier under the title *From
Reimarus to Wrede*.   In it there was no compromise.   The
attempts to make Jesus intelligible to modern men were
described and ruthlessly exposed.   " The Jesus of Nazareth
who came forward publicly as the Messiah, who preached the
ethic of the Kingdom of God, who founded the Kingdom of
Heaven upon earth, and died to give His work its final con-
secration, never had any existence.   He is a figure designed by
rationalism, endowed with life by liberalism and clothed by
modern theology in an historical garb ".[2]

If the " eschatological " interpretation has shown the inadequacy of the " liberal " presentation of the mission and
teaching of Jesus, in its " consistent " form it is as one-sided
as the view it sought to displace.   Neither view is adequate to
the total data of the Gospel records.   The problem remains
insoluble so long as it is presented in the alternatives, Was the
Kingdom present or future, immanent or transcendent ?   It is
necessary to look again at the meaning of " the Kingdom of
God " and to seek an interpretation which shall be more adequate

[1] pp. 134 f.   [2] p. 396.

to the facts ; this more recent scholars have done, and there is increasing agreement as to the meaning of this phrase.[1]

In the Old Testament, as in the New, " the Kingdom of God ", as Gloege has shown, has not the static sense of a realm, but the dynamic sense of God's rule. " This rule of God is never something separated to an extent from God ; it is a pregnant expression for God Himself ". It is God regnant and redemptive. In His parables and sayings Jesus uses many a figure to describe the Kingdom, but He " never compares it with a dead object or with anything immobile but with a man who is doing something, or with something which finds itself in movement, or with which something is done ". Since the Kingdom of God denotes God regnant, we never find in the Gospels the common phrases of modern Christian piety about " building " or " extending " the Kingdom. The words the Gospels use are, " entering ", or " going in ". Men are invited to enter the Kingdom as into something already existing (Matt. v. 20 ; vii. 13, 21). They go in as to a marriage feast (Matt. xxv. 10) ; they are like those summoned by a king to a banquet at which all things are ready (Matt. xxii. 4). For those who do the works of love the Kingdom is prepared " from the foundation of the world " (Matt. xxv. 34). The Kingdom is thus at once a possession and a hope. It is present for already God's redemptive activity may be experienced ; it is future for God's kingly activity will be unconditioned when the Kingdom comes in power (Mark ix. 1).[2]

Since in the teaching of Jesus, the conception of the Kingdom was throughout " theocentric ", " the relation between present and future is not antithetic but organic. In the activity of Jesus the future had already broken through into the present ". " The Bridegroom was already in men's midst ; the banquet had begun ".[3] When John the Baptist, in the weariness of his

[1] For the interpretations of Gloege, *The Kingdom of God and the Church in the New Testament*, 1929 ; T. W. Manson, *The Teaching of Jesus*, 1931 ; Otto, *The Kingdom of God and the Son of Man*, 1934; Dodd, *The Parables of the Kingdom*, 1935 : see the writer's *The Doctrine of the Work of Christ*, pp. 18–21.

[2] *Reich Gottes und Kirche im Neuen Testament*, pp. 36, 55, 75, 80.

[3] *Op cit.* pp. 110 f.

captivity, sent disciples to ask Jesus whether He was He that should come, Jesus bade them tell him of these signs of the Kingdom's presence, " The blind receive their sight and the lame walk, the lepers are cleansed, and the deaf hear and the dead are raised up and the poor have good tidings preached to them " (Matt. xi. 5). Already the powers of evil were suffering defeat. The works of healing done by the seventy were a sign that Satan was " fallen as lightning from heaven " (Luke x. 18), and His own healing of the dumb man was a proof that the Kingdom of God was already operative (Luke xi. 20). There was no need to look here and there for the coming of the Kingdom. It was already in men's midst for He was there, and in Him God's rule was already manifest in its redemptive power.

In the Old Testament, the coming of the rule of God was connected with the two conceptions of the people of God and of the Messiah. God was regarded as the King of His people, but it became clear that not all the people were willing to be His subjects, nor would the nation as a political entity be saved from the menace of foreign powers. Elijah had been comforted with the thought that, although the nation as a whole was faithless, he was not alone in his fidelity ; the nation would not be totally destroyed, for there were still the seven thousand who had not bowed unto the Baal.[1] By Isaiah the doctrine of the Remnant was clearly taught. It is expressed in the name he gave his son Shear—jashub—" a remnant shall return ". The nation as a whole would be dispersed but a remnant should return whose stay should be " upon the Lord the Holy One of Israel ".[2] This thought was developed in Jeremiah's teaching on the New Covenant, and found sublime expression in the Servant-Songs of the later part of the Book of Isaiah. This conception of the Servant of God, who by his sufferings should fulfil God's saving work for men, was ignored by the Judaism of our Lord's time, and the Messiah for whom men looked was a Messiah who should triumph over the enemies of God's chosen people.[3] It is this which may explain the reserve with which Jesus spoke of Himself as the Messiah.

---

[1] 1 Kings xix. 18.   [2] x. 20 f.   [3] See earlier, pp. 34 f.

The turning point in the ministry of Jesus came with Peter's confession of Him as the Messiah. Our Lord accepted the term, but warned His disciples against making their discovery public. At once He began to speak of His rejection and death, and Peter began to " rebuke " the Man whom he had confessed to be the Messiah, for Peter, too, could not conceive of a Messiah who should suffer. That " rebuke " was a revival of the temptation in the wilderness to seek to bring in the Kingdom by some way more likely to achieve success, and Jesus rebuked Peter : he was doing Satan's work ; he was thinking not God's thoughts but men's.

From the time of Peter's confession, Jesus spoke of Himself often as the Son of Man. Some, though not all, Aramaic scholars say that the Aramaic equivalent *bar-nasha* means merely " man ". Son of Man is used in Daniel to denote the Kingdom of God on earth which would succeed the four pagan empires. These pagan tyrannies were symbolized by " beasts ", the purified Israel, " the saints of the Most High ", by one " like unto a son of man ". In the *Similitudes of Enoch*, Son of Man is used of the " Elect of God " who should be the agent of God's judgment and mercy. " The son of man " may mean " man " but, if, with many scholars, we interpret son of man by its use in Enoch then it denotes not merely a man, but the mysterious " Man " of Jewish apocalyptic expectation.[1]

Our Lord thus connects two conceptions which by others were held in isolation. He was the Son of Man, the vicegerent of God in the bringing in of God's Kingdom, the Messiah designated for this task, and, at the same time, He was the Servant of the Lord who should accomplish His work not in outer glory but through suffering. And in that suffering His disciples were called to share. They were the " little flock ",

---

[1] Dr. T. W. Manson gives to the phrase a collective meaning, connecting it with the conceptions of the Remnant and the Servant of Jehovah, but even so it denotes in the end Jesus alone. Jesus " sets out to create in Israel that Son of Man. But not many can be found to go with him any part of the way, and none to follow him to the end. The last part of the way he travels alone, and at the cross he alone is the Son of Man, the incarnation of the Kingdom of God on earth ". *The Teaching of Jesus*, p. 235.

to whom it was God's good pleasure to give the Kingdom. But even when Jesus spoke later of His death, the disciples did not understand His meaning and were afraid to ask Him. Still they were disputing as to their own standing, each desiring to have pre-eminence, and Jesus warned them that the only pre-eminence was that of service.[1]

Jesus went up to Jerusalem, there to challenge the Jewish leaders and to die. He did so because He knew that this was the way in which His work for men would be fulfilled. We read that, as Jesus and the twelve were going up to Jerusalem, " Jesus was going before them ; and they were amazed " and " were afraid ". A third time He warned them of what lay before Him, and, when James and John came to ask the chief places of honour in the Kingdom, He spoke of the cup that He must drink and of the baptism with which He would be baptized. He, the Son of Man, was come, not to be ministered unto but to minister, and to give His life a ransom for the many.[2] It was as the Suffering Servant of the Lord that He would fulfil His task. His formal entry into Jerusalem was a hint of His Messiahship, and His purification of the temple a further challenge to the religious leaders of the people. The last days are sombre with the sense of crisis ; our Lord tells the parable of the husbandmen who, having wounded their master's envoys, kill his son and are themselves destroyed ; Mary anoints Him with precious ointment ; Judas arranges for His betrayal. At length He partakes His last meal with the twelve, and gives to it sacramental significance. Judas goes from the Lord's Supper to complete His work of betrayal. There follow the agony of Gethsemane, the arrest, the trial and condemnation of Jesus by H s own nation and by Pontius Pilate, and, at last, the Crucifixion. Had that been the end, we should not have heard of Jesus, for crucifixion was too frequent for a further instance of it to be recorded. But Good Friday, Black Friday as it seemed, was followed by Easter Day, and later came Pentecost, and the full realization of the first believers that not only was the Man they had followed risen from the dead but that His

---

[1] Mark ix. 32–7.   [2] Mark x. 32–45.

Spirit was with them bringing them a strange new power and joy.

The contribution of Christianity to the problems of personal character and corporate activity does not lie merely, or even chiefly, in the teaching of Jesus. It lies in the significance of God's action for men in Jesus Christ. That action was the culmination of those acts which the Old Testament records. The holy God of whom the prophets spoke had manifested that salvation which they foretold. In the Life and Death and Resurrection of Jesus the Messiah the early Church found its *kerugma*, its " proclamation ", which was every man's concern, and the great events which that *kerugma* announced were not merely events of the past ; they were facts of present significance. Theology and ethics, history and moral judgment, were inseparably one, for the grace of God in Christ demanded and received the response of faith, and gratitude to God for what He had done in Christ became the inspiration and the norm for Christian character. To know what God would have us do, we need to remember what God Himself has done.

CHAPTER III

THE TEACHING OF JESUS

THE attempt in modern times to isolate the teaching of Jesus has ended in failure. He cannot be understood merely as a teacher. And yet that teaching may not be ignored. There have been periods in the history of the Church when men were far more eager to call Jesus " Lord, Lord " than to do the things which He commanded. We think e.g., of the means St. Cyril of Alexandria used to secure the victory of what he held to be a correct Christology, or of those persecutions of heretics in which many earnest and zealous men took part. And even in sections of the Church which long ago renounced the claim to persecute, there have been those whose Christian orthodoxy has had little influence over many aspects of their conduct.

A Swiss novelist has depicted the following dialogue between Henry II and Thomas à Becket.

" To whom do you appeal, Thomas," laughed the King, " To the Holy Trinity ? "

" I appeal to the Gospels," whispered Thomas, " which are the record of Him in whom there was found no un-righteousness ".

" These are the words of no true Bishop ! " cried the King in noble disgust. " These are the words of a wretched heretic. The sacred Book of the Gospels belongs to a pearl-embroidered altar-hanging and has nothing to do with the order of the world or with things as they really are ".[1]

That story contains a warning we do well to heed. It was no part of our Lord's vocation to be a social reformer, and we may not claim His authority for any particular attempt to solve

---

[1] From Conrad Ferdinand Mayer's *The Saint*, quoted by Dr. Deissmann in his letter to the Conference of German and British Theologians held at Canterbury in 1927. *Theology*, May 1927, p. 249.

our social problems, nor put His name on the banner of any political party.   And yet His revelation of God and His concern for men have much to do " with the order of the world ", and " with things as they are ".   To refuse to seek for social better-ment is to acquiesce in social evils, and this those may not do who profess to believe in Him who healed the sick and fed the hungry, and who spoke of anxiety as if it were the deadly enemy of the soul of man.

Our Lord's teaching was not abstract but concrete ; He dealt with individual men and women in their needs.   He did not compile a doctrinal statement on the Doctrine of God or the Doctrine of Man, nor issue a nicely balanced code of conduct. Instead, in His parables and pointed sayings, He expressed with dazzling finality one aspect only of eternal truth, and that the aspect which on the particular occasion needed to be emphasized. That is why His teaching cannot be systematized.   Books on *The Teaching of Jesus* are many and varied.   It was worth while to have read even the longest and dullest of them if they threw light on even a single saying of our Lord's, whilst the best of these books are monuments of patient skill.   Yet there is one great difference between reading these books and reading the Gospels themselves.   Books which seek to systematize " The Teaching of Jesus " can, we find, be read without discomfort. They do not drive us to penitence and shame and hope, as does the Gospel record of the words of Jesus ; in generalizing their meaning, they rob His words of their sharp poignancy.   A Christ presented as a greater Plato is not the Christ who either wins us to an allegiance such as no man can claim, or else repels us so that, like the rich young man of old, we turn away sorrowful, or, like St. Peter say, " Depart from me, for I am a sinful man, O Lord ".

When some years later I read Dr. Lowrie's life of Kierkegaard I was interested to find that, a century ago, that great Danish writer had had the same misgiving.   " The Biblical interpreta-tion of mediocrity goes on interpreting and interpreting Christ's words until it gets out of them its own spiritless (trivial) meaning —and then, after having removed all difficulties, it is tran-quillized, and appeals confidently to Christ's words.   It quite

T.C.W.

escapes the attention of mediocrity that hereby it generates a new difficulty, surely the most comical difficulty it is possible to imagine, that God should let himself be *born*, that the Truth should have come into the world . . . in order to make trivial remarks. And likewise the new difficulty as to how one is to explain that Christ could be crucified. For it is not usual in this world of triviality to apply the penalty of death for making trivial remarks ".[1]

Presentations of " The Teaching of Jesus " inevitably bring together His teaching and arrange it in separate divisions. It has to be remembered that this is only for convenience of description, and no such presentation can take the place of the vivid records of the Gospels in which the words of Jesus derive their authority from Him who spoke them, and their significance from the circumstances of those whom He addressed. He dealt with men and women in their concrete need and sin ; He was not a lawgiver nor an ethical philosopher, and to generalize His words is to misrepresent them.

Some modern philosophers have sought to establish the validity of moral standards, whilst ignoring, or rejecting, belief in God. Speculations of this kind were alien from our Lord's thought. His estimate of what man was, and what man should be, is based throughout on His certainty of God. The God of whom He spoke was not an idea of God required to substantiate our highest ideals. God was for Him the living God, at once our King and our Father.

God is our King. In the strongest terms our Lord asserts God's power, His knowledge and His majesty. He did not, indeed, speak of God's omnipotence and omniscience. That was not His way. Instead, He spoke in concrete terms of the heavens as God's throne, and the earth as His footstool. The flowers of the field owe to God their beauty, and He has regard even to a sparrow's fall. The parables depict God's authority over men as that of a master over his slaves, or of an oriental despot over his ministers of state.[2] God, and no one else, is to

---

[1] Walter Lowrie, *Kierkegaard*, p. 580. The translation given above is from Dr. Lowrie's more recent translation of Kierkegaard's *Attack upon Christendom*, p. 197.

[2] Matt. xviii. 23–35 ; xxv. 14–27 ; Luke xvi. 1–13 ; xvii. 7–10.

be feared. Men may kill the body but they cannot kill the soul; God can cast both soul and body into Gehenna.[1] Yet the power of God is not arbitrary. He bestows sunshine and rain not on the good alone but on all. But Jesus recognized that God's rule is hard for men to understand. God seems at times like an unjust judge, or like a master who forces new tasks on slaves already tired. Yet our Lord speaks throughout in utter confidence of God's goodness. God is not only our King; He is our Father.

To call God " Father " was to use a phrase already familiar to Jewish piety. The beautiful *Ahabah* prayer of the morning service of the Jewish Prayer Book was probably already in use in the Temple,[2] with its invocation of " our Father, our King " ! " O our Father, merciful Father, ever-compassionate, have mercy upon us ". " Father " has become the characteristic Christian description of God, and yet, as Dr. T. W. Manson has shown, our two primary authorities, Mark and Q. " agree in their testimony that Jesus speaks of ' the Father ' or ' my Father ' or ' your Father ' only in His prayers or in conversation with His disciples, and that only in the period subsequent to Peter's Confession ".[3] God's Fatherhood was for Him the expression of His unique filial experience of God. That Fatherhood was illustrated to His disciples by His own trust in God. This unique relationship found expression in His words, " I thank thee, O Father, Lord of heaven and earth, that thou didst hide these things from the wise and understanding, and didst reveal them unto babes : Yea, Father, for so it was well-pleasing in thy sight. All things have been delivered unto me of my Father ; neither doth any know the Father save the Son, and he to whomsoever the Son willeth to reveal him ".[4] And because of His knowledge of the Father, He could utter His stupendous invitation " Come unto me, all ye that labour and are heavy laden, and I will give you rest ".

[1] Matt. x. 28.

[2] So Dr. Israel Abrahams surmises, *A Companion to the Authorized Daily Prayer Book.* Revised Edition, p. xlix.

[3] T. W. Manson, *The Teaching of Jesus*, p. 96. Q. is the Collection of the Sayings of Jesus found in both Matthew and Luke.

[4] Matt. xi. 25 ff. Luke x. 21 f.

The Fatherhood of God was not for Jesus a platitude nor a commonplace, and the Fatherhood of which He spoke was Fatherhood as Orientals understand it—a Fatherhood not of love only but of authority. What that Fatherhood may denote for us is shown in the familiar words of the Lord's Prayer, in which we are bidden first to pray for the hallowing of God's name, the coming of His Kingdom, and the doing of His will on earth as it is in heaven. Our Lord brings home to His hearers the Father's care by reference to the kindness human parents show. A father does not give his son a stone when he asks for a loaf, or a serpent when he asks for a fish, " If ye then, being evil, know how to give good gifts unto your children, how much more shall your Father which is in heaven give good things to them that ask him ? " Yet human fatherhood, even at its best, is an inadequate symbol of the Fatherhood of God. Thus the Parable of the Prodigal Son is not interpreted aright if the love of the father, who welcomed back his wastrel son, be taken as the expression of ordinary human love. St. Luke tells us that the parables of the lost sheep, the lost coin and the lost son were spoken after the Pharisees and Scribes had complained that Jesus received sinners and ate with them. That seemed to them a menace to morality and contrary to Divine justice. To argue, as Jülicher did, that our Lord in this parable uses a simple analogy from human life to prove that it is self-evident that God welcomes back the repentant sinner,[1] makes that parable, as Nygren says, " singularly unconvincing ". It would be open to a Pharisee to cite cases where such con-donation of wrongdoing often works out very badly, and to refer to a wiser father who, when his wastrel son returned, knowing how little good intentions may be worth, put him on probation that his son might prove the genuineness of his repentance by honest work, and the son thus tested later thanked his father " for the strictness that had led to his amendment ".[2] Our Lord spoke less of the love of God than much popular

---

[1] *Die Gleichnisreden Jesu* [2], I. p. 102, and II. p. 361.

[2] *Agape and Eros*, I. p. 59. Cp. the writer's *Doctrine of the Work of Christ*, pp. 24 f. There is an interesting parallel in a parable of a prodigal son, where the father thus tests his son, in the Mahayana Buddhist book, *The Lotus of the Good Law*, S.B.E. XXI. pp. 98–108.

preaching would suggest, and nowhere does He speak of that love as if it were self-evident. That the holy God loves men, was not for Him a truism but a paradox. What we call forgiveness is often the expression not of love but of lovelessness. We condone an offence because we care too little for the offender to be indignant at the wrong which he has done. What does it matter to us if some stranger we employ for a few hours' casual job lies to us or cheats ? But if it were a son who so acted, we should be deeply grieved. God does not view our sin with the indifference of such lovelessness. We, and those whom we wrong, are alike meant to live as the children of our heavenly Father. God's love is stern ; " Whosoever shall cause one of these little ones who believe on me to stumble, it were better for him if a great millstone were hanged about his neck, and he were cast into the sea ". Sin is an evil so grave that even self-mutilation would be better than to fall under the judgment of God ; to enter the Kingdom maimed is better than not to enter it at all.[1]

In our Lord's teaching man's relationship with God ceases to be legal. The elder brother of the Parable, and the Pharisee who, going to the temple to pray, gave God particulars of his good deeds, are types to be shunned not copied. Reward there is, but it may be reward " with persecutions ". The man who has toiled all day in the vineyard gets his stipulated pay, but he has no right to complain if others who have not " borne the burden of the day and the scorching heat " receive as much for one hour's work as he receives for twelve.[2] God's relationship with man thus transcends that of human justice. Judgment He uses, but above judgment there is grace. The love of God is not meted out according to human merit.

It was this abandonment of legalism which accounts in part for the opposition to Jesus of the religious leaders of His time, the Scribes and Pharisees. Jewish scholars, like Dr. C. G. Montefiore and Dr. Abrahams, have complained with justice of the indiscriminate condemnation which the Pharisees have received from many Christian writers. There were good Pharisees as well as bad. As we read the denunciation of them

[1] Mark ix. 42–7 (cp. Matt. v. 28 f. ; xviii. 6 ff.). [2] Matt. xx. 1–16.

in the Gospels, it is often well to substitute for " Pharisees " " religious people ", for their sins were not merely the sins of a particular type of Jew, but sins to which all religious persons are tempted—to put religious observance before humanity, and to use religion for the gratification of vanity.   If Dr. Lukyn Williams was right, " hypocrite ", though a transliteration of the Greek word used in the denunciation of the Pharisees, is not an accurate translation, for the word meant not " hypocrite ", but " play-actor ".   As Dr. P. T. Forsyth put it, Pharisaism " did not begin as conscious duplicity, but as unconscious unreality, as a disease not of the conscience but of the soul. It is not an ethical complaint but a religious ".   " It is a false form less of conduct than of sanctity.   It is less inconsistent conduct than self-conscious sanctity, which takes itself as seriously as its salvation ".   " It is not moral inconsistency, therefore, professing one thing and living another, so much as it is conscious, superior, censorious, and therefore spurious religion ".   " It was, in the classic form, the evisceration of religion by people intensely devoted to it ; people, indeed, more concerned about the piety of their religion than about the truth of their revelation, people engrossed with holiness but spending more on the cultivation of their own than on the understanding of God's.   It is devoted, subjective, and even egoist piety, at the cost often of moral judgment ".[1]

Religion may hide from men their need of penitence and love.   Devout Pharisees, like devout Jews to-day, might rejoice in obeying *minutiae* of the Law and prize such amplifications as a " fence " about the Law, protecting its major requirements from infringement, but a legalistic conception of religion, whether it be Christian or Jewish, tends to the quest of a sanctity which neglects the weightier demands of justice and of love. Such precisians are in special danger of being *hypocritai*, play-actors, living a life of unreality and using religious observances as a substitute for social justice.   Some of the Pharisees came themselves to realize this peril.   Thus in the Jerusalem *Talmud* we read, " Who is the pious fool ?   He who sees a child strug-

[1] *The Justification of God*, pp. 113 ff.   Here, as often, Dr. Forsyth anticipated by his spiritual genius later conclusions of scholarship.

gling in the water, and says, ' When I have taken off my phylac-
teries, I will go and save him ', and while he does so, the child
breathes his last. Who is the crafty scoundrel ? R. Huna
says : He is the man who, lenient to himself, teaches others
the hardest rules ".[1]

Our Lord attacked those Pharisees who utilized their piety
to increase their self-esteem and by their casuistry falsified
moral values ; who were scrupulous to pay their tithes of
" mint and anise and cummin " and " left undone the weightier
matters of the law, judgment and mercy and faith ". Such
were blind guides, straining out the gnat and swallowing the
camel.[2] But it was not only such unworthy Pharisees who were
repelled by the teaching of Jesus.

The words of Jesus, like His actions, expressed a different
conception of God's relationship with men than that of Pharisaism. He, too, spoke often of rewards, and sometimes of
punishments, and yet the very rewards of which He spoke
were different from the rewards men usually seek. The man
who has abandoned for His sake home and kin, " shall receive
a hundred fold now in this time, houses and brethren, and
sisters, and mothers and children, with persecutions ; and in
the life to come eternal life ".[3] It is clear that the rewards
are not to be literally interpreted (no man can receive a hundred
mothers !), whilst the words added in St. Mark, " with persecutions ", show that the early disciples found that the reward
for fidelity was not of the kind which pleasure-lovers seek.
Each of the Beatitudes speaks of a reward. The reward of the
pure in heart is to see God, but only the pure in heart would
find in that vision a reward. Jesus gives no guarantee that the
good will be prosperous and the bad be poverty-stricken. The
wastrel son is welcomed back by his father ; the labourers who

---

[1] *A Rabbinic Anthology* by C. G. Montefiore and H. Loewe, p. 487 ;
cp. the reference to the seven classes of Pharisees of whom the first is
" the shoulder-Pharisee " ; *i.e.* the man who packs his good works on his
shoulder in order that they may be seen. G. F. Moore, *Judaism* II.
p. 194.   [2] Matt. xxiii. 5-7, 16-24.

[3] Mark. x. 29 f. Luke xviii. 29 and some texts of Matt. xix. 29
refer to " wife " which occasioned Julian the Apostate's sneer : " are
.the faithful to have one hundred wives ? "

work in the vineyard for one hour only receive the pay of those
who have worked for a full day.   All legal or commercial ideas
of God's relationship with men are thus abrogated.   If we did
all the things commanded us, we should have done nothing
extra, and would still be " unprofitable slaves ", for we should
have done merely " that which it was our duty to do ".[1]
Jewish theologians spoke sometimes of " the chastisements of
love ", sufferings which were sent to men not in punishment for
their sins, but for their testing and refinement.   But they spoke
more of " no chastisement, no guilt ; where there is suffering,
there was first sin ".[2]   Jesus, though He spoke at times of
rewards and punishments, refused to make retribution the sole
principle of explanation.   The Galileans whose blood Pilate had
mingled with the sacrifices, or the eighteen on whom the tower of
Siloam fell, were not sinners more than others.[3]   All alike needed
to repent.   The highest good men could receive was the Kingdom
of God.   This was not gained by human merit, it was God's
gift.   Not recompense but grace was the full expression of
God's relationship with men.

Since God is a God of grace, Jesus enjoined on His followers
forgiveness of their enemies.   He bade His disciples, " Love
your enemies, and pray for them that persecute you ; that ye
may be sons of your Father which is in heaven ; for he maketh
his sun to rise on the evil and the good, and sendeth rain on the
just and the unjust ".[4]   It is interesting to notice how differently
two modern Jewish scholars comment on this command.   Dr.
C. G. Montefiore refers his " Jewish readers more especially to
the first twenty pages of a little book called *Tales of Tirah
and Lesser Tibet* by Lilian Starr ".   After her husband, Dr.
Starr, had been murdered by a Pathan in 1917, she returned in
1920 " to show in practice the Christian revenge in contrast
to the system of blood-feuds, or vendetta, prevalent without
exception among all the frontier tribes ".   Dr. Montefiore
adds, " One may differ profoundly from dogmatic Christianity ;

---

[1] Luke xvii. 10.
[2] Strack and Billerbeck, *Kommentar zum Neuen Testament aus
Talmud und Midrasch.* II. p. 193.
[3] Luke xiii. 1–5.   [4] Matt. v. 44 f.

one may even criticize certain portions of the teaching of Jesus, but who will not pay his homage to Mrs. Starr, and who must not allow that the motive power of her life has been the love of her Master and that part of his doctrine which demanded all for the highest and urged men to love, *i.e.* to do good to their enemies ? "[1]

Very different is the comment of Dr. Klausner of the University of Jerusalem. He regards the teaching of Jesus on loving our enemies, and the reason given for the injunction, as " an element in Jesus' idea of God which Judaism could not accept ". It follows from it " that God is not absolute righteousness ". " He is not the God of justice, in spite of His day of Judgment : in other words, He is not the " God of history ". Klausner speaks with praise of Jesus as " a great teacher of morality and an artist in parable ", and yet holds that the Jews did well to reject Him not only because of His " exaggerated nearness to God ", which led Him to His " constant emphasis and insistence on ' But I say unto you ' as opposed to ' them of old time ' ", but because of the very nature of His teaching. Jesus did, indeed, observe the ceremonial laws, yet " he so decries " their value as " to make them of secondary importance compared to the moral laws, and *almost* to nullify them ".[2] He holds that " throughout the Gospels there is not one clear item of ethical teaching " for which a Jewish parallel cannot be found, but complains that it was not " an advantage but a drawback " that " his ethical teaching was not lost in a sea of legal prescriptions and items of secular information ". " Judaism is not only religion and it is not only ethics : it is the sum-total of all the needs of a nation, placed on a religious basis " but Jesus " set up nothing but an ethico-religious system bound up with his conception of the Godhead ", and thus " he both annulled Judaism as the life-force of the Jewish nation, and also the nation as a nation. For a religion which possesses only a certain conception of God and a morality acceptable to all mankind, does not belong to any special nation and consciously or unconsciously breaks down the barriers of nationality ".[3]

---

[1] *The Synoptic Gospels* [2], II. p. 418.
[2] *Jesus of Nazareth*, pp. 379, 381, 370.   [3] *Op. cit.* pp. 384, 390.

Jesus lived as a Jew, and His mission was " to the lost sheep of the house of Israel ", and yet, when a pagan woman asked His help, He gave it and healed her daughter. As Dr. C. Anderson Scott wrote, " What but a smile, half ironical, half inviting could have provoked her retort—' Truth, Lord, I am nothing but a poor pet dog ; all I ask for is the scraps ' ".[1]

His teaching was universal in its scope, for He dealt with men as men, and not as members of a class or nation. All the injunctions which He gave are summed up in the one command, relevant for those of every nation and every age, " Thou shalt love the Lord thy God with all thy heart, and with all thy soul, and with all thy mind " and " thy neighbour as thyself. On these two commandments hangeth the whole law and the prophets ".[2]

In the application of this double command, our Lord uttered those striking sayings which to-day haunt men's minds and cause much perplexity. As we have seen, Jesus spoke as a Jew to Jews and those whom He addressed had already learnt from the Old Testament that there is but one God and He is just and holy. That He was a Jew influenced not only the content but the form of His teaching. He was incarnate as an Oriental and a Jew, and that meant that He used Oriental modes of speech.[3] We English, and still more the Scots, have, as our characteristic mode of speech, what the old grammarians call litotes or meiosis. We say less than we mean, and the more our feelings are moved, the more we understate our meaning. During the Battle of London, I was talking to an Eastender about the damage done to his home and neighbourhood. When he wanted to express how horrible was the desolation caused by a big bomb, he said, " It didn't 'arf make a mess ". The Scots surpass us in this, and if they wish to express superlative praise they will probably say, he or she is " na' bad ". In school and university we are trained to avoid generalizations and to say less than we imply. But Jesus was an Oriental

---

[1] *Dominus Noster*, p. 24, on Matt. xv. 21–8.   [2] Matt. xxii. 37–40.

[3] In the following paragraph I have utilized some sentences from my article on *The Teaching of Jesus and Christian Preaching* in *Theology To-day*, April 1946.

and, as an Oriental, expressed His meaning not by meiosis but by hyperbole. He did not say, as we might, great wealth may in certain circumstances hinder spiritual receptivity. He said, " It is easier for a camel to enter in through a needle's eye than for a rich man to enter into the kingdom of God." [1] How that has troubled some western commentators ! Some, following Cyril of Alexandria,[2] tell us that the word translated " camel " denotes a rope or cable ; others, that the needle's eye is really a postern gate which a camel could manage to squeeze through. But somehow not even the most prosaic commentator has succeeded in getting rid of the humorous exaggeration of the other saying about " straining out a gnat and swallowing a camel ". Failure to understand the Oriental exaggeration of such words merely makes a commentator absurd. It is more serious when people have taken, as if it were sober prose, the warning of our Lord, " If any man cometh unto me, and *hateth* not his own father, and mother, and wife, and children . . . he cannot be my disciple ".[3] In doing so they have used these words to justify an inhumanity alien from His meaning. Thus in Cassian's *Institutes*, that great text-book of Western monasticism, we read of a monk " who was intent on purity of heart, and extremely anxious with regard to the contemplation of divine things ". " After an interval of fifteen years ", he received a pile of letters from his parents and friends and burnt them without opening them, in order that he might not be distracted by reading letters from those who loved him.[4] *The Institutes* narrate a still more distressing story of how the devotion of a monk to Christ was tested by having his little son beaten and starved so that, whenever he saw his son, his son was in tears, and, in the end, the monk was ordered to throw him into a river ; this he did, not knowing that the other monks would rescue the poor child.[5] And we are asked to believe that

---

[1] Mark x. 25. I used to notice in India that an Indian preacher, preaching on the danger of avarice, would use the Tamil proverb, " Say cash (*paṇam*) and even a corpse (*piṇam*) will open its mouth ". Not even the most ignorant in the congregation would imagine that a corpse would so act.

[2] *Comment in Matt.* Migne, *Cyrilli Opera*, Tom. V. Col. 430.

[3] Luke xiv. 26.   [4] V. xxxii.   [5] IV. xxvii.

this cruelty was approved by Him who when on earth was the friend of little children.

Yet these words of Jesus do demand an allegiance which, if necessary, must override all ties of family. We remember what John Bunyan wrote about going to prison in loyalty, as he believed, to Christ. " The parting with my wife and poor children hath often been to me in this place as the pulling the flesh from the bones, and that not only because I am too fond of these great mercies, but also because I should have often brought to my mind the many hardships, miseries and wants that my poor family was like to meet with should I be taken from them, especially my poor blind child, who lay nearer to my heart than all beside. Oh, the thoughts of the hardship I thought my poor blind one might go under would break my heart to pieces."[1] And there are still those for whom following Christ means thus " hating " loved ones. I think of an Indian Christian belonging to a high caste and very influential family. Someone gave him a New Testament. He read it and, in the end, decided that he must be a Christian. He put himself in touch with a Christian Church and was baptized. When he returned home, his younger brother spat on him, his father disinherited him, and forbade him to enter again his home, and his mother, weeping passionately, told him he was no longer her son. That man, to preserve his loyalty to Christ, had thus to " hate " the father whom he honoured and the mother whom he deeply loved. And not converts only, but many a missionary learns in his own experience the import of these words of Jesus. A man feels the call to serve his Lord in a distant pagan land. He is an only son and his parents feel he ought not to leave them, or parents have to return to the mission-field leaving their children behind. Special tasks entail special obligations. In the recent war conscription saved many a man from such mental conflict, but in the early years of the 1914–18 war, before conscription was introduced, how many had to make a like grim choice. They felt they ought to join the army, but to do so meant leaving a wife with a young child. They loved their families, and yet felt constrained to act in a way which in

[1] *Grace Abounding*, § 327.

ordinary times would seem harsh and cruel. And our Lord still calls some to tasks which involve separation from their loved ones as do the hard tasks of war.

We have dwelt at length on our Lord's reference to " hating " loved ones, as it affords a clear instance of the folly of interpreting His words as if they were clauses in a code of law. In His sayings, as in His parables, He so spoke as to startle men from their complacency, and compel them to ponder on His teaching. His words were relevant to a particular situation. He dealt with men one by one, and that meant that He spoke of one aspect of truth at a time. We have an illustration of this in those three sayings of Jesus which St. Francis read out to his companions, and made the basis of his order : Matt. xix. 21 ; Luke ix. 1–6 ; Matt. xvi. 24–7.[1]

The first, Matt. xix. 21, is our Lord's command to the rich young man who wanted to join His little company of disciples. " If thou wouldest be perfect, go, sell that thou hast, and give to the poor, and thou shalt have treasure in heaven : and come, follow me ". Our Lord warned men against being the slaves of Mammon, and in His parable of Dives and Lazarus made clear how severely He condemned those who were indifferent to others' needs. When the young man with great possessions " turned away sorrowful ", Jesus spoke to His disciples of how hard it was for " a rich man to enter into the kingdom of heaven ". But it is clear from the Gospels that He did not bid all His friends renounce their property. This young man wished to follow Jesus—to accompany Him at a time when He was going up on His last journey to Jerusalem there to experience rejection and death. That he could not do so long as he was encumbered with possessions. Not all were called in this sense to follow Jesus ; most had to meet the ordinary obligations of home and livelihood, and show their trust in God not, indeed, by taking " no thought about to-morrow ", but by being free from that anxiety which springs from distrust in God and servitude to Mammon.[2]

[1] P. Sabatier, *Vie de S. François d'Assise* [28], p. 85.
[2] The verb translated in Matt. vi, 25, 27, 31, 34 in the A.V., " take thought " denotes " be anxious ". Our Lord forbids not forethought but distracting anxiety.

The second passage, Luke ix. 1–6, gives our Lord's commands to the Twelve as He sent them out to go swiftly from village to village, " preaching the gospel and healing everywhere ". They were to " travel light ", and take nothing with them for their maintenance. This, too, was a special command. Jesus and the disciples did not normally go penniless. There was the " bag " of money which Judas carried.[1]

The third passage, Matt. xvi. 24–7, was addressed to the Twelve, after Peter's confession that Jesus was the Messiah. Jesus accepted that designation, but at once warned His disciples that He would be a very different Messiah from what they hoped. He was going up to Jerusalem, not to reign in splendour, but to suffer and be killed. And when Peter " began to rebuke him ", Jesus not only rebuked Peter with passionate severity, but warned His disciples that if they wished to go with Him to Jerusalem, they must be ready to deny themselves, take up their cross and follow Him. Luke, by adding the words translated " daily ", generalizes the injunction to take up the cross, and by so doing robs the words of their tragic meaning. No man is called " daily " to be crucified, for Jesus meant by " taking up his cross " readiness to endure actual crucifixion, not the endurance of life's usual ills. It would have been well if Judas had heeded the warning and not gone up to Jerusalem for, had he done so, he would not then have betrayed his Master.

All these sayings are related to special circumstances. St. Francis could not have done his great and gracious work among peoples estranged from Christianity by the rapacity of many of its representatives had not his companions, like himself, lived in joyful poverty, free from all attachments. The radiant life of St. Francis and his companions are a priceless treasure, but some who praise the Poor Man of Assisi do so not to honour his Lord, but to discredit Him. To be a Christian, they say, is to live a life such as St. Francis lived. That means that to be a Christian is impossible for almost all, and thus Christianity may be relegated to the realm of lovely fantasy. These sayings of our Lord do imply that He claimed an obedience which may

[1] John xii. 6 ; xiii. 29.

be very costly. Our age has seen this possibility become actual for many, for whom loyalty to Christ suddenly involved the concentration camp. All are called to obey ; not all are called at all times to make such sacrifices. · From the ordinary villagers of Galilee He did not require renunciation of home that they might accompany Him, if need be, to death. Instead, He reminded them of their Father's care, and bade them live their lives without anxiety for to-morrow's food. " Sufficient unto the day is the evil thereof ", which is much the same as our homely English proverb, " Don't trouble trouble till trouble troubles you ".

These sayings of Jesus are not to be interpreted as items in a legal code. What then of the Sermon on the Mount ; is not that a new Law ? In Matthew's Gospel it is so presented as to call to mind the promulgation of the Law at Sinai which, too, was given on a mountain, and yet, even in Matthew's compilation, there is the complete, and not merely, as with some Rabbis, the partial rejection of the idea that man could merit salvation by obedience to the commands of law.

True blessedness is not to be won by the method employed by many to secure worldly success. " It is the poor in spirit " who possess the kingdom, the meek who inherit the earth, the mourners who are comforted, those that hunger and thirst after righteousness who shall be filled, the merciful who shall obtain mercy, the pure in heart who shall see God, the peacemakers who shall be called the sons of God, whilst the persecuted for righteousness' sake are still blessed for theirs is the Kingdom of Heaven. We have here a transformation of values, for all life is judged by its relation to God's character and purpose. The truly blessed are those who seek God's grace, who show His mercy, whose hearts are pure and who are ready, if need be, to suffer persecution because of their loyalty to Him. As Dr. Oman wrote, " Blessedness concerns a gospel and not merely a morality ; and yet it manifests itself as a gospel only as it calls forth a profounder morality ".[1]

There follows the section in which our Lord contrasts the better righteousness, demanded of those who would " enter the

[1] *Grace and Personality* [2], p. 105.

kingdom of heaven ", with the righteousness of the scribes and
Pharisees. In it the commands of the Jewish law are so
deepened as to forbid not only acts of murder and adultery but
thoughts of revenge, all words of contempt and all impure
desires. By some this passage is interpreted as the promulgation of a law of terrible severity, for who is there who can
claim never to have had a revengeful or an impure thought ?
Thus Klausner, writing as a Jew, declares that " Judaism will
never allow itself to reach even in theory the ethical extremeness
characteristic of Christianity ; this extremeness has no place
in the world of reality ". Judaism " could receive into the
Holy Scriptures both the book of Jonah with its love for the
enemy, and the book of Esther with its hate of the enemy.
This fact comes from two deep causes. First, Judaism knows
that the nature of man will always be human nature and not
angel nature. Second, the God of Israel is the God of history ;
and in history there is justice ". So he claims that " Judaism
is a more practical faith than Christianity, it is more capable
of realization in actual life ".[1] It is reported that Kierkegaard once said to a Jewish friend that it was lucky for him that
he (as a Jew) was free from Christ, and in his *Journal* he wrote,
" With God the Father I could get along easier than with the
Son, for He (the Son) is the example that must be followed ".[2]
Certainly, if the sayings in this section are interpreted as
commands, then we are all condemned. " It is well ", as
Barth has said, " that in all ages there have been the so-called
fanatics (*Schwärmer*) who have understood these commands and
the whole Sermon as a law to be literally fulfilled ", for " occasionally some have declared too clearly and confidently that the
radicalizations of the Old Testament Law, formulated in the
examples given in Matt. v. 21–48, are not meant, and are not
to be understood, legally, *i.e.*, not as precepts to be literally
fulfilled by us ". " And yet ", he adds, " it is true that they
are only examples. It is no less true that in these examples it
is made clear that the grace of God, the grace of the Kingdom
of Heaven, which has drawn near, makes a claim upon the whole

[1] *From Jesus to Paul*, p. 609.
[2] W. Lowrie, *Kierkegaard*, p. 123.

man ".[1] This section is not so much the promulgation of a new law, but, as Strack and Billerbeck have shown, the *reductio ad absurdum* of the whole legal conception of God's relationship with men. " By the explanation that He gave of the divine commands, Jesus sought to bring home to the conscience of His hearers that their own power was inadequate to fulfil God's will as God willed that it should be fulfilled ".[2] The section ends with the words, " Ye therefore shall be perfect as your heavenly Father is perfect ", or as St. Luke puts it, " Be ye merciful even as your Father is merciful ".

If, in His extension of the scope of the Ten Commandments, Jesus had been putting forth a new law, on obedience to which our salvation depends, then it would be absurd to speak of His message as a Gospel, for what He taught was in that case not Good News but bad. Who is there anywhere who can say that he has kept these demands ? If Christianity be in this sense a new law, we all alike are damned. But, as we have seen, the section ends not with God the Judge but with God the Father. That means that the whole relationship is changed. A law-giver or judge is concerned with what men do. The children of the heavenly Father have to seek to be what He is. That involves a demand which none of us in this life can perfectly fulfil. We know of One alone who on earth has lived a life of perfect sonship with God. These sayings reveal what perfect sonship is, and, in doing so, uncover our own sin. Yet Christianity, as the Germans say, is *Gabe* as well as *Aufgabe*, a gift as well as a demand. As Brunner puts it, " The indicative of the Divine promise becomes the imperative of the Divine command ".[3] Jesus revealed what God is, and in doing so showed what His children must seek to be.

The Law marked an immense advance on that lawless period when " every man did what was right in his own eyes ".[4] The

---

[1] *Kirchliche Dogmatik*, II. ii. p. 777.

[2] *Kommentar zum neuen Testament aus Talmud und Midrasch*, IV. pp. 1–21.

[3] *The Divine Imperative*, p. 80. Or, as von Hügel used to emphasize, there is an " interaction " between " the *Isness* of Religion " and " the *Oughtness* of Morals ". *Essays and Addresses*, II. p. 164.

[4] Judges xvii. 6.

Law was like a map showing the roads on which men might travel. But God has not willed to give us in Christ such a map. Had He done so, we should not have escaped the complacency of the legalists, for we might then feel that we were finding our own way and earning our own salvation. And since maps grow out of date, we should be again entangled in the sophistries of legalism. Had Jesus brought us " truths ", then we might have advanced beyond Him, as the pupils of a brilliant researcher may advance beyond their teacher. But in Him God has given us not mere " truths " but the Truth. Truths require development and correction, but Christ the Truth never becomes out of date for in every age men find Him, as Kierkegaard used so often to say, their " Contemporary ".[1] He has not provided us with the immediate answers to our modern perplexities. But He remains, and in Him we may know what God is, and what His children must seek to be and do.

We shall have to consider later the application of New Testament Ethics to the " Orders " in which we live—Marriage, Industry and the State.[2] In our discussion it will not be possible to win from the words of Jesus a direct answer to our modern problems.

The Sermon on the Mount condemns divorce. In Matthew's version, and in Matt. xix. 9, divorce is permitted in the case of fornication. This exception is not found in the parallel passages in Mark and Luke,[3] and probably reflects the attempt of the Jewish Christian Church to turn the Divine ideal into a law.[4] The Pharisees came to Jesus asking Him about the lawfulness of divorce. The rival schools of Hillel and Shammai, as Dr. Abrahams says, " differed materially, the former gave the husband a legal right to divorce his wife for any cause ; the school of Shammai limited the right to the case in which the wife was

[1] *Training in Christianity*, (published in 1848) pp. 104 and 9. Cp. p. 38. " In Christianity there is perpetual Sunday twaddle about Christianity's glorious and priceless truths, its sweet consolation ; but it is only too evident that Christ lived 1800 years ago."
[2] See later, pp. 171–259.   [3] Mark x. 11 ; Luke xvi. 18.
[4] For the view that Matthew is to be followed, see R. H. Charles, *The Teaching of the New Testament on Divorce*. For the contrary view, G. H. Box and C. Gore, *Divorce in the New Testament*.

unchaste ".[1] It is significant that our Lord did not base His
answer on an interpretation of the Law about divorce in Deut.
xxiv. 1, which permits the husband to divorce his wife for
" some unseemly thing ".   Instead, He went back to the divine
intention in creating man male and female, so that a husband
" shall cleave to his wife : and the twain shall be one flesh ".[2]
Some there are who for " the kingdom of heaven's sake " have
to renounce marriage and be as " eunuchs ", but nowhere do
our Lord's words imply that the unmarried life is, in itself,
" purer " or " higher " than the married.   The life-long union
of man and wife is an " order of creation " ; that is how God
meant men and women to live.   The Law had, indeed, permitted
divorce but that was due " to the hardness of men's hearts ".
God's children have no need for such a concession and must
conform to God's creative will.   This they can do because,
living by the divine forgiveness, they have learnt to forgive.
To-day, as when the Law was given, there are those whose
hearts are " hard ".   What kind of law ought a sub-Christian
society to make for such ?[3]

The problems of industry and of its rewards are to-day acute.
It is God's intention that we should work to live but who of us
dare claim that the industrial order in which we live is an adequate expression of the divine intention ?   We cannot go out
of that order, whilst abruptly to annihilate it would show not
love but lovelessness.   We may not claim the authority of Christ
for our pet schemes of economic change, for He has left us no
direct commands which would give us here the solution that we
need.   Yet we remember how He condemned those who refused
to respond to others' needs, how He bade us pray for *our* bread
for to-morrow,[4] bread not for ourselves alone, but for others,

[1] *Studies in Pharisaism*, I. p. 71.   Dr. Abrahams adds, " The ' schools '
or ' houses ' of Hillel and Shammai belong to the first century.   It is
uncertain whether this particular difference of opinion goes back to Hillel
and Shammai themselves and thus to the very beginning of the Christian
era."

[2] Matt. xix. 4 f.   Cp. Gen. i. 27 ; ii. 24.

[3] See later, pp. 200–5.

[4] The rare word translated " daily " in the Lord's Prayer seems to
mean " for the coming day ".

and we remember, too, how our Lord warned men against anxiety more than against any other sin. How then can His disciples be content that others should live in conditions of insecurity and poverty which make anxiety almost inevitable.[1]

Most acute of all our problems is the relation of the Christian to the State. Here, too, we may not claim to find in Christ's words the clear and immediate answer to our perplexities. Those whom He addressed lived under a Quisling prince or in an " occupied " land. He disappointed His hearers by bidding them render unto Caesar the things which are Caesar's and unto God the things which are God's. He spoke to men who had not, as we have, some share of responsibility for the action of their Government. We think, for instance, of His parable of the Good Samaritan. In the priest and Levite who, seeing a man wounded by violent men, did nothing about it, lest they should soil their hands and mar their sanctity, we have the prototype of those who thus act to-day. It is not fanciful to see in the Good Samaritan the prototype of those who help others distressed by violence, and who, like those in the Friends' Ambulance Unit and the Red Cross, have sought to assuage the pangs of the wounded. But here the story stops. What of the government official responsible for keeping good order on the road from Jericho to Jerusalem ? Ought he to have been content merely to help those who had fallen among thieves, or should not he, by just force, have put down the robbers and thus made the road safe for travellers ? The story gives us no guidance here, and in our discussion on the Christian attitude to the State we shall not be able to claim the immediate relevance of the words of Jesus.[2]

The significance of our Lord for Christian Ethics may not be confined to the words He spoke. His teaching presupposes the stern teaching of the Old Testament with its demand for social righteousness and its affirmation of the sole supremacy of God, whilst His mission was the climax of God's redemptive acts. The significance of Jesus lies in the *kerugma* as well

[1] See later, pp. 217–21.   [2] See later, pp. 234–8.

as in the *didache*, in the proclamation of what God has done in Him, as well as in the record of what He taught. We know what God has done, and in the deeds, as well as in the words of Jesus, we discern the character of God who is at once our King and our Father. We may receive the Kingdom, experience God's gracious reign, and we are called to live as those who are God's subjects and His children. In one sense we cannot imitate Him. His vocation was to be the Messiah and Saviour, and that vocation excluded those vocations of home and livelihood in which most have to live their lives. Yet His fidelity in His vocation we have to seek to imitate in our very different vocations. The impulse to Christian character comes from what He was, as much as from what He taught and what He was reveals what we must strive to be.

The Gospels end with the story of the Cross and Resurrection. The representatives of religion and of civilization joined together to crucify Him. His disciples, who had listened to His teaching, left Him to face alone His agony; Peter denied Him and Judas betrayed Him. His fidelity to God did not win Him the reward of safety or immunity from suffering. Instead, it led Him to His rejection and a cruel death. I have heard men speak as if love would always melt the hardest heart. Those who thus speak forget that it was Judas who had lived with Jesus and seen His love, who sold Him to His enemies, and enabled them to secure His death. There are times when in our lesser sorrows we find it hard to trust in a heavenly Father's care. At such times we remember the prayer of Jesus in Gethsemane and learn to say after Him, though it be in faltering speech, " Father, not my will but Thine be done ". And when we find it hard to forgive those who have done us wrong, it is not His command that we must forgive of which we chiefly think, but of His prayer upon the Cross, for those that put Him there, " Father, forgive them for they know not what they do ".[1] We remember His promise to the penitent thief and His prayer to the God who seemed to have deserted Him. And God raised Him up. In that Life and Death and

---

[1] Luke xxiii. 34. The prayer is omitted by some ancient texts, but may be confidently accepted as genuine words of Jesus.

Resurrection we find those great redemptive acts of God which inspire that gratitude from which our Christian conduct springs. He is to us not a dead but a living Lord, and His Spirit promised to His Church [1] takes of His words and deeds, and makes them significant for the present as for the past.   In the other books of the New Testament, to which we have now to turn, are shown the amazing changes made in man's lives through their response to God's supreme gift to men in Him.

[1] For the common Christian tradition that our Lord had promised the Spirit, see Acts i. 4 ; ii. 33 ; Gal. iii. 14 ; and cp. John xiv. 16, 26 ; xv. 26.

CHAPTER IV

SOME NEW TESTAMENT
INTERPRETATIONS

T HE Gospels are at once the simplest and the most difficult of the books of the New Testament. They are the simplest, for their narrative of astounding things and their record of the pointed, and often pictorial, teaching of Jesus make an immediate appeal to men and women of every age and at every level of education. And yet these books baffle us by their difficulty. Jesus, as Matthew Arnold said, " was above the heads of His reporters ", and, for all the seeming simplicity of His language, He is above our heads also. We can only partly understand the significance of His career, and we find it hard to be sure how He would have us relate His words to the tasks of our complex modern life. Yet many who are attracted by the Gospels find some of the other books of the New Testament unintelligible and even repellent. Thus the letters of the converted Rabbi Paul show at times the influence of his Rabbinic training, and his involved arguments seem to many modern men tedious and unconvincing. In his eagerness to become all things to all men St. Paul pressed into his service words and ideas familiar to those to whom he wrote, but hard to be understood by those who live not in the first but in the twentieth century. And this difficulty is not confined to the Epistles of St. Paul. Such books as the Epistle to the Hebrews, or the Book of Revelation, cannot be understood without some knowledge, in the one case of Alexandrian Judaism, in the other of the bizarre, and yet conventional, symbols of Jewish Apocalypse.

It is not surprising that some would have us turn at once from the Teaching of Jesus to the problems of our modern world. But the Gospels may not thus be isolated. Much that is implicit in them becomes explicit in the other books of the New Testament. As we seek to relate the significance of Jesus to the moral problems of our time, we have much to learn from those who proclaimed the Christian Gospel not only to Jews but to Gentiles. Their hard task it was to show how the Christian life should be lived not in Palestine alone but throughout the Mediterranean world, and to bring into the unity of the Church those separated by the ancient antagonisms of Jew and Gentile, free-born and slave.

(1) THE FIRST BELIEVERS

It is customary to speak of the Church being " born " on that Day of Pentecost when " the promise of the Father " was fulfilled and the presence of the Spirit realized. But that Church was already founded in the lifetime of Jesus. As we have seen, the hope of a glorified nation had been transformed by Isaiah into the hope of a faithful remnant (*sār*), and by the Prophet of the Exile it was taught that this " remnant " would be the servant of the Lord, fulfilling His purposes even though it be by suffering.[1] When St. Peter confessed Jesus to be the Christ, there was the beginning of the Church, the *ecclesia*. This was that " little flock " to whom it was the Father's good pleasure to give the Kingdom.[2] But when Jesus was crucified, the hope that He was the Messiah faded away. Not till He rose again, did that hope revive and then with a new certainty. On the Day of Pentecost the power of the Spirit was received. The early disciples saw in their experience the fulfilment of the prophecy of Joel, and St. Peter proclaimed the Jesus, whom the Jews had crucified, as both " Lord and Christ ". Very many believed and were baptized. The intense experience found expression in the " speaking with tongues ", uttering sounds of emotional but not of conceptual content. But these first believers were not distinguished by emotion only. " They were steadfastly adhering to the teaching of the apostles and to the

---

[1] See earlier, p. 40.   [2] Luke xii. 32.

fellowship (*koinonia*), to the breaking of bread and the prayers ".[1] From the first, teaching was one of the functions of the Church. Excitement there was, but there was more than excitement; there was the desire to know the truth. The words of Jesus, embodied in the Gospels, owe their preservation to the interest taken in them from the first by those who sought to learn from the Apostles about the words and deeds of this Man whom God had sent, whom now they knew to be the Messiah, their risen Lord and Saviour. These first disciples felt impelled to be together. They adhered steadfastly to the Fellowship, and their sense of belonging together found expression not only in the common meal and in the prayers, but in their eagerness to provide for each other's needs. " And all that believed were together and had all things common; and they sold their possessions and goods and parted them to all, according as any man had need ".[2]

Some have seen in this an early instance of communism. But the case of Ananias and Sapphira shows that no one was compelled to give to others. If this spontaneous generosity be " communism ", then, as Troeltsch says, " It was communism which differed from all other kinds of communism and can only be described as the religious Communism of Love ". " It was a communism composed solely of consumers, a communism based upon the assumption that its members will continue to earn their living by private enterprise, in order to be able to practise generosity and sacrifice ". " There was also no attempt at any organization on business lines such as a joint group of producers would have desired ".[3] Communism seems too formal a word to describe the spontaneous generosity of these first believers. Their newly found faith and joy led them to share, and not to hoard, their possessions. This was not due to any economic theory; it was due to the unity of interest which made the Christian Fellowship like a family in which the needs of any were the concern of all. In the light of their great

[1] This, the translation of C. A. Scott, *The Spirit* (edited by B. H. Streeter), p. 137, seems to represent the meaning better than the R.V.
[2] Acts ii. 44 f. Cp. iv. 32, 34 f.
[3] E. Troeltsch, *The Social Teaching of the Christian Churches*, I, p. 62.

experience, and in their hope of the speedy return of Christ, worldly possessions seemed of little value, except in so far as they provided the means by which the needs of the poor in the Fellowship might be met. Some have thought that this " communism " was responsible for the later poverty of the Church at Jerusalem which made it necessary for St. Paul to raise collections for the " saints " at Jerusalem. But it has to be remembered that Jerusalem was a city of religion, dependent in large measure on the Temple for its wealth, and in Jerusalem then, as in Benares in modern times, it would not have been easy for one who had severed himself from the city's religion to earn a livelihood.

At first the believers in Jerusalem seemed to have enjoyed popular favour and many priests were added to their number. But with the preaching of St. Stephen the radical difference between the new religion and the old became clear. Persecution followed, and the leader of the persecutors was Saul the Pharisee.

(2) THE TEACHING OF ST. PAUL

At St. Paul's conversion the Church gained one uniquely fitted by gifts, experience and early training to become the missionary of Jesus Christ not to Jews alone but to Gentiles. Brought up in Tarsus, he understood the life of those provincial cities in which Christianity was to win its most conspicuous triumphs. If, as seems likely, he had his schooling there, he would have known something of the paganism of the time, its cults and aspirations and of that Stoic philosophy of which Tarsus had had some famous teachers. But it is possible to exaggerate the influence on him of his pagan environment. Little as we know of the paganism of the Tarsus of Paul's youth, Paul's knowledge of it was probably no greater than that which is provided for us by modern scholars.[1] Like other Jews of the

[1] The evidence is set forth in full by H. Böhlig (who exaggerates the influence on Paul of the paganism of his boyhood), *Die Geisteskultur von Tarsos im augusteischen Zeitalter mit Berücksichtigung der paulinischen Schriften.* Cp. the writer's *The Gospel of St. Paul. A Reinterpretation in the Light of the Religion of his Age and Modern Missionary Experience,* pp. 21-5.

Dispersion, he would have learnt to speak Greek and had the Septuagint for his Old Testament, and, although his Greek was influenced by its Hebraisms, he had not, as have modern missionaries, to learn a language, but could use Greek with the ease of one who had spoken it from childhood. Yet, as Paul tells us, his was a strictly Jewish home ; he was a Hebrew of the Hebrews, brought up, that is, in a home where parents and children spoke Aramaic, and his intense devotion to his ancestral faith would have been not less but more because he lived in a pagan city. His interest in religion was not interest in the paganism of his surroundings but in the Judaism which had his devotion. He observed the law with Pharisaic strictness and, in reference to its righteousness, was " blameless ".[1] It was this zealous young Pharisee, this pupil of the famous teacher Gamaliel, who " consented " to St. Stephen's death.

St. Paul gives no explanation of his conversion. It was enough for him that God had called him through His grace and had revealed His Son to him that he might be the apostle to the Gentiles.[2] But those satisfied with their ancestral religion do not change it. Little as we know of the events which preceded his conversion, it is hard to believe that Loisy was right when he said, " The conjecture that Paul, like Luther, had an unquiet soul is entirely gratuitous " ; " Paul gives no evidence at all that he was ill at ease under the Law, that he had anguish of conscience before his conversion, and that he found insufficient the salvation which the Pharisaic faith afforded him ".[3] Although it is true, as Loisy said, that " St. Paul was not one to analyse himself for the benefit of posterity ",[4] yet he has given us evidence that he was ill at ease under the Law. The famous passage in Rom. vii. 7–25, has an intensity which shows that Paul was not writing abstractly but from his own at first bitter, and then glad, experience. He tells us that it was through the Law that he first knew sin. The forbidden becomes the attractive and it was the command, " Thou shall not covet (or lust) ", which gave sin its " occasion ". That was

---

[1] Phil. iii. 5 f. [2] Gal. i. 15 f.
[3] Les Mystères Païens et le Mystère Chretien, p. 324.
[4] Op. cit. p. 305.

a command which affected not acts alone, but feelings. It
may well have been some report of the teaching of Jesus which
brought to him the realization that more than outward obedience was required. No longer could he claim to have earned
salvation for, although he could control his actions, his feelings
he could not control. He willed to do the good but evil was
present with him. Other Jews might feel that, although salvation was to be earned, yet God was merciful. But Paul was
not one who could be content with compromises. For him, as
for Brand in Ibsen's play, if was " all or nothing ". Thus his
very earnestness drove him to despair. " Who shall deliver
me out of the body of this death ? " What if the followers of
Jesus were right ? And yet, if retribution was, as he believed,
the final principle of God's rule, how could a crucified man be
the Messiah ? It is doubt that makes the persecutor, and Paul
persecuted, as he says elsewhere, " exceedingly " the Church
of God. He had his part in Stephen's death and witnessed
Stephen's radiant confidence. For a man of his intense temperament, it was either hate or love. His conflict was resolved ;
in the Man who had been crucified He found His Lord and gave
Him henceforth the intense devotion of his life. Those who had
followed Jesus in His earthly life passed too gradually from
perplexed loyalty to Christian faith to realize to the full the
implicates of their confession that the crucified Jesus was the
Messiah and Lord. But for Paul that discovery not only meant
that he had gained a new Lord ; it involved a radical change in
his conception of God and of God's relationship to men. He
now knew that not law but grace was the full expression of
God's character and purposes, and this discovery made him the
ambassador of God's reconciling word not to Jews alone but to
Gentiles.

St. Paul at his conversion not only gained in the crucified
and risen Lord a new Lord whom it was his delight to serve.
He also experienced God in a new way, and felt within him the
energizing power of the Spirit. His transformed religion meant
a radically different approach to ethics. Religion ceased to be
primarily a demand, and right conduct resulted not from the
strained attempt to obey detailed commands, but from the

response of faith to God's supreme gift to men in Jesus Christ. Paul's ethical teaching can be understood only as it is related to his faith and his experience.

For St. Paul the decisive fact of this Christian experience was this : that God had revealed His Son to him.[1] Henceforth he was Christ's " slave ", belonging to Him, eager at all times to serve Him. To express his relationship with Christ, Paul uses, time after time, a phrase which apparently he coined. He was " in Christ Jesus ", " in the Lord ". The phrase denotes, as Deissmann says, " the most intimate conceivable communion between the Christian and the living Christ ".[2] It was " in the Lord " that he did his work and lived his life and in a moment of exaltation he could even claim " I live, and yet no longer I, but Christ liveth in me ".[3] It is customary to speak of Paul's " Christ-mysticism ". But if mysticism be used of the esoteric experience of a spiritual élite, Paul was not a mystic, whilst if by mysticism we mean the personal experience of spiritual realities, Paul would have all his converts in this sense be " mystics ". As a Jew he had not only sought to win salvation by the way of righteousness ; he had also looked for God's redemption in the coming of the Messianic age. That New Age had dawned. To be a Christian was to share already in its powers. That was not an experience meant only for spiritual adepts. It was for all Christians, and there were those who learned from Paul to enter into this experience. Thus we find Tertius, Paul's amanuensis, who was probably a slave, saluting " in the Lord "[4] the readers of the Epistle he was transcribing. All alike were meant to live in time as in the eternal for the eternal was not now the unknown ; its content was given in Jesus Christ. The Gospel which Paul preached was, like the message of his Lord, a Gospel which spoke, not of forgiveness

[1] Gal. i. 15 f.

[2] *Die neutestamentliche Formel " in Christo Jesu "*, p. 98. Deissmann shows that of the 196 times the phrase occurs in the New Testament 164 are in St. Paul's Epistles (or 155, if we omit the Pastorals).

[3] Gal. ii. 20. What follows is based in part on the writer's *Gospel of St. Paul*, pp. 170–5. [4] Rom. xvi. 22.

only, but of deliverance from bondage to the seen and the temporal. It is a deliverance which on earth is incomplete. But even in this present age, we may look not at the things which are seen but at the things which are not seen, knowing that, while the things we see are transitory, the things that are unseen are eternal [1] and to that unseen world we in part belong for Christ is there and we belong to Him.

The living Christ is known in the historic Jesus. The Lord in whom Paul lived, was one with the Jesus who had been crucified whom many of Paul's fellow-believers had known in His earthly life. He was the One whose " considerateness " and " magnanimity " were known even to the crudest of Paul's converts.[2] Paul's writings were not theological treatises but missionary letters, written to meet the special needs of converts who already knew something of the words and deeds of Jesus. Explicit quotations are naturally few, and yet the influence of the words of Jesus is unmistakable, and his grateful references to the character of Jesus show that his theology was not only that of the cradle and the cross. In " flesh like our flesh ", Jesus yet was sinless ; He was one of " tender mercies " ; even He " pleased not Himself ".[3] The clearest evidence of Paul's knowledge of the character of Jesus is to be found in his famous description of love. Paul was by nature choleric and hypersensitive. The love, the *Agape*, of which he wrote is not the love he found easy to exhibit—it is the love made manifest in Jesus Christ.[4] The supreme expression of that love Paul found in the cross. He " loved me and gave himself up for me ".[5] In these words we may discover the content of Paul's faith and the inspiration of his service.

In the crucified Christ Paul gained a new conception of God as a God of grace. He had thought of Him as the Judge whose commands he found he could not fulfil ; now he knew that the glory of God could be seen " in the face of Jesus Christ ". God had in Christ taken the initiative in reconciliation. " God was

---

[1] Cor. iv. 17 f.

[2] 2 Cor. x. 1. I adopt Anderson Scott's suggestion that ἐπιείκεια should be translated not " gentleness " but " magnanimity ".

[3] Rom. viii. 3 ; 2 Cor. v. 21 ; Phil. i. 8 ; Rom. xv. 3.

[4] 1 Cor. xiii. 4–7.   [5] Gal. ii. 20.

in Christ reconciling the world unto himself, not reckoning "
unto men " their trespasses, and having committed unto us the
word of reconciliation ".[1]   " While we were yet sinners, Christ
died for us ".   That is how God commends His love to men.
All is of God's free grace, for it was while men were hostile to
God that He reconciled them to Himself through the death of
His Son.[2]   Paul uses the legal terms of his Judaizing opponents,
and speaks of God as " just " and " justifying " ; but he uses
them to express a forgiveness which is alien from human justice.
We are justified " freely " ;   God " justifies the ungodly " *i.e.*
" acquits the guilty ".   That is what a judge may not do, but a
father may.   The very strangeness of Paul's terms serves to
remind us of the paradox of forgiveness.   Men had thought they
needed to offer sacrifices to appease an angry God.   Instead,
we know God as " just and justifying " because He has set
forth His Son to be the means of reconciliation.[3]   God freely
forgives those who turn to Him in faith.

To denote his new relationship to God, Paul uses the meta-
phor of " adoption ".   That, too, is a legal term.   Paul uses it
to denote not a legal relationship with God but the reception
of the believer into a life of filial trust and love.   His awe of
God remained, and yet the holy God was the God whom with
childlike confidence he could call Abba, Father.[4]   As Paul's
letters show, he learnt to see God's fatherly care not only in the
work of the Church and the redemption of the race, but in all
the circumstances of daily life.   God was the Father of our
Lord Jesus Christ, and " the God and Father of our Lord Jesus
Christ ", he found to be the " Father of mercies and the God of
all comfort ".   Not only was he confident of God's forgiveness,
he was enabled to find even in sorrow a larger equipment for
service, for God so comforted him in every kind of trouble that

---

[1] 2 Cor. v. 19.

[2] Rom. v. 8 and 10.

[3] Rom. iii. 21–8.   The word translated " propitiation " in our versions
is probably an adjective.   As Dr. Dodd has shown, the word is not used
in the Septuagint in the classical sense of placating a man or a god, but
means expiation in the sense of removing guilt.   So here " the sending
of Christ is the divine method of forgiveness ".   *Comm. in loc.* and cp.
The Bible and the Greeks, pp. 82–95.   [4] Rom. viii. 15.

he was able to comfort others through the comfort he had himself received.[1]

St. Paul described the Christian experience not only as Life in Christ and Adoption into sonship but as the possession of the Spirit, and in this he used the ordinary language of early Christian piety. As we have seen, the great experiences at Pentecost were interpreted as the fulfilment of Joel's prophecy that God would pour His Spirit upon all flesh. The first believers were Jews, and the experience of the Spirit was stabilized by teaching and by prayers. In the Graeco-Oriental world there was the danger that the extraordinary accompaniments of enthusiasm should be more prized than the transformation of character. Paul's raw converts at Corinth could easily have turned Christianity into an orgiastic cult. It must have been a strange Church meeting at which a man could in his ecstasy declare that Jesus was " accursed ", and yet believe that he was inspired by the Spirit. Paul provides the necessary test. No man so speaking was inspired by the Spirit of God.[2] Yet Paul, too, spoke " with tongues ", and would not have such enthusiasm forbidden, but he knew that ecstasy was no test of truth, and bade his converts seek first those gifts which built up the Church and helped to make Christ known, and, above all, to seek the higher gifts of faith and hope, and that love which is the greatest gift of all.

St. Paul relied on the Spirit to produce those fruits which are the tokens of the Christian character. Instead of living " in the flesh ", fulfilling its desires, he and all believers were " in the Spirit ". They were sealed with the Holy Spirit. This possession of the Spirit he describes by a commercial term (ἀῤῥαβών), not Greek but Phoenician in origin, translated in our versions by " earnest ", and denoting a first instalment guaranteeing the delivery of the rest.[3] The possession of the Spirit was the proof that the powers of the age to come were already in part experienced and one day would be fully theirs. The Spirit was not the source of a new revelation. Its possession was the means by which Paul could claim to have " the mind of Christ ".[4]

[1] 2 Cor. i. 3 f.   [2] 1 Cor. xii. 1–3.
[3] Eph. i. 14.   [4] 1 Cor. ii. 16.

The Christian life could be equally well described as a life of faith, or as life in the Spirit, for faith is man's response to the Spirit's work. " Where the Spirit of the Lord is, there is liberty ", but the liberty is not the liberty of license for the revelation which the Spirit gives is a revelation implicit in Christ. The liberty of the Spirit is not the liberty to do what we like, but the liberty to will and to do what is well-pleasing to God. The preaching of Christ, without the experience of the Spirit, might have made Christianity traditional and legal, concerned with the past and not the present, whilst, without its association with Christ, belief in the Spirit's guidance would have led some to fanaticism, and others to a vague religiosity without moral meaning or power.[1] Both these dangers were overcome in Paul's teaching. The Spirit was the Spirit of God and the Spirit of the Lord. The Spirit did not bring a new revelation ; instead, it enabled the revelation of God in Christ to be realized, and gave energy and power to live according to what Christ had taught and done.

In this new experience of adoption into sonship, life in Christ, and the present, though partial, possession of the power and illumination of the Spirit, Paul found the impulse to the Christian life. No longer was he in bondage to the Law. Religion ceased to mean the attempt to earn salvation by obedience to commands and prohibitions ; the obedience he could not render by his own striving became possible when it was the response to his experience of God's grace. Ideally that obedience should have been complete. Paul did not find it so. He uses the strongest terms to describe the self-discipline he required to use, lest, having preached to others, he should be himself disqualified.[2] In what is one of the latest, and may be the last, of his Epistles, Paul the aged, awaiting death in prison, speaks of himself as not " having as yet obtained ", and not being " already made perfect ". Still he had to " press on toward the goal ", seeking to become what God meant him to be.[3]

---

[1] Cp. R. Winkler, *Das Geistproblem*, p. 28, and the writer's *The Gospel of St. Paul*, p. 180. [2] 1 Cor. ix. 24–7.

[3] Phil. iii. 2, with its fierce abuse of the Judaizers, illustrates the imperfection of this loving and yet passionate man.

T.C.W.

St. Paul summoned his converts to become what they already were. As sons, they were " heirs " " heirs of God and joint-heirs with Christ " ; God had foredained them " to be conformed to the image of his Son, that he might be the firstborn among many brethren ".[1] Converts from paganism were no longer aliens but " fellow-citizens with the saints ", members of the household of God.[2] As such, they must be " imitators of God as beloved children ", " blameless and harmless, children of God without blemish ", so living as to shine as " lights " amid the darkness of the world.[3] Christ was their Lord ; let them then seek that love made known in Him—that love without which all other gifts are profitless.[4] Christ " pleased not himself " ; let the strong therefore bear the infirmities of the weak. Let them put " on the Lord Jesus Christ ", clothe themselves with His character, and " make not provision for the flesh, to fulfil the lusts thereof ".[5]

Many of St. Paul's converts came from the dregs of paganism and they lacked the moral discipline which Paul himself, like other Jews, had gained from Judaism. He was under no illusions as to the vices of the pagan world, and yet he sought to meet the needs of his converts not by giving them a code of laws but by urging them to live by the Spirit and to bring forth the fruits of the Spirit. In Galatians Paul puts first among the works of the flesh, fornication, for, like his Master,[6] he condemned not only adultery, which all condemned, but fornication which then, as now, many thought unimportant. But the works of the flesh were not for him only what men call " carnal " sins. They included not only drunkenness, but also idolatry, quarrelsomeness, and outbursts of temper.[7] In another passage, he adds " covetousness the which is idolatry ".[8] " Covetings " also were among the things our Lord said defiled men. A better rendering than " covetousness " ($\pi\lambda\epsilon o\nu\epsilon\xi\iota a$) would be, as Dr. Anderson Scott pointed out, " insatiableness " ; such " absorption and exclusive trust in the material things of life " is " idola-

---

[1] Rom. viii. 17 and 29.   [2] Eph. ii. 19.
[3] Eph. v. 1 ; Phil. ii. 15.   [4] 1 Cor. xiii.
[5] Rom. xiii. 14.   [6] Mark vii. 21 f.
[7] Gal. v. 19 ff.   [8] Col. iii. 5.

try ".[1] With the works of the flesh St. Paul contrasts the fruit
of the Spirit : love, joy, peace, good-temper, kindness, goodness,
fidelity, consideration for others, self-control.[2] Those that live
by the Spirit have no need of Law.

" The natural man ", as Sohm says, " is a born Catholic ",[3]
and converts from paganism then, as now, could more easily
conceive of Christianity as a doctrine to be learnt and a teaching
to be obeyed, than as a creative experience of forgiveness, sonship with God, and life in Christ under the guidance of the
Spirit. To Paul's amazed surprise some of his converts in
Galatia yielded to the propaganda of the Judaizers and, Gentiles
as they were, desired to be circumcised and fulfil the requirements of the Jewish Law. To Paul that seemed a relapse into a
servitude like that of paganism. Obviously Paul was not
referring here to the Law's moral demands. By Law he here
means legalism, the system in which righteousness is regarded
as something to be earned. In this sense Law meant servitude.
It was a tyrant like the spiritual tyrants which were believed to
oppress the pagan world.[4] Paul could not understand how
Gentile converts should put themselves under its bondage.

St. Paul's immediate success might have been greater had he
issued orders to his converts. His Epistles naturally contain,
not doctrinal teaching only, but warnings against the sins
which marred the life of the Churches he had founded, and
exhortations to live the Christian life. But, though he gave
warning and exhortation, he refused to legislate. Instead, he
reminded his converts of the great Christian facts that so they
might be impelled to worthy Christian living.

It is significant that some of St. Paul's greatest statements
of Christian truths—statements which later acquired immense
importance in the development of Christian theology—were
written to secure the performance of ordinary Christian duties.
Thus when he wanted to get Christians at Corinth to give gener-
ously to the collection for the poor at Jerusalem, he does not

---

[1] C. A. Scott, *New Testament Ethics*, p. 114 f.
[2] Gal. v. 22.   [3] *Outlines of Church History*, p. 25.
[4] Gal. iv. 3, 9. τὰ στοιχεῖα, which the A.V. translates " the elements " and the R.V. " the rudiments of the world ", seems to denote
astral spirits. Cp. *The Gospel of St. Paul*, pp. 135 f.

say, " You ought to give such and such proportion of your
income to this good cause ", he writes, " Ye know the grace of
our Lord Jesus Christ that, though he was rich, yet for your
sakes he became poor, that ye through his poverty might
become rich ".[1]

At Corinth at the common meal which preceded the Lord's
Supper, some ate and drank to excess whilst others went hungry.
It was to his rebuke of this vulgar greed that we owe St. Paul's
famous account of the Lord's Supper,[2] whilst it was to warn
his Corinthian converts against fornication that he wrote his
poignant words, " Ye are not your own for ye were bought
with a price ".[3]   At Philippi there was bickering in the Church,
and Paul, to secure the unity of the Christians there, wrote those
sublime words on Christ's self-emptying and exaltation on
which much Christological speculation has been based.[4]

To St. Paul, with his passionate sincerity, the great Christian
facts seemed sufficient to secure Christian character, for Christian faith would be active in Christian love. He discovered
that some of his converts were but " babes in Christ ". They
needed to be fed not with " meat " but " milk ".[5] Against his
wish, the great Apostle of Christian liberty was compelled to
give not only warning and exhortation but definite instruction
on particular issues.   Those whom he thus described as " babes "
were members of the Church at Corinth—the least satisfactory
of all the Churches he had founded. The First Epistle to the
Corinthians is of peculiar interest. In the first six chapters,
Paul has to rebuke the scandals of which he had been informed
—the party-strife, the condonation of an incestuous marriage,
the litigation of Christian against Christian before pagan courts,
and the toleration of fornication, as if it were no more wrong
than eating and drinking. Chapters vii–xv deal with problems
in regard to which the Corinthian Church had consulted him
and these chapters provide a vivid picture of moral weaknesses,
genuine perplexities, the greed shown even at the Lord's Supper,
the disorders in public worship, and the denial by some even of
so fundamental an article of faith as the resurrection of believers.

[1] 2 Cor. viii. 9.   [2] 1 Cor. xi. 23–9.   [3] 1 Cor. vi. 19 f.
[4] Phil. ii. 5–11.   [5] 1 Cor. iii. 1 f.

Against his will Paul was compelled to be a casuist, as every missionary has to be who is responsible for the guidance of immature Christians. Yet, with it all, Paul sought to avoid being a legislator.

St. Paul did not write for anchorites or monks but for those called to live the Christian life in their homes, in the environment of a pagan society and under a pagan government, and to do so as those within the Christian Fellowship. It is instructive to see how he related the Gospel to these aspects of the life of his converts.

Life in the home means for Christians life in a mutual loyalty which excludes sexual relations outside marriage. That to us is a truism ; it was not so regarded by converts from paganism brought up to regard sexual indulgence as a natural concomitant of manhood. Time after time, St. Paul had to warn Christians against fornication. God willed their sanctification, and that meant that they must abstain from fornication. Let each man live with his own wife in sanctification and honour. So Paul wrote in what seems to be the earliest of his extant letters.[1]

The Graeco-Oriental view that matter was evil led not only to license but to asceticism. In the Church at Corinth both these tendencies were found. The scandals with which St. Paul had to deal included, as we have seen, that of an incestuous marriage. St. Paul bade the congregation meet together for the expulsion of the offender from the Church.[2] In a letter which is not extant, he had urged the Corinthian Christians " to have no company with fornicators ". He explains that he did not mean that they should not associate with pagans who were fornicators, for then must they " needs go out of the world ". But fornicators could not be allowed to remain within the Christian Fellowship.[3]

One of the problems on which the Church at Corinth had

[1] Thess. iv. 3 f., interpreting as " wife " the word translated in our versions by " vessel " (σκεῦος)—a vulgar usage for which there are Rabbinic parallels.

[2] 1 Cor. v. 1–5. From 2 Cor. ii. 5–11 it appears that later he repented and with Paul's approval was readmitted.

[3] 1 Cor. v. 9–13. It is possible that 2 Cor. vi. 14–vii. 1 is part of the lost letter.

written to St. Paul for his advice was that of marriage. Some
Christians there, though married, had abandoned normal marriage relationships, and others thought they ought to remain
unmarried. St. Paul was compelled to give a ruling, but he
did so with much reluctance and with unusual hesitancy. He
himself was too absorbed in his work to feel the need for marriage,
and he could wish that others were as he was. But each man
had his own grace-gift from God, and must act accordingly.
He advised his converts that they were better married and, if
married, should not run into temptation by refraining for more
than short periods from conjugal intercourse. He reminded
the married of our Lord's prohibition of divorce, and forbade
a husband to leave his wife, or a wife her husband, even although
the other partner in marriage was a pagan. In regard to the
unmarried, Paul's own feeling was that it would be well for
them, if they could, to remain unmarried.[1]

There follows St. Paul's answer to the question about
" virgins ". In the second and third centuries the Church had
to condemn the " spiritual " marriage in which a man and a
woman lived together, but as brother and sister, not as man
and wife. Some have thought that such " spiritual " marriages
existed in the Corinthian Church. It seems improbable that
Paul, who had warned married couples of the peril of any pro-
longed interruption of marriage relationships, would have
tolerated a custom so provocative of temptation. He is careful
to state that he had " no commandment of the Lord ". If
virgin or widow wished to marry, let her do so, but his own
judgment was that it was better to make no change. The reason
he gave is significant. It was not because marriage is a lower
state than celibacy. It was, to use the translation of the
Revised Version, " by reason of the present distress ", *i.e.*
because of the impending Tribulation. When Paul wrote this
letter, he was expecting ᵗhe speedy return of Christ, and
believed that that return would be preceded by a great Tribulation. Since all human relationships would thus soon be at an
end, it would be better to face the time of trouble without the
cares that family life involves.

[1] 1 Cor. vii. 1–24.

St. Paul retained to the end his belief that the Day of the Lord was at hand, and yet the thought of the end of the age ceased to dominate his thought, and he no longer looked for it to come within his own lifetime. The Christian home thus gained a new significance, and in two of the Epistles written when he was a prisoner in Rome, St. Paul speaks again of the relation of husband and wife, parents and children. The deference of wives to husbands was fitting " in the Lord ", and husbands were bidden to " love their wives and be not bitter against them ". Children are told to be obedient to their parents, to their mothers as well as to their fathers ; but parents must not " provoke " their children, lest they be " discouraged ".[1] The relationship of husband and wife is used to express Christ's relationship with the Church—a sure sign that Paul did not regard that relationship as something impure, differing from that of lust only by being legalized ; husbands were bidden to love their wives even as Christ had loved the Church, and given Himself up for it. Husbands and wives are " one flesh ". Let each man love his wife even as himself.[2]

The Christian life had to be lived not only in the home but in the social structure of that age. Some Christians were slave-owners ; more were slaves. In 1 Corinthians, the expectation that Christ would speedily reappear, made Paul think of slavery, like other secular institutions, as of only transient importance. As a man was, so he should remain. Before Christ there was no difference. In Him free men were bound and slaves were free men.[3] In the " House Rules " of his later Epistles, slaves are bidden to obey their masters as " fearing the Lord ", and masters to " render to their servants that which is just and equal " as those who know they have themselves " a Master in heaven ".[4] Masters must refrain from threatening their slaves. Masters and slaves have a master in heaven, and " there is no respect of persons with him ".[5] How little social distinctions counted with Paul is shown in his letter to Philemon. Philemon's slave, Onesimus, like the typical slave of Roman comedy, had robbed his master and fled to Rome. There he had some-

---

[1] Col. iii. 18–21. [2] Eph. v. 22–5. [3] 1 Cor. vii. 21–4.
[4] Col. iii. 22–iv. 1. [5] Eph. vi. 9.

how met Paul, been converted by him, and thus become his
" child ", begotten in his bonds. Paul would have liked to
keep him with him ; instead, he sent him back to his Christian
master with a lovely little letter in which he told Philemon that
Onesimus who had been " unprofitable " was now what his
name denoted, " profitable ", and offered to make good what
Onesimus had stolen and begged Philemon to receive him, not
as a slave, but as a " brother beloved ".[1] Paul had had " much
joy and comfort " in Philemon's love ; let him receive Onesimus
as he would have done Paul to whom he had owed his own
conversion.

The Christian life had to be lived within the framework
of the Roman State. Paul had spoken to his converts of their
liberty in Christ, and liberty could easily lead to insubordination.
Some in his congregations were of Jewish stock and among
Jews there was already that political unrest which later cul-
minated in the Jewish rebellion. When Christians at Thes-
salonica had used Paul's teaching of the Second Coming of Christ
as an excuse for idleness, he had bidden them to get back to
work. The end was not yet. Before Christ returned, Antichrist
would appear, and that could not be so long as Antichrist was
kept in check by the restraining power. He thus in this Epistle
regarded the Roman Empire as the means by which for the
time peace was maintained.[2] Writing several years later to
the Church at Rome, he bade its members be in subjection to
the government. The State was the instrument of what Paul
calls " the Wrath "—that inexorable principle of retribution
which, although it does not adequately represent the character
of God, yet by His appointment rules over those not redeemed
by Christ. The State secured order and a measure of peace,
and he bade men pay their taxes in words which seem to reflect
the command of Jesus about rendering to Caesar the things
which are Caesar's and to God the things which are God's.[3]
The little groups of Christians he addressed had no responsi-

---

[1] John Knox in his *Philemon among the Letters of St. Paul*, suggests
that Onesimus became the Bishop of Ephesus whom Ignatius describes
as " a man of inexpressible love ". Ignatius, *To the Ephesians*, I. If
so, he did, indeed, become " profitable ".

[2] 2 Thess. ii. 1–9.   [3] Rom. xiii. 1–7.

bility for the action of the State. What they were responsible for was the condition of the Christian Fellowship.

Christians were not called to live their Christian life in solitariness. Instead, they were called to live as members of the Church and to do so worthily. For St. Paul the Church was " the Israel of God " in contrast with " the Israel after the flesh ".[1] Our Lord had called His disciples the " little flock ", a phrase suggestive of the reference in Isaiah to the " Remnant " who should be faithful. St. Paul identifies this " remnant " with the Church,[2] and uses words which suggest that the Church is the suffering Servant of the Lord.[3] The Church is one because it is the Church of the one God. He speaks of it as the body of Christ,[4] or as the body of which Christ is the head.[5] So strongly was the unity of the Church realized that the persecution of any of its members was the persecution of " the Church of God ".[6] It was Paul's great ambition to make the Church what it ideally was, and this childless man lavished his affection on the churches he had founded and had in them the supreme joy and sorrow of his life. He strove to make the Church indeed a fellowship where love was the only law, and where secular differences of race or sex or status ceased to divide. Jew and Gentile, slave and free, male and female ; all were one in Christ Jesus.[7] The strong must bear the burden of the weak the enlightened be tolerant of the prejudices of the over-scrupulous, and abstain from things indifferent, if thereby they could avoid causing their brethren to stumble.[8] St. Paul felt himself " debtor both to Greeks and to Barbarians, both to the wise and the foolish ". At all costs he must preach the Gospel to all whom his words could reach, but he was not a Hebrew prophet, feeling responsible for a nation's actions and denouncing its social evils and political blunders. Instead, he was the missionary leader of obscure congregations, having no responsibility for the secular affairs of the great world outside the Church, and desiring from the State only those conditions of stability and

---

[1] Gal. vi. 16.   [2] Rom. ix. 27.   [3] Col. i. 24.
[4] 1 Cor. xii. 12 ff. ; Rom. xii. 4 ff.
[5] Eph. iv. 15.   [6] Gal. i. 13.   [7] Gal. iii. 28.
[8] e.g. of food offered to idols (1 Cor. viii. 10–13 ; x. 23–33), of vegetarianism and Sabbatarianism (Rom. xiv. 1–8).

peace which would enable the Gospel to be preached, and the Church's task fulfilled. His situation is not ours ; we have a responsibility for social and international justice such as no Christian of Paul's time had. But had the Church become, and remained, what St. Paul sought for it to be, the life of the Church would be a witness, more powerful than any political action, to the possibility of a society bound together by faith and hope and love.

As we have seen, the teaching of Jesus was concerned with the Kingdom of God ; St. Paul refers only occasionally to the Kingdom of God, and speaks much more of Christ's Cross and Resurrection. Some have supposed that St. Paul refrained from speaking of the Kingdom for prudential reasons. The Roman Empire was ready to tolerate Christianity as yet another oriental religion, until at length it discovered that the loyalty Christians gave to Christ was incompatible with that Caesar-worship which was to become a test of loyalty to the State. At no time would it have been ready to tolerate a rival sovereignty, and this the words, " Kingdom of God ", might be understood to imply. That may account in part for the paucity of Paul's reference to the Kingdom of God, and yet, as Paul did not entirely avoid that phrase, this explanation seems inadequate. It was not a matter of mere expediency. Christ crucified and risen was for him a more poignant expression of his own faith, and, at the same time, a summary of the Gospel more intelligible to converts from paganism who, unlike Jewish converts, were not looking for the coming of the Kingdom. The days are gone when Paul could be regarded as too indifferent to the earthly life of Jesus to trouble to gain knowledge of His words. Occasional as are his letters, they show an unmistakable acquaintance both with the words and character of the earthly Jesus. Why then did he not use more the phrase which more than any other sums up the teaching of Jesus as recorded in the Synoptic Gospels ?

If the Kingdom of God be interpreted as an earthly Utopia, which Christians are called to " build ", " create " or " extend ", then, indeed, there would be an irreconcilable contradiction between the ethical teaching of Paul and of his Master. But for Jesus the Kingdom meant not a realm but a rule ; it was, as we have seen, a periphrasis for God regnant and redemptive.[1] It is something we may " find ", " receive " or " enter into ", not something we " create" or " extend ". It was in the Cross and Resurrection that God's kingly rule has been most clearly manifested. We live in a world where acts go on to their effects, where retribution is a reality, where what a man sows that he also reaps. And yet the retributive order in which we live is not the full expression of the character of God. God is a God of grace, of love (*agape*), and the Cross is the final expression of that grace and love, and so the inspiration of Christian faith and the greatest incentive to Christian character and conduct. That Cross is the vivid expression of God's forgiveness, the supreme manifestation of a love which will not let us regard our sin as unimportant. That love of Christ has constraining power, and, since He died for all, we may not willingly harm our neighbour for he, too, is " the brother for whose sake Christ died ". Free, we are in bondage, for we are not our own, we are " bought with a price ".[2] From that love of God which is in Christ Jesus our Lord, nothing in life or death, or external circumstances can separate us. We can be " more than conquerors through him that loved us ".[3] These are tremendous claims. The influence of them can be traced not only in Paul's service but in the service of devoted Christian men and women in every age. And the proof that God so reigns Paul found in Christ's Resurrection. Because of that Resurrection, he could bid even his Corinthian converts be " steadfast, unmovable, always abounding in the work of the Lord " as those that know that their " labour is not in vain in the Lord ". [4] Proclamation and teaching, *kerugma* and *didache*, are thus one. The primitive Christian creed of Christ's Death and Resurrection, which formed the essential elements of the Proclamation, was, at the same time, the supreme impulse and test of that Christian character which the teaching of Jesus described and enjoined.

[1] See earlier, p. 39.
[2] 2 Cor. v. 14 ; 1 Cor. viii. 11 ; Rom. xiv. 15 ; 1 Cor. vi. 19 f.
[3] Rom. viii. 37 ff.   [4] 1 Cor. xvi. 58.

(3) THE FIRST EPISTLE OF ST. PETER

Great as was the contribution of St. Paul to the application
of the Gospel to the varied needs of the ancient world, we may
not so isolate his teaching as to forget that in its essentials he
was speaking not for himself alone, but for many within the
Church of his time.   The First Epistle of St. Peter is an illustration of this common faith.   Written, as we may believe, for
St. Peter by Silvanus (Silas) [1] from Rome to Christians scattered
throughout Asia Minor, this lovely little letter shows the clear
impress of the character of Jesus and the power of His example
to inspire ordinary men and women to be loyal to Him, even
though loyalty meant suffering, and to be so not only with courage
but with joy :—" whom not having seen ye love ; on whom,
though now ye see him not, yet believing, ye rejoice greatly
with joy unspeakable and full of glory ". [2]   Once they had lived
in pagan lusts ; now they were redeemed by the precious blood
of Christ.   As such must they live.   Pagans as they had been,
they were now " a royal priesthood, a holy nation " ; let them
so live among their pagan neighbours that they too may learn
to glorify God.   Christians were already suspected and slandered
and yet they must not give way to resentment and insubordination.   Let them be submissive to the Emperor, and to the
provincial governors whose task it was to restrain the evil and
reward the good.   In Christ they were free, and yet they must
not use their freedom as a pretext for wrong-doing for they were
the servants of God.   Let them honour all men ; love the
brotherhood ; reverence God and honour the Emperor. [3]

Some whom Peter addressed were house-slaves, and thus
subject to the capricious cruelty of pagan masters.   Even if
they were unjustly punished, they must bear it patiently for
Christ also suffered, leaving an example, and by His stripes we
are healed.   There were women married to husbands who were
pagans ; let them so live in modesty and gentleness that their
husbands might be gained.   And Christian husbands ought so

---

[1] v. 12—this would account for what has seemed to some the strongest
argument against Peter's authorship—the excellence of its Greek.
         [2] i. 8.   [3] ii. 9–18.

to live with their wives that their prayers together might not be hindered.[1]   Christians might have to suffer for their faith. If they suffered not for wrong-doing but for loyalty, let them glorify God.[2]   The letter ends, apart from the salutation, with the words, " to him be the dominion for ever and ever ".   On earth there was persecution, but still God reigned, and even in persecution He could be trusted and obeyed.

(4) THE EPISTLE TO THE HEBREWS

The Epistle to the " Hebrews " was also written to confirm the faith of Christians tempted to abandon a Christianity which some thought too costly.   Written at a time when the Old Testament had become the Bible of the Church, its writer sought to demonstrate the unique dignity of Christ and the perfect adequacy of the Christian religion.   This " word of exhortation " speaks of those who in the past had been loyal in all difficulties, and its readers are bidden to remember again Jesus " the pioneer and perfecter " of their faith, who had endured the Cross and despised the shame.   They had received a Kingdom which cannot be moved ; let them therefore serve God with reverence and awe ; helping one another in their needs, and in purity of life be ready to bear the reproach of Christ.[3]

(5) THE EPISTLE OF ST. JAMES

No book of the New Testament is so exclusively ethical in its teaching as this Epistle.   If its author was James, the brother of our Lord, then it was probably a very early book written before the Epistles of St. Paul.[4]   More probably, it was written by another James, a teacher of the Church, who, as Dr. Moffatt said, wrote " this tract for the special purpose of recalling Christians to the *agenda* of their faith ".[5]   He warns his readers against instability, and denounces the social snobbery which

---

[1] iii. 1–7.   [2] iv. 16.   [3] xii. 28–xiii. 13.
[4] If so it was probably addressed to Jews of the Dispersion, as Dr. A. T. Cadoux suggests : *The Thought of St. James*, pp. 10–18.
[5] *The General Epistles*, p. 3.

flattered the rich ; refers at length to sins of speech, to worldliness, pride and avarice, and the tract ends with an appeal to seek to save the sinner. Very famous is its attack on faith apart from works.[1]   The phrase is St. Paul's, but not the meaning ; Paul meant by faith the personal response to the grace of God in Christ—a faith which leads inevitably to obedience and to love. A faith which is " dead " would have seemed to Paul no faith at all. Doubtless, as James says, the demons also " believe and tremble ", but the belief that God is, which demons also hold, is not what Paul meant by faith. Yet, as the history of the Church shows, there are always some who think of faith as mere assent, and the Epistle of St. James remains as a needed warning against every attempt to make religion a substitute for goodness. How necessary such a warning was is shown by the evidences of antinomianism which the New Testament itself affords. The opening chapters of Revelation, the Pastoral Epistles, Jude and 2 Peter alike had to condemn the lawlessness of some who claimed the Christian name and yet lived loveless and licentious lives.

(6) THE JOHANNINE WRITINGS

The First Epistle of St. John

The most deadly peril came to Christianity not from Jewish legalism, or from Roman Caesar-worship, but from the " Gnosticism " of those who, using Christian terms, sought so to " improve " Christianity as to rob it of its essential meaning. The Christian proclamation of the Son of God become for our sakes man and dying like a crucified criminal upon the Cross, seemed to many in the pagan world not only incredible but ridiculous. Graeco-Orientalism regarded matter as evil. How then could one truly divine become incarnate ? The Christian proclamation seemed to such a childish tale, and there were those within the Church who sought to make the Gospel more impressive by adapting it to the culture of the age. Ordinary Christianity might do well enough for ordinary Christians, but it was too crude for those who prided themselves on their

[1] ii. 14–16, and 26.

gnosis, their " Knowledge ". Since spirit and matter were opposed, some sought to free themselves from the material by asceticism,[1] whilst others, holding that things done by the body could not affect the self, spoke as if it did not matter what their body did ; they themselves did not sin.   It was this that aroused John's indignation, and accounts for the apparent contradiction of his words.   " God is light and in him is no darkness at all. If we say that we have fellowship with him, and walk in darkness, we lie, and do not the truth ".   " If we say we have not sinned, we make him a liar ", for the Gospel is a message addressed to sinful men who need forgiveness.[2]   Yet elsewhere John says, " Whosoever abideth in him sinneth not ; whosoever sinneth hath not seen him, neither knoweth him ".[3]   The contradiction is resolved as we remember the false teaching John was seeking to combat.   Those who claimed to have a superior Christianity could say, " We do not sin, for nothing done in the body can affect the self of the man who has *gnosis* ".   Against this comes John's rebuke.   To say we have no sin is self-deception.   But the Gnostic could also say, " What does it matter what I do ? By my illumination I have passed into a realm where deeds are of no importance, so I can sin if I like, and still be a Christian ". But that, says John, is what a Christian may not do.   We cannot claim to be the children of God and yet be content to indulge in sin.   " God is righteous ", and righteousness is the test by which we may know whether we are begotten of him.[4] To this test of righteousness, John adds the test of love.   We may know whether " we have passed out of death into life ", by this, do we love our brethren ?   We know what love is : " He laid down his life for us, and we ought to lay down our lives for the brethren ".   The letter was written during a lull in persecution, when there might be no occasion to show love in the extreme form of martyrdom.   John adds a homelier test of more general application.   If we see our brother in need and refrain from giving him help, how can we claim to have the love of God ?   Fine words are not enough ; we have to love in deed

[1] Cp. 1 Tim. iv. 3 (" forbidding to marry and commanding to abstain from meats ").

[2] i. 5–10.   [3] iii. 6–10.   [4] ii. 29.

and truth.[1]   Useless is it to speak of knowing God if we do not
show love, for God is love.   The absolute of love is to be seen
not in any love of ours but in the love of God who sent His Son
to be the means of our salvation.   As God loved us, so must we
love.   We may not claim that we love God if we do not show
love to the brother whom we have seen and whom we can
help.[2]

To the tests of righteousness and love John adds the test of
right belief.[3]   Regarding matter as evil, the Gnostics denied the
reality of the Incarnation, and refused to believe that the
Divine could have endured so shameful an experience as that of
crucifixion.   The earthly Jesus and the heavenly Christ were
two, not one.   The earthly Jesus was a good man on whom the
heavenly Christ—one of the many aeons who bridged the gulf
between the supreme God and the world of men—had descended
at his baptism but left him before the crucifixion.   Such an
interpretation robbed the Gospel of its saving power.   Those
who are begotten of God are meant to overcome the world—to
expel from their lives the notes of the pagan world around them :
sensuality and selfishness (the lust of the flesh), covetousness
and ostentation (the lust of the eyes), the overprizing of material
success (the vain glory of life).[4]   For that victory we need the
fullness of the Christian faith—to believe that Jesus is the Son
of God, and that the Son of God came " not with the water only
but with the water and with the blood ".   The Son of God was
not a visitant on earth untouched by sorrow and shame ; He
died for men upon the Cross.[5]

This Epistle ends with the words, " Guard yourselves from
idols "—keep yourselves from all false substitutes for God.
These words may be the last which have come down to us from
any who had seen our Lord on earth ;[6] the events of recent
years provide a grim commentary on their solemn warning.

---

[1] iii. 14–18.   [2] iv. 7–2.
[3] Cp. the title of R. Law's suggestive exposition of this Epistle, *The
Tests of Life.*   [4] ii. 15 f.   [5] v. 4 ff.
[6] Many scholars believe it was written by John the Elder who as a
young man had known Jesus in Jerusalem.   The words of the opening
verses seem to speak of actual, and not merely mystic, seeing of Christ,
" the Word of life ".

The Gospel of St. John

In the Gospel of St. John the Christian revelation finds consummate expression in simple and familiar words like Light and Life and Truth and Love, which yet prove of inexhaustible significance. " God so loved the world that he gave his only begotten Son, that whosoever believeth on him should not perish but have eternal life "[1]—these words are a summary not only of this Gospel but of the Good News itself. The love of God is manifested in the love of the Son. He was the good Shepherd ready to lay down His life for His Sheep.[2] The commandment, " Thou shalt love thy neighbour as thyself ", has gained a new and deeper meaning for the love enjoined is the love Christ showed. " This is my commandment, that ye love one another, even as I have loved you ".[3] That love must show itself in simple, humble service. As Jesus washed His disciples' feet, even so must His disciples serve one another.[4]

St. John has been called the Apostle of love, and in Christian art he has often been depicted as gentle and, indeed, effeminate. That is due to a misunderstanding of this Gospel. No book of the New Testament puts more sternly the antithesis between good and evil, light and darkness. Christ's coming meant " crisis ", judgment, and the narrative depicts how men and classes judged themselves by their attitude to Him and their sin was not merely foolishness. They had both " seen and hated " both Him and His Father.[5] From those who believed in Him was required a love which was not sentimentality but the love which obeyed His word. Only as men abide in His word, can they be truly His disciples, and they alone shall know the truth, and by the truth be made free.[6] The disciples, who do the things which He commands them, are those whom He calls His friends and to whom He reveals His secret.[7]

This obedience is not to a detailed law. Christ promised to His disciples the Spirit of truth, who would bring to their remembrance all that He had taught them and guide them into all truth, bringing no new revelation, but making clear to them the meaning of His words and deeds.[8]

[1] iii. 16.   [2] x. 11.   [3] xv. 12.   [4] xiii. 13 ff.
[5] xv. 24.   [6] viii. 31 f.   [7] xv. 14 f.   [8] xvi. 13 ff.

T.C.W.

PART II

METHODS AND MOTIVES

CHAPTER V

THE METHOD AND SCOPE OF CHRISTIAN ETHICS

BRIEF and inadequate as has been our survey of Biblical Ethics, it should at least suffice to show that the New Testament knows nothing of a "simple teaching of Jesus" which has only to be systematized to provide the solution of all our problems. Many of our problems receive in the New Testament not only no solution but no attention. Were the Jesus of the New Testament merely that supreme Teacher whom many modern scholars have depicted, that would seriously affect our estimate of His significance, for His teaching, as teaching, seems not only irrelevant but self-contradictory. The words of Jesus were remembered and prized by the writers of the New Testament but we cannot depict Him simply as a teacher without departing radically from their estimate of Him. As Dr. F. R. Barry has said, " Any discussion of Christian Ethics starts from mistaken premisses, if it begins, as so many discussions do, by collecting the sayings in the Synoptic Gospels, grouping them under various headings and then proceeding to 'apply' them to contemporary moral perplexities. Because, frankly, they will not apply. They belong to His world, not to ours ".[1] We cannot in this sense compile a summary of " Christian Ethics ", and claim for it the allegiance of modern men. The world into which Jesus came was not lacking in moral philosophy or ethical admonition, and the uniqueness of the Christian Gospel is not to be found in the nobility of its ideals but in its story of what God has done for men in Christ's Life and Death and Resurrection.

The Jews among whom Jesus lived had already learnt to think of God as just and holy, and belief in the righteousness of

[1] *The Relevance of Christianity*, pp. 72 f.

God remains as the presupposition of the Christian message. Already some had learnt the necessity not only of just action, one to another, but of a love which showed itself in forgiveness.[1] Our Lord did not need to tell men to " be good ". Instead, as we have seen, He summoned them to " enter into " or " receive " the Kingdom of God, to come, that is, into a relationship with God in which God is known and experienced as King and Saviour. Even the twelve disciples were baffled by Him. He was a teacher, but they could not understand His teaching ; they saw Him heal the sick, they heard Him speak of God's power and God's forgiveness. At length, St. Peter saw in Him the Messiah, but he could not conceive that the Messiah would accomplish His work in suffering. Yet the Cross, which was at first the end of the disciples' hopes, became luminous with a new and gracious meaning. The Resurrection proved Him to be the agent of God's salvation, and they discovered that the way of the Cross was, indeed, the way which God approved. The words of Jesus had now a new significance for they were not prized merely as the sayings of a great teacher ; instead, they had the authority of One whom they knew to be their risen Lord, and whom they came to confess as the Son of God. The Christian message was not Good Advice ; it was News, Good News of God. Even the words of Jesus were preserved in the context of His deeds. The compiler of St. Matthew's Gospel might bring together sayings of Jesus so that the Sermon on the Mount looks, at first sight, like a Christian counterpart of the Law given at Sinai. Yet even the Sermon on the Mount, as we have seen, is not a new law ; instead, it involves an abandonment of the legal conception of religion, for the disciples of Jesus are called not merely to do what God commanded but to be like their Father in heaven. And in the Epistles the most moving appeals for Christian character spring not from the reiteration of commands of Jesus but from the recital of what Christ was, of what He suffered and of what God had done in Him.

Since the New Testament is more concerned with what God has done than with what men ought to do, it is not possible to

[1] See earlier, p. 32.

speak adequately of Christian Ethics except in relation to the Christian facts. The Teaching is dependent on the Story; it cannot be understood except in relation to these great redemptive acts of God which the New Testament proclaims.

But if this be so, certain problems immediately emerge:

(1) What is the relation of Christian Ethics to other ethical teaching?

(2) If Christian Ethics be dependent on Christian faith, is there a moral obligation resting upon all; in more technical language, is there a Natural Law the recognition of which makes possible the co-operation of Christians and non-Christians in the quest for justice within and without the nation?

(3) If Christian Ethics cannot be systematized, what is its sphere and function?

(1) THE RELATION OF CHRISTIAN ETHICS TO OTHER ETHICAL TEACHING

In a very suggestive article Professor E. S. Waterhouse has pointed out the loss sustained in the study of Christian Ethics by its isolation from " other ethical systems, either those of the moralists or of the non-Christian religions ", and the no less loss suffered by General Ethics from this separation. " Whether we like it or not, it remains that the ethics of modern Europe are to be understood only in the light of the profound influence which Christianity has had upon them. If they react against Christian standards, it does not alter the fact that the reaction must be measured with reference to those standards. Yet the unhappy division of secular and sacred has led to the methodological blunder of approaching modern ethics with no special reference to its principles. In this country for the last fifty years, the young student of ethics has usually started with the familiar text-books of Muirhead or Mackenzie. Muirhead has three incidental references to Jesus in his book and none to St. Paul. Mackenzie makes one reference to Jesus, remarking that He was neither recluse nor ascetic, and quotes St. Paul twice. But Mill is referred to eighteen, and Kant nineteen times, often at length. If we ask ourselves which has had the greater influence upon both the theory and the practice of morals, the Sermon on the Mount, or what Carlyle called the ' pig-philosophy ' of Hedonism, the Epistle of St. Paul or the *Critique of Pure Reason*, the absurdity of such disproportion leaps to the eyes ".[1]

For this separation there are many reasons. As, Dr. Waterhouse himself points out, " Morality at last resort depends upon the philosophy of life which underlies it ". And many books on General Ethics are written by men whose philosophy of life is not compatible with Christianity. The Christian Ethic cannot be presented simply as a system of moral demands. Not even the Teaching of Jesus can thus be isolated and systematized. The Christian Ethic rests on historical facts. It shows what men must do in connexion with what God has done, and, until there is a readiness to explore the Christian facts, there cannot be an understanding of Christian Ethics. But it ought in fairness to be added that the moralist desiring to understand the significance of Christian Ethics is inevitably perplexed by the difficulty of determining what Christian Ethics is. Christians differ at least as much in regard to Christian Ethics as they do in regard to Christian Theology and, until there is a greater consensus of opinion, we have little right to complain that Christian Ethics is misunderstood, or ignored, by many who write on morals.

A great New Testament scholar has said, " The unchanging element in our religion has been its ethical teaching. Its doctrines have been variously understood in every generation ; its institutions and ritual have assumed many forms and have given rise to countless divisions. But the ethical demands have never varied. They were set forth two thousand years ago, and, in the interval, the whole framework of man's life has been remodelled, but they are still valid in practically their whole extent for all sections of the Church. It is this permanence of the moral teaching which has secured the identity of the religion

[1] *Ethics and Christian Ethics* in *Philosophy*, April 1943.

amid all changes ".[1]   If this claim could be accepted, the writer on Christian Ethics would have an easier task, for it would then be sufficient to describe that moral teaching which has always, everywhere, and by everybody, been accepted as Christian.   In every age where the Gospels have been known and prized, the words of Jesus have indeed shown their strange power to drive men to penitence, aspiration, hope and love.   But it cannot rightly be claimed that " the ethical demands have never varied ", or that these demands have been identical with those " set forth two thousand years ago ".

Some continuity there has been throughout the Christian centuries, for the remembrance of God's gift to men in Christ has at no time been completely lost.   Christian parents have told their children of God and of His Son, and the Church, even in the darkest ages, has borne witness to Him by Scripture, Sacrament and public worship.   No century, and no section of the Church, has a monopoly of those who, as St. Bonaventura said of St. Francis, have lived " a life of sacrifice inspired by the desire to pay back somewhat unto Christ who died for us, and to stir up others to the love of God ".   The faithful followers of Jesus recognize each other across the ages, and feel themselves one in Him.   But even Christians of the same generation have differed much in their conceptions of His ethical demands. Tertullian and Clement of Alexandria, St. Augustine and Julian of Eclanum, Melanchthon and St. Ignatius of Loyola, Joseph Butler and John Wesley, Cardinal Newman and R. W. Dale of Birmingham—how varied is the conception of the Christian life these great names recall, and how much each differed from his contemporary in his interpretation of the ethical demands of Christianity.   There has been, and is, at least as much difference among Christians on questions of ethics as on questions of theology, and, since differences in moral demands have a more obvious relation to practical issues, these differences are more acutely realized than are differences in theology.

On the history of theology there is no lack of adequate textbooks and monographs.   The influence on the formulations of theology of current philosophy and praxis, has long been

[1] E. F. Scott, *The Ethical Teaching of Jesus*, p. ix.

realized so that it is possible to distinguish the *kerugma*, the Christian proclamation, from the intellectual expressions of it which have varied from age to age. The interrelation of Christian Ethics to current culture has been far less adequately explored and, admirable as are some of the histories of Christian Ethics,[1] much still remains obscure. History affords many an instance of the blindness of Christians in the past to what seem to us to-day obvious implicates of the Christian message. It is not only that Christians have failed to do the right ; influenced by national interests or class prejudice, they have called wrong right, and have claimed for contemporary cruelties and injustices the sanction of religion. And we have no reason to assume that we are so much wiser than our forefathers as to be immune from the infection of our environment. It is easy to claim the Christian name for demands which are unrelated to the Christian Gospel, whilst, at the same time, ignoring other demands which are inherent in the Christian message. In every age Christian Ethics has been distorted by accretion and accommodation.

That accretion and accommodation have been due in part not to the isolation of Christian Ethics but to its undue dependence on contemporary conceptions. Thus, even in New Testament times, the current conception of matter as evil led not only to errors of doctrine but to an asceticism which forbade marriage, and to a moral laxity which regarded sins of the flesh as unimportant for they did not affect the soul.[2] The Church opposed the ethical dualism of its Graeco-Oriental environment, but its own ethics was increasingly influenced by the intellectualism of the Greeks, and by that depreciation of the material which led to the overprizing of virginity.

---

[1] The most comprehensive book in English is *The History of Ethics within organized Christianity*, by T. Cuming Hall. The first volume of Luthardt's *History of Christian Ethics* (to the Reformation) has been translated and is still useful. H. H. Scullard, *The Ethics of the Gospel*, covers the whole period, and his *Early Christian Ethics in the West*, gives a more detailed account of the period from Clement to Ambrose. Very suggestive and valuable are E. Troeltsch, *The Social Teaching of the Christian Churches*, and R. Newton Flew, *The Idea of Perfection in Christian Theology*. Much useful material is to be found in F. R. Barry, *The Relevance of Christianity*, and K. E. Kirk, *The Vision of God*.

[2] See earlier, pp. 90 f.

It is significant that the first Christian treatise on Ethics, St. Ambrose's *On the Duties of the Clergy*, is avowedly based on Cicero's *De Officiis*. It assumes, as not requiring proof, that the traditional Greek virtues, Prudence, Justice, Fortitude and Temperance, are the Cardinal Virtues of Christianity, and refers to the heroes of the Old Testament as illustrations of their possessors. By St. Augustine these Cardinal Virtues are interpreted as forms of love ; " Temperance is love keeping itself entire and incorrupt for God ; Fortitude is love bearing everything readily for the sake of God ; Justice is love serving God only, and therefore ruling well all else, as subject to man ; Prudence is love making a right distinction between what helps it towards God and what might hinder it ".[1]

The most influential attempt to combine Christian and general Ethics was provided by St. Thomas Aquinas in whose vast *Summa Theologica* the traditions of the Fathers of the western Church, and especially of St. Augustine, are combined with Church praxis, and expressed in the framework of that Aristotelianism which was the " New Learning " of his age. Virtues are defined as " habits ". Quoting " the Philosopher " (*i.e.* Aristotle), St. Thomas enumerates the three Intellectual Virtues of Wisdom, Science and Understanding,[2] and adds to them the four Cardinal, or Moral, virtues of Prudence, Justice, Temperance and Fortitude,[3] and the three Theological Virtues of Faith, Hope and Charity.[4] St. Thomas's immense synthesis is a masterpiece of systematization, but Christian Ethics cannot be forced into the mould of Aristotelianism without distortion. We may learn much from the cool scrutiny of moral concepts to be found in the great writers of secular ethics. How much it meant to some of us in our youth to read the Socratic dialogues with their probing into the meaning of high-sounding words, and their witness to a quest for truth even at the cost of death ; to study the exposition of Justice in Plato's *Republic*, and to see how he sought to plan an ideal state in which that Justice should be embodied ; to read the *Nicomachean Ethics* of Aristotle with its shrewd analysis of human character ; and later

---

[1] *On the Morals of the Catholic Church* (an Anti-Manichean treatise), XV.   [2] II. i. 57. 2.   [3] II. i. 61. 2.   [4] II. i. 62. 3.

to read Butler's *Sermons* with their affirmation of the authority of Conscience, or to study Kant with his rigorous delineation of the awful obligation of duty. But Christian Ethics cannot be adequately expressed in alien systems. Conscience, as Butler emphasized, has authority, but conscience itself can be perverted. Kant's maxim, " I ought therefore I can ", is not the language of Christian, or, indeed, of human experience, nor can a Christian be content to regard God merely as the necessary postulate of the practical reason.[1] Philosophies come and go, and with them the ethical systems dependent on them. And to-day there is no philosophy, and so no system of ethics, which can claim to be the recognized world-view of our age. The Christian Ethics propounded by Protestant writers, under the influence of great philosophers, of Spinoza, of Hegel or of Kant, have only historic interest, for these philosophers no longer hold the allegiance of modern men. Thomistic Ethics still claims the allegiance of Roman and some Anglo-Catholic moralists. That is possible because in the Roman Church not only the study of theology but the study of philosophy " and the teaching of these sciences to their students must be accurately carried out by Professors [in seminaries, etc.] according to the arguments, doctrine, and principles of St. Thomas which they are inviolately to hold ".[2] In other words the modified Aristotelianism of St. Thomas is normative for all Roman Catholic teachers, and, in this way, permanence can be claimed for the ethical system of St. Thomas as well as for his theology.

To Protestant Christians no such way is open. The only body of knowledge, whose influence in the modern world is

[1] Kant himself before his death seems to have realized the inadequacy of this position. See T. M. Greene, *Kant. Selections*, pp. 370–4, with its reference to the notes found in manuscript at Kant's death and not published till 1920.

[2] Canon 1366 para. 2 of the new Codex of Canon Law issued by Authority of Pope Benedict XV, 1917. In his Encyclical, *Aeterni Patris* of 1879, Leo XIII had enjoined " the Restoration of Christian Philosophy, according to the mind of St. Thomas Aquinas, the Angelic Doctor ". To " youths engaged in study " should be given " the pure streams of wisdom which flow from the Angelic Doctor as from a perennial and copious spring ". The Encyclical and Canon are given in vol. I of the Dominican translation of the *Summa Theologica*, pp. i–xxxiii.

comparable to the influence of Aristotle in the time of St. Thomas, is that of Natural Science. But, in spite of Dr. Julian Huxley's attempt to prove the contrary, Natural Science cannot, even with the help of the New Psychology, provide the modern world with a system of ethics. Scientists may be as concerned with moral values as any other serious-minded men, but such values are not to be derived from Natural Science. The patient researches of scientists may serve to remind us of the importance of the intellectual virtues, and these, as Baron von Hügel wrote, " are no mere empty name : candour, moral courage, intellectual honesty, scrupulous accuracy, chivalrous fairness, endless docility to facts, disinterested collaboration, unconquerable hopefulness and perseverance, manly renunciations of popularity and easy honours, love of bracing labour and strengthening solitude : these and many other cognate qualities bear upon them the impress of God and of His Christ ".[1] As Bishop Butler wrote, " It is as easy to close the eyes of the mind, as those of the body ".[2] It is terribly easy to mistake prejudice for principle, to use impressive words without examining their meaning, and to try to further the cause of class or party by claiming that its interest or programmes have the support of Christianity. Christian Ethics does not make Moral Philosophy superfluous, for the concepts of ethics need to be scrutinized and their validity discussed.

Yet Christian Ethics and Moral Philosophy inevitably differ in method and approach. Christian Ethics is a deduction from Christian theology and expresses in the imperative mood what theology states in the indicative. And that is only another way of saying once again that the " teaching ", the *didache*, is dependent on the proclamation, the *kerugma*. To the Christian believer some of the problems of Ethics are solved in advance. He has not to consider whether goodness is merely a convenient social convention, for he knows that it expresses the very character of God. Christian faith does not make a man a competent economist or sociologist, but the Christian believer knows, or should know, that economic values are subordinate to human,

---

[1] *The Mystical Element of Religion*, I. p. 79.
[2] Sermon X. *Upon Self Deceit*, para. 11.

and that the authority of the State is limited, for the State, too, stands under the judgment of God. Christian ethical judgments are inevitably theocentric ; moral problems are to be explored from the standpoint of God's will—a will which is not arbitrary, for it is the will of the God whose holy love we may already discern in Christ. With the recognition of God goes the remembrance of human sin. The Christian who speaks or writes on Ethics may not do so as if his conscience was clear, and his moral judgment unimpaired by sin. It is not as the good but as the forgiven, that he has to seek to judge of the problems of his time.

In some of their more extreme statements great Christian teachers, like St. Augustine and Calvin, have spoken as if our race was so totally depraved that outside the Christian sphere there was no goodness and no right discernment of good and evil. This view has in recent years found a zealous, and, at times, a fierce advocate in Karl Barth.[1] Against the Nazi attempt to find in race and blood, or in the utterances of Hitler, a new source of revelation, the Confessional Church at Barmen, under Barth's brave leadership, affirmed at the Synod of Barmen in 1934 : " Jesus Christ as witnessed by the Scriptures is the one true Word of God which we hear and obey, and in which we trust in life and death. We condemn the false doctrine that the Church should recognize as God's revelation, besides this one Word, as source of its message, other facts or powers, forms or truths ". That affirmation was as necessary as it was courageous. There is a sense in which Barth's words are true, " The right Ethics can only be Christian Ethics, and this Christian Ethics, if it would speak scientifically, cannot be distinguished from theological Ethics ".[2] The Christian believes that in Christ alone has God's Will been fully revealed. But he cannot be content to survey the human conflict from an ivory tower, nor can he restrict moral insight to those who understand and accept the affirmations of Christian faith. The history of Christian Ethics shows how much the Church's ethical teaching has needed to be criticized, and the teacher of Ethics,

[1] Cp. his attack on Brunner, *Nein*, E.T. in *Natural Theology*, comprising " Nature and Grace " by Professor Emil Brunner and the reply " No ! " by Dr. Karl Barth.   [2] *Kirchliche Dogmatik*, II. ii. p. 603.

even of Christian Ethics, needs to take note of such criticism, whilst Christian philosophers, using the language of philosophy and engaged in its arena, are required to expound and defend an ethical teaching which is congruous with Christian values. It is right that there should be a Moral Philosophy, scrutinizing ethical principles and motives, and Christian Ethics cannot be established only by authority. There may be those who, like those well-informed religious leaders about whom our Lord uttered His most solemn warning, have so identified themselves with evil that they cannot recognize good when they see it.[1] And yet there has been given to all some power of discerning good and evil. Ethical aspiration and achievement are not confined to the sphere of Christian faith. There has been everywhere some knowledge of the good. And the recognition of this has often been expressed by the conception of the Law of Nature, binding on all alike, whether they be Christians or not.

(2) CHRISTIAN ETHICS AND THE " LAW OF NATURE "

Sir Norman Angell reports that a German student one said to him, " My professor is a very learned man. You can take to him a quite simple matter ; and in ten minutes he will have made it completely incomprehensible ".[2] It would not need that German professor's learning to make a statement on the Law of Nature " incomprehensible ", for it is no " simple matter ", and it cannot be discussed without some reference to its involved and elusive history.[3] Christians are a minority even in so-called Christian countries and " Christian " countries

---

[1] Mark iii. 29. [2] *The Steep Places*, p. 70.

[3] Recent discussions in English include the illuminating booklet by A. R. Vidler and W. A. Whitehouse, *Natural Law, A Christian Reconstruction*, and C. H. Dodd's pamphlet, *Natural Law in the Bible* ; Troeltsch, *The Social Teaching of the Christian Churches*, I. pp. 150–61 ; 193–9 ; 257–327 ; II. 528–44 ; 602–25 ; 673–7 ; N. Micklem, *The Theology of Politics* ; E. Brunner, *The Divine Imperative*, pp. 269 ff. ; 627–33 ; *Justice and the Social Order*, chapter 12 ; L. Dewar in *Christian Morals*, chapter 3 ; Christopher Dawson, *Religion and the Modern State* ; *Christian Faith and the Common Life* (*Church, Community and State*, vol. iv), especially the essays by Reinhold Niebuhr and Werner Wiesner. Of older books, A. J. Carlyle, *A History of Medieval Political Theory in the West*, 1903, is of special importance.

have to seek to establish a world-order which shall include not only Hindus, Japanese and Muslims, but also Communist states on whose rulers Christianity has no influence. Is there any possibility of securing at least a minimum of agreement as to the nature of the common good and so of the " natural " rights of men ?

" Law of Nature " suggests to modern men the " laws " of natural science. That is not the older use of this term. As Dr. Vidler and Dr. Whitehouse's little book puts it, " the English terms ' Natural Law ' and ' the Law of Nature ' are derived from the Latin *lex naturae* or *naturalis* and *ius naturale*, which were used by Cicero, Seneca, etc. and the Roman jurists, and which were ultimately derived from the *phusikon dikaion* of Aristotle. ' A rule of justice ', says Aristotle (*Eth. Nic.* V. vii), ' is natural that has the same validity everywhere, and does not depend upon our accepting it '. ' True law ', says Cicero, ' is right reason in agreement with Nature ; it is of universal application, unchanging and everlasting . . . Whoever is disobedient is fleeing from himself and denying his human nature ' (*De Rep.* III. xxii) ".[1] This conception of Natural Law had great importance in Stoicism, going well with its belief in the immanent Soul of the world (*anima mundi*). From Stoicism it passed into Christianity, and enabled Christian thinkers to conceive of secular life as governed by a divine law, though not under the Christian law of love. This teaching of Natural Law, like so many other teachings, received its most influential expression in the *Summa Theologica* of St. Thomas.

In his *Treatise on Law*, St. Thomas speaks first of Eternal Law, which is " not distinct from God Himself ", and then of the Natural Law. Under the head of Natural Law, he writes " A gloss on Rom. ii. 14 : ' Where the Gentiles who have not the law, do by nature those things which are of the law ', comments as follows : ' Although they had no written law, yet they have the natural law, whereby each one knows, and is conscious of, what is good and what is evil ' ". St. Thomas adds, " The natural law is nothing else than the rational creature's participation of the eternal law ".[2] In his more

---

[1] *Natural Law*, pp. 12 f.   [2] II. i. Q. xci. 1. 2.

detailed exposition of the Natural Law, he writes, " The first principle in the practical reason is one founded on the notion of good, viz., that *good is that which all things seek after*. Hence this is the first precept of law, that *good is to be done and ensued, and evil is to be avoided*. All other precepts of the natural law are based on this." He includes under this head, " whatever is a means of preserving human life and of warding off its obstacles "; " those things which nature has taught to all animals, such as sexual intercourse, education of offspring and so forth "; and, since " man has a natural inclination to know the truth about God, and to live in society ", " whatever pertains to this inclination belongs to the natural law, for instance, to shun ignorance, to avoid offending those among whom we live, and other such things regarding the above inclination ". To the Question, " Whether the Natural Law is the same for all ? " St. Thomas answers, " yes ", " as to general principles ", " both as to rectitude and as to knowledge ". Yet in detail it may fail " both as to rectitude, by reason of certain obstacles ", and " as to knowledge, since in some cases the reason is perverted by passion, or evil habit, or an evil disposition of nature ". This Natural Law is " unchangeable ". It may, indeed, be added to, but it cannot be subtracted from, except in some rare cases. Quoting St. Augustine's words (*Conf.* ii), " Thy law is written in the hearts of men which iniquity itself effaces not ", he writes, " the natural law cannot be blotted out "; " its most general precepts " are " known to all ", although, as to its " secondary precepts ", it " can be blotted out from the human heart, either by evil persuasions ", or " by vicious customs, and corrupt habits, as among some men, theft, and even unnatural vices, as the Apostle states (Rom. i), were not esteemed sinful ".[1]

St. Thomas's teaching on Natural Law is normative for the Roman Church, and has been used, at times, with beneficent effect. Those outside the Christian sphere, and so not bound by the Positive Law revealed in Christianity, are yet under obligation to obey the Natural Law, and to that Natural Law the Positive Laws of States must be subordinated. Thus it is

[1] II. 1. xciv. 2, 4, 5, 6.   Quotations are from the Dominican Translation (vol. viii).

by the recognition of Natural Law that modern Roman Catholic philosophers like Jacques Maritain have powerfully asserted the inalienable rights of men, and it was on the basis of Natural Law that Pope Pius XI in his Encyclical *Mit brennender Sorge* of 1937 denounced not only the Nazi persecution of Catholics but also the Nazi claim that Hitler, the Nazi Party, or the State, had absolute authority, and that the supposed good of Germany was the sole criterion of justice.

" He who takes the race, or the people, or the State, or the form of Government, the bearers of the power of the State or other fundamental elements of human society— which in the temporal order of things have an essential and honourable place—out of the system of their earthly valuation, and makes them the ultimate norm of all, even of religious, values and deifies them with an idolatrous worship, perverts and falsifies the order of things created and commanded by God. . . . Every positive law, from whatever lawgiver it may come, can be examined as to its moral implications and consequently as to its moral authority to bind in conscience, in the light of the commandments of the natural law. The laws of man that are in direct contradiction with the natural law bear an initial defect, that no violent means, no outward display of power, can remedy. By this standard must we judge the principle, ' What helps the people is right '."

As Dr. Micklem has written, " This notable document is not merely a protest against indubitable persecution, and a firm reassertion of the Christian Gospel ; it also counters the romanticism of National Socialism with a coherent, catholic and Christian philosophy of law and of the State ".[1]

In Protestantism the conception of Natural Law has caused much perplexity. The Reformers emphasized strongly the effects of the Fall. The traditional theology of the West, following Irenaeus, had distinguished between the likeness (*similitudo*) and the image (*imago*) of God in which, according to Gen. i. 26 f., man had been created, and had taught that at the Fall only the likeness of God was lost ; man was still in God's image.

[1] *National Socialism and the Roman Catholic Church*, p. 172 f. The Encyclical is quoted from the translation published by the Catholic Truth Society. *The Persecution of the Church in Germany.*

Luther, instead, identified " likeness " and " image ", and taught that, after the Fall, only a small relic of the image remained with man. Yet, however small be that relic, it still was true that all men had " the Law written by nature in their hearts ", and this law, following Irenaeus, Luther identified with the Decalogue. " Even if Moses had never written the Law, yet still all men have the Law written by nature in their hearts ".[1] Calvin, too, for all his emphasis on the total depravity of man, spoke of the things contained in the Decalogue as being " dictated to us by that internal law ", which " is in a manner written and stamped on every heart. For conscience, instead of allowing us to stifle our perceptions, and sleep on without interruption, acts as an inward witness and monitor, reminds us of what we owe to God, points out the distinction of good and evil, and thereby convicts us of departure from duty ".[2] Nor did his belief in man's total depravity prevent his recognizing goodness wherever it is to be found. " In reading profane authors, the admirable light displayed in them should remind us that the human mind, however much fallen from its original integrity, is still adorned and invested with admirable gifts from its Creator. If we reflect that the Spirit of God is the only fountain of truth, we will be careful, as we would avoid offering insult to Him, not to reject or contemn truth wherever it appears. In despising the gifts, we insult the Giver ". Among these gifts he mentions those which lead to the achievement of civic justice.[3] The " human soul is, indeed, irradiated with a beam of divine light, so that it is never left utterly devoid of some small flame, or rather spark, though not such as to enable it to comprehend God ",[4] and " in every age there have been some who, under the guidance of nature, were all their lives devoted to God ".[5] Calvin thus recognized that there remained with men some power of moral choice, and that

---

[1] *W.A.* XVI. p. 431.

[2] *Institutes*, II. viii. 1. The paragraph goes on to speak of " our dullness and contumacy " because of which God gave us His written Law which " removes the obscurity of the law of nature " and stirs us up from our lethargy.

[3] *Op. cit.* II. ii. 14 f.   [4] II. ii. 19.   [5] II. iii. 3.

the light which flickers in every human soul comes from Him who is the Light.

In the seventeenth and eighteenth centuries, at a time of much religious scepticism, some of the great moralists sought to establish the independent authority of ethics, and so the law of nature came to be interpreted as something which conscience, or the practical reason, could discover and obey. This confidence in man's power to know and do the right, reached full expression in the Deist movement, and it was on the ground of the Natural Law that the American Declaration of Independence of 1776 declared, through Jefferson's influence : " We hold these truths to be self-evident ; that all men are created equal ; that they are endowed by their Creator with certain unalienable rights ; that among these rights are life, liberty and the pursuit of happiness ".

In the nineteenth century, outside the domain of the Roman Church, the influence of Natural Law waned. Whereas the great Jurists had affirmed that Positive Law, the statutes promulgated by the State, was based on Natural Law and derived from it its authority, some Jurists taught, instead, that law was derived solely from the authority of the State. Where the conception of Natural Law lost its divine reference, it lost also its authority. If law has for its sole sanction the authority of the State, by what means can the Nazi subordination of justice to the alleged good of the people be condemned ? The conception of law as merely the expression of the will of the State seems inadequate, and the conception of " the Law of Nature "—whether that term be used or not—as the expression of an obligation binding upon all, and requiring that Positive Laws shall be in accordance with its dictates, is gaining increasing influence even with those outside the Roman Church.

It is necessary to distinguish the two conceptions of Natural Law. The first, the classical and Christian based on the conception of a divine Law of which Natural Law is the impress in the mind of man ; the second, that which ignores God and thinks only of the competency of human reason. Those who rely on human reason tend to forget what Kant called " radical evil ". Our reason is distorted by sin. Yet, although Christians think first of God and His will, and see in man's power to distinguish between good and evil the gift of God his creator, it is possible for them to co-operate with men of other faiths, or no faith at all, in the quest of justice and humanity.

It is not only within the Christian sphere that goodness is prized. Karl Barth once accused those who speak of the higher elements of non-Christian religions as " howling with the wolves ". If he had known more of the non-Christian religions he condemned, he might have spoken differently. Doubtless God might have made the world in black and white. He has not done so. There are greys and greens and blues. Thus in India how great have been the contrasts. In the ancient *Rigveda*, there is the conception of the just God, Varuna, the guardian of the moral order, the punisher of sin, as well as the less worthy conception of Indra, who became the more popular deity. There is the noble Krishna of the *Gita* as well as the lewd Krishna of the *Puranas* ; there are *bhakti* poets whose devotion to their gods may make us ashamed of the coldness of our zeal, and, even among animist outcastes there is the love of parents for their children, kindness to strangers, and much patience in privation. Gautama the Buddha taught the way of pity and self-discipline, and later Mahayanist Buddhists the way of self-sacrificing love. In China, Confucius taught " reciprocity ", and Confucianism has bidden men not do to others what they would not have them do to them. *The Confessions of al-Ghazali* show how a Muslim may love God and seek to serve Him. There is not unrelieved darkness. And yet there is no *consensus gentium*, no common conception of the content of the good. The Highest Common Factor of non-Christian ethics is small. Yet there is some power in men to recognize and prize the good. And, to come nearer home, who of us who lived in London during the air-raids could fail to realize the fidelity and devotion of many who, having little or no religion, yet did their duty with unselfish courage ?

The Bible itself does not speak as if only within the sphere of its revelation was there any appreciation of the good. The Covenant made with Abraham was not the first Covenant ; there was earlier the Covenant with Noah, and Jewish Rabbis were later to point out that the sons of Noah were given seven commands—commands obligatory on all men. These " Noachide commands " forbade idolatry, incest, shedding of blood, profanation of the Name of God, injustice, robbery and the cutting off of flesh or limb from a living animal. These sins, as Dr. C. G. Montefiore comments, " are regarded as repugnant to fundamental human morality, quite apart from revelation ".[1] Thus Amos uttered his words of judgment against neighbouring nations, not on the ground that they were aliens or heathens, but because their cruel acts in war were rebellion against God. Even the writer of " Malachi " declares, " In every place incense is offered unto my name, and a pure offering : for my name is great among the Gentiles ".[2]

In the New Testament there are many passages which assume that pagans also can distinguish between right and wrong. Thus in 1 Peter Christians are bidden so to live that Gentiles may see their good works and glorify God ; let them have a good conscience that, when they are slandered, " they may be put to shame who revile your good manner of life in Christ ".[3] " The implication ", as Dr. Dodd says, " is that there is in pagans a capacity for sound moral judgment, a *communis sensus* which will lead them to recognize as good that which the revealed Law of God declares to be good ".[4] And with this St. Paul agrees, for he bids Christians " take thought for things honourable in the sight of all men ", whilst his praise of magistrates as ministers of God, rewarding the good and punishing the evil, assumes that there is a Law of Nature which enables men to judge between good and evil.[5] The conception of the Law of Nature finds its clearest expression in Rom. i. 19 ff. and ii. 14 f. St. Paul condemns, as without excuse, the idolatry of the pagan world with its intimate connexion with moral degradation. The Gentiles might have known God, indeed, they had known Him, through the created world ; but they had turned away from Him. Yet with God there is " no respect of persons ". It is " the doers of a law " that shall be " justi-

---

[1] *A Rabbinic Anthology*, p. 556.

[2] Amos i. 3–ii. 3 ; Mal. i. 11.   [3] 1 Peter ii. 12 ; iii. 16.

[4] *Natural Law in the Bible*, p. 6.   [5] Rom. xii. 17 ; xiii. 1–6.

fied ", and Gentiles who, " do by nature the things of the law, these, having no law, are a law unto themselves ".   They show " the work of the law written in their hearts ", their conscience condemning or excusing them.

Our Lord, as we have seen, spoke concretely not abstractly, whilst His mission was almost entirely restricted to His own people.   Yet it was of a pagan centurion that He said, " I have not found so great faith, no, not in Israel ".[1]   Men are " evil " ; yet, even so, they know how " to give good gifts " unto their children, and our Lord used this fact to assert God's still greater generosity.   With care of children goes marriage, and our Lord, as we have seen, bases the sanctity of marriage not on the Jewish law, nor on any special revelation He himself had brought, but on God's " order of creation ".   As male and female had God created man.   And St. John's Gospel declares that in the Word " was life ; and the life was the light of men ", and that the Word who is the true light, " lighteneth every one coming unto the world ".   The Word did not at the Incarnation first begin His work for men.   We remember Origen's apt reply to Celsus, who had sneered that " if God, like Jupiter in the comedy, should on awaking from a long sleep desire to rescue the human race from evil, why should He send this Spirit of whom you speak into a little corner of the earth, and (of all peoples) to the Jews ? "   " It was not as if awaking from a long sleep that God sent Jesus to the human race, Jesus who not only in the incarnation but always has conferred benefits upon men.   For no noble deed has ever been done by men, without the divine Word who visited the souls of those who were capable for a while of receiving Him ".[2]

" Natural Law " is not a happy phrase.   Brunner, while recognizing the truth for which it stands, would have us abandon the term because of the inevitable misconceptions of its meaning. " Anyone who attempted in our day to revive and apply the old doctrine of the law of nature in any of its forms would find that no definition " " of his conception of nature and of the law of nature would safeguard him from the misunderstanding that he wishes to subject law to the forces of nature.

[1] Matt. viii. 10.   [2] *Contra Celsum*, VI. 78.

The man of to-day, whether jurist or theologian, seems incapable
of eliminating from the concept ' the law of nature ', the association ' the laws of nature ', ' natural instinct ', and so on, and
that misunderstanding will flood away all the barriers of
definition, no matter how securely erected.   Hence, on account
of its later history, the terms must simply be abandoned ".
These dangers certainly exist, but old terms have a way of
coming again into current speech, and, however it may be
among the German-speaking peoples, the term is again becoming
current coin in the Anglo-Saxon world.   Whether the term be
used, or not, the idea for which it stands is necessary and
relevant.   As Brunner says, " the opposition to the law of
nature has not only prepared the way for the totalitarian State
but made it possible ".   We need to assert that there are rights
which are not dependent on the caprice of State-laws but on
that justice which is determined by the conception of God's
order of creation.   That a child should have the care a child
requires, that an adult should not be despised because of his
race, that marriage should be respected—behind all these rights
stands the will of God in Creation.   To quote Brunner once
again, " The totalitarian State, which arose on the ruins of the
law of nature, has been the means of bringing it to life again ".[1]
To the Christian the natural law, obedience to which secures
the elementary rights of men, is based upon the holy Will of
God ; and justice is not merely of man's creation.   However
obscured by personal or by corporate sin, some power to know
right from wrong remains with all, unless it be with those, if
such there be, who have so identified themselves with evil that
they can no longer distinguish it from good.   The Christian
derives his knowledge of the good not from the surmises of his
" practical reason " but from the revelation of God in Jesus
Christ.   When the sun is shining, we do not need other lights.
But if we are in darkness even a dimmed torch is better than
no light at all.   The Church's prime task in the world is that
of evangelization—to bring to those who know it not the light
which comes to us in Jesus Christ.   But He it is who lighteneth
every man coming into the world.   There remains in man some

[1] *Justice and the Social Order*, pp. 82–9.

power to know the good. We have the right to demand that none should wantonly injure others, and in that quest for justice and fight against oppression, there can be co-operation between Christians and non-Christians. It is this that the concept of Natural Law expresses and, as such, for all its obscurity, it needs to be asserted and preserved. Difficult as this discussion has been, it is closely related to modern needs. Only by the recognition of Natural Law can we assert that Justice of the State on which the peace of the world depends.[1]

(3) THE SPHERE AND FUNCTION OF CHRISTIAN ETHICS

In the moral chaos of our time many are more concerned with the question, What ought I to do ? than with the question, What ought I to believe ? The New Testament seems, at first sight, disappointing for, as we have seen, it gives us no immediate answers to many of the pressing problems of our age, but proclaims God's great acts in Christ's Life and Death and Resurrection. The Gospels tell us of our Lord's call to men to repent and receive the Kingdom, to experience, that is, in Him the redemptive power of God, whilst St. Paul and St. John alike rely on the supreme facts of Christ's Cross and Resurrection to change men's lives, and on the presence of the Spirit to guide into all truth and to enable Christians to know and to do the will of God revealed in Jesus Christ.

Christianity, as the New Testament presents it, is not a legal religion, and does not provide us with a code of regulations dealing with every case of conduct. Instead, it speaks of the grace of God in Christ which evokes the response of a faith which leads inevitably to love. That is why Christianity in its New Testament form seems incomplete to those who want precise answers to every moral problem. But then, as Brunner says, this " demand for Ethics ", " may be—like the cry for a strong man—merely an expression of shrinking from responsibility, which desires an authoritative promulgation of a law which will settle all difficulties once for all, which will lay down beforehand what everyone has to do or leave undone in every situation—

[1] On the " Justice of the State " see later, pp. 246-9.

in a word : the demand for the doctrinal authority—binding on the conscience—of the Roman Catholic Church ".[1] If it is a Christian law-book that is wanted, neither the New Testament nor a Protestant Ethics which is based upon the New Testament, can meet this want.   For that it would be necessary to turn to the manuals of Moral Theology provided by the Roman Church, which are comprehensive in their range, and impressive in their precision.   The Moral Theology of the Roman Church assumes not only the authority of the Gospel but the authority of a Church infallible in the sphere of morals as of dogma. Where the Curia has given decisions, these decisions have the force of law ; where no decision has been given, the appeal is made to ecclesiastical tradition, the teaching of the Fathers and Doctors of the Church, and especially to that of St. Thomas Aquinas or St. Alphonsus de Liguori.   Where counsels differ and there is no decision, recourse is had to systems of casuistry, ranging, according to the degree of strictness, from Tutiorism, through Probabiliorism and Aequiprobabilism to Probabilism, which seems to-day the most popular system.   Probabilism is exposed to the dangers which Pascal attacked in his famous *Provincial Letters,* but a legal system inevitably involves some kind of casuistry for its interpretation.   As Professor Henry Davis, S.J., writes, " It is precisely about law that Moral Theology is concerned.   It is not a mirror of perfection, showing man the way of perfection.   It shows him the way of salvation, which will be attained by the observance of the Commandments of God and of the Church.   It must, at the same time, be admitted that a man who aims only at keeping within the four corners of the law, will sometimes wander outside the pale, and will find himself in a very perilous situation, may even jeopardize his salvation, not because Moral Theology offers him the broad road and lax principles, but because man himself does not act up to the principles offered ".[2]

The Moral Theology of the Roman Church is the necessary adjunct to the work of priests in the confessional, and has behind

---

[1] *The Divine Imperative,* p. 9.

[2] *Moral and Pastoral Theology,* I. p. 4.   This four-volume work, first published in 1935, is quoted from the fifth edition of 1946.

it the supposed infallibility of the Church which claims to be the only true representative of Christ on earth. It is strange that the methods of this Moral Theology should be copied by a recent Anglican writer, Professor Mortimer. As he says, " For Roman Catholics the Church has spoken finally on a great number of issues. For Anglicans there are authoritative statements on comparatively few questions and the rest are left to the conscience of the individual to decide for himself what is his lawful course ". He adds, " Hence the importance for Anglicans of a correct understanding of the principles of probabilism ".[1] The authority most quoted by Professor Mortimer, as by Roman Catholic writers, is St. Thomas Aquinas. St. Thomas's *Summa Theologica* is, indeed, a masterpiece of systematization, and he was a man as devout as he was gifted. Yet, when he is quoted as the supreme authority on moral issues, it should be remembered that his acceptance of the authority of the Latin Church led him to endorse the most dreadful error that the Church has made—its persecution of heretics, and he did so after the institution of the Inquisition and the bloody crusade against the Albigensians.[2] When we read of the Authority of the Church as a guide to morals, we remember that it was only in 1917 that the canon authorizing persecution was omitted from the Canon Law. Protestants to their shame have persecuted, but, whereas at Champel near Geneva there stands the expiatory monument erected by the children of Calvin to Servetus, the Roman Church has not yet retracted nor apologized. The sin of persecution, in which so many in the past have shared, is in itself a sufficient warning that great names give no security for right judgment. In his wonderfully skilful synthesis of Aristotelianism, Church praxis and Augustinian Christianity, St. Thomas conceals, he does not resolve, the difference between Aristotelianism and Christian teaching. Impressive and instructive as is his presentation of

[1] *The Elements of Moral Theology*, p. 95.
[2] *Summa Theologica*, II. ii. xi. 3, 4. Those in error are after two admonitions to be delivered " to the secular tribunal to be exterminated thereby from the world by death ". Those who, after being taken back, relapse are admitted to Penance if they return, " but are not delivered from the pain of death ".

Virtues and Vices, of Sins Mortal and Sins Venial, he has obscured the insight of the New Testament that Christian Ethics is concerned in the first place not with deeds but with the doer, and, although he asserts the primacy of Grace, he yet retains that conception of merit which is irreconcilable with the Gospel. If by Christian Ethics we mean the provision of a detailed legal code, then it is to St. Thomas and the Roman Church that we must go. From the New Testament no such legal code can be obtained. It speaks, instead, of the divine Initiative in men's salvation and proclaims God's redemptive acts in Christ's Life and Death and Resurrection. It puts to us the question, What sort of men ought those to be, who have experienced God's grace in Christ ? and, although it gives no direct answer to the social and political problems of our time, it impels us to judge of these in the light of what we know our God to be.

Not only the method but the scope of Christian Ethics is very variously conceived by Protestant writers. Should Protestant Ethics deal only with the personal life of the Christian or should it deal with those Ordinances or Orders of Creation, Marriage, Industry and the State, within which the Christian life has somehow to be lived ? It is usual to distinguish between Individual and Social Ethics. That distinction is convenient for the purposes of exposition, but it may be misleading. We have to live our lives not as anchorites but in society. We come into the world as members of a family, and our life is in part conditioned by the life of the larger units of which we form a part. Brunner in his great book *The Command and the Ordinances*—in English called *The Divine Imperative*—rejects this distinction. " There is ", he says, " no individual Christian ethic ". " God's command places us in relation to our neighbour not to ourselves ". " To believe means ' Don't bother about yourself any more ! '   God has put all your affairs in order. Whoever lives in faith, in justification, is free from all anxiety about the ' I '. It is true that we are to ' hallow the Self ' but what does this mean save that we are to turn it towards God—

in service?"[1]   Martin Kähler, on the other hand, in his treatment of Christian Ethics concentrates on the personal life of
the Christian and deals with the communities of Family,
Industry and State only in so far as they are spheres in which
Christians have to seek to do God's will.[2]   There is point in
each contention.   Christian Ethics is concerned with the ethics
of Christians and the Christian life is not to be lived in solitude.
Yet Christian teachers have differed much in their conception
of the Christian Life, and in the following chapter an attempt
will be made to discuss its Motives and its Sanctions.   The
natural communities of Marriage, Industry and State are not
merely spheres in which Christians, like others, live.   They are
communities which stand under God's judgment, and Christians
are called not merely to live in these communities as Christians,
but to take their part in making them more in accord with
God's just rule.

After a discussion of the Motives and the Sanctions of
Christian Ethics the attempt will be made to relate what we
may learn from the New Testament to the perplexing problems
which life in these communities present.   But for Christians
there is yet another community in which to live—a community
not of Nature, but of Grace, the community of the Church, in
whose fellowship we share, and by whose help we may attempt
tasks too great for any to achieve alone.   A final chapter will
deal with *The Church's Task*, the task of continuing Christ's
work for men.

[1] pp. 189 f.
[2] *Die Wissenschaft der Christlichen Lehre* [3], pp. 467–670.

CHAPTER VI

THE MOTIVES AND SANCTIONS OF CHRISTIAN ETHICS

THE New Testament, as we have seen, has as its prime concern not what men must do, but what God has done for men in Christ's Life and Death and Resurrection, and in the writings of St. Paul the attempt to earn salvation by obedience to law is vigorously denounced. This teaching could easily be misunderstood, and the New Testament itself shows how the rejection of legalism led some to antinomianism.[1] The old controversies on the motives and sanctions of the Christian life are not of merely historic interest. They are still relevant to modern needs and Christians differ much in their answers to the issues which they raise.

If God's relationship to man be one of " grace ", what then is the place of " law " ? If salvation be by faith, what of " works " ? If monasticism be rejected, what place has asceticism in Protestantism ? If the Christian life has its fulfilment in the life beyond the grave, what is the relevance of the eternal to the moral tasks which confront us as we seek to live as Christians in our present state of imperfection ? It is to these four problems that we have now to turn.

(1) LAW AND GRACE

As we have seen, our Lord had no need to assert God's sole supremacy and righteous will, for He addressed those who had for their Bible the Old Testament, and who had already learnt to think of God as just and holy. The most influential religious

---

[1] The word seems first to have been used by Luther, who denounced Agricola's rejection of law as " antinomianism ".

leaders of the people were the Scribes and Pharisees who found in the Law their joy and pride, and sought to obey not only the six hundred and thirteen precepts of the Pentateuch but refinements of these precepts designed to secure that none of them should be violated. The Gospels record the words of the scribe who said that to love God " with all the heart, and with all the understanding, and with all the strength, and to love his neighbour as himself, is much more than all whole burnt offerings and sacrifices ", and to the scribe who thus spoke Jesus said, " Thou art not far from the kingdom of God ".[1] Jesus was Himself a " practising " Jew, and, although He seems to have preferred the simple congregational worship of the Synagogue to the elaborate ceremonies of the Temple, He paid the temple tax, observed the Jewish feasts, and bade the leper He had healed show himself to the priest and " offer the gift which Moses commanded ".[2] He did not condemn the Pharisees for their tithing of " mint, and anise and cummin ", but for their neglect of " the weightier matters of the law, judgment and mercy and faith ".[3] Yet for Him the Sabbath was made for man, not man for the Sabbath. Ceremonial ablutions before eating were to Him of no importance, and He rejected the Levitical distinction between foods which were " clean " and " unclean ". Defilement does not come from externalities. It is what a man is, not what he eats, which determines whether he is defiled or pure, and the casuistry of the Pharisees He sternly condemned.[4] For Him there was but one supreme command, to love God and to love our neighbour as ourselves, and, as the Parable of the Good Samaritan shows, our neighbour is anyone whom we can help.

Our Lord expressed His message in terms of " the Kingdom of God ". That, as we have seen, is another way of saying, God regnant and redemptive. He called men to " enter into ", or " receive ", the Kingdom, and spoke of it as a treasure so great that the wise man would seek to secure it at any cost. The regnant and redemptive powers of God were already present among men for He was there. The Pharisees spoke much of

---

[1] Mark xii. 33 f.   [2] Matt. viii. 4.
[3] Matt. xxiii. 23.   [4] Mark vii. 1–23.

the " yoke " of the Law. Jesus bade men, instead, take His yoke upon them and learn of Him ; His yoke was easy and His burden light and those that take His yoke would find rest unto their souls. Jesus thus put Himself in place of the Law, the *Torah*. It was His yoke, not the yoke of the Law, that His disciples were to bear. The service to which they were called was not the service of a detailed law, but service such as He showed, who did not desire such " lordship " as " the kings of the Gentiles " used, but was amongst men " as he that serveth ".[1] Legalism was thus abrogated, and personal devotion to our Lord takes the place of the strained attempt to obey the Law's demands.

The rigorist tends to be harsher to others even than to himself. Like the elder brother in the parable, he thinks he has transgressed none of his Father's commands, even although he has entirely failed to give him the response of understanding, and, because of his self-complacency, is indignant that the prodigal should be forgiven. Like the Pharisee in the Temple, he can thank God that he is not as other men are, and yet it was the despised " publican " whose only prayer was, " God, be merciful to me a sinner ", " who went down to his house justified ".[2] Our Lord thus conceived of man's relationship with God in a different way than did the Pharisees. He had come to seek and to save that which was lost. He was the friend of " publicans " and sinners—of those whom the religious leaders of the people were content to condemn and scorn. Salvation was not something men could earn. When we have done all, we are still " unprofitable servants ". We have done at best no more than we were bound to do, and may not claim to have earned for ourselves any merit.

Our Lord thus rejected all legalism ; yet He retained to the full the Jewish tradition of God's awful majesty and stern judgment. If antinomianism means doing as we please, there is no trace of it in His teaching. The Ten Commandments are not abrogated but deepened in their demands. There is a retributive order in which actions go on to their effects, and God's judgment is a dreadful reality. Rather than " cause one

[1] Luke xxii. 24–7.   [2] Luke xviii. 13 f.

of these little ones that believe " on Him " to stumble ", it were
better for a man " if a great millstone were hanged about his
neck, and he were cast into the sea ". It would be better to
enter the Kingdom of God maimed and mutilated, than not to
enter it at all.[1] As for individuals so is it for nations. When
Jesus " wept ", it was not because of the agony of the crucifixion
which a few days later He would undergo ; it was because of
the ruin which would inevitably befall the Jerusalem at which
He gazed, through the people's rejection of Him, and their
choice of the way which would lead to its destruction. At the
trial scene and at the crucifixion, men judged themselves by
their attitude to Him. Yet on the Cross He prayed for those
that put Him there, " Father, forgive them for they know not
what they do ". And after the Resurrection, His disciples
discovered in that Cross the supreme expression of the love of
God.

To express that love of God, St. Paul and St. John speak
of God's grace. " Grace " reminds us at once of the Greek ideal
of beauty, and, although loveliness in art did not in itself bring
loveliness of character, there was one kind of moral beauty
which the Greeks prized and described as grace—the beauty of
ungrudging generosity. Love is a word of many meanings, and
the early Church used to describe the love of God not the
familiar words for love and friendship, but a word that was
little known. They needed the unfamiliar word (*Agape*) to
describe a love which is not of the lovable only but of the
unlovely. Grace is that love, but that love seen from the angle
of men's sin and need. As St. John's Gospel puts it, " The
Law was given by Moses ; grace and truth came by Jesus
Christ ". The incarnate Word, whose glory had been seen on
earth, was " full of grace and truth ".

The glory, the splendour, of the Divine, had been manifested
in the grace of the earthly Jesus, and this glory, which was
full of grace, was not, as were the fables of the gods, a figment
of the imagination. It was full of truth, reality, and expressed
the final secret of the character of God for to see the Son is to
see the Father. The disciple's relation to his Lord was one of

[1] Mark ix. 42-7 ; cp. earlier, p. 61.

T.C.W.

love and not legality and yet to love Him meant to do the things that He would have us do. " If ye love me ye will keep my commandments ". As Dr. Temple commented, " If we don't, we shan't. Let no one deceive himself about that. There is no possibility of meeting His claim upon us, unless we truly love Him. So devotion is prior to obedience itself ".[1]

It has been from the writings of St. Paul that the great controversies on Law and Grace have derived their battle-cries. And that is natural for, as we have seen, St. Paul's teaching on Law and Grace was expressed in words of deep emotion, and was influenced both by his own inner conflict and by his struggle with the Judaizers.[2] He had sought to be " just " before God, but since, as he discovered, the Law concerned not only deeds but desires, he found he could not meet its demands. Other Jews might share his belief that salvation was dependent on complete obedience to the Law, and yet comfort themselves with the thought that God, who knew man's frailty, would not deal severely with those who had failed in part to meet the Law's demands. But for Paul such a compromise was impossible. Those of the Way claimed that the crucified Jesus was the Messiah of Jewish hope. If that was true, legalism was annulled, for, from the standpoint of the Law, a crucified man was accursed. Paul persecuted more fiercely the Church of God until at last, this man, who had consented to Stephen's death and seen his strange confidence and joy, felt himself confronted by the Christ whose followers he had persecuted. His conversion meant for him not only that he had gained a new Lord but that he had learned to think of God in a new way. God was now for him the God of grace, not a God who needed to be appeased, but the God who in Christ had reconciled the world unto Himself. " While we were yet sinners, Christ died for us ". That is how God proves His love towards us. In Christ's death upon the Cross, God had shown Himself at once " just and the justifier ". Thus a new way of salvation was revealed.

---

[1] *Readings in St. John's Gospel*, on John xiv. 15.
[2] See earlier, pp. 71 f.

We are saved not by obedience to Law, but by our response to the grace of God in Christ. Grace became for St. Paul the supreme word of religion, and every one of his Epistles begins, and most end, with the prayer that grace may be with those whom he addressed.

The grace of God evoking gratitude, the love of Christ with its constraining power, the present, if partial, experience of the Spirit's power—in these St. Paul found the sources of the Christian life. He could not understand how converts at Galatia who, as Gentiles, had never known the burden of the Jewish Law, should desire to be circumcised. To Paul that seemed to him a reversion to servitude like that of the paganism they had renounced. Still less could he understand how his converts from paganism, who lacked the discipline of the Law, could turn their liberty into licence. They were not their own, they were " bought with a price ", how then could they depart from purity ? St. Paul was compelled to answer his converts' inquiries and advise them on the perplexing problems that beset small Christian communities living in the midst of paganism. He gave instructions on how to live the Christian life as parents, children, slave-owners or slaves. But he refused to be a legislator. Salvation did not come by law but by grace. Yet retribution was a reality, and what men sow that they reap ; there is " the Wrath "—the retribution, which, although it does not adequately express the character of God, yet holds sway over those who refuse to do His will. In Christ men may know God as He is, the God of grace whose love took action in the Cross.

By converts from paganism St. Paul's proclamation of God's grace was almost inevitably misunderstood. Law they could understand, for paganism had its many enactments ; licence, too, they understood, for they had not had the moral discipline of Judaism. If not law, then why not licence ? So, as Jude puts it, some turned " the grace of our God into lasciviousness " " denying our only Master and Lord, Jesus Christ ", and, as the writer of 2 Peter complained, " the ignorant and unsteadfast wrested to their own destruction " things in St. Paul's Epistles which " were hard to be understood ".[1] The opening chapters

[1] 2 Peter iii. 16.

of the Book of Revelation, and the First Epistle of St. John, likewise show how great was the danger of that rejection of all law which later came to be called Antinomianism.

Antinomianism has recurred at times in the history of the Church.   Some of the Gnostics of the second century, like those of the first century whom the First Epistle of St. John attacked, claimed that because of their *gnosis*, their illumination, they were free from the obligations of morality.   Luther, who, by reason of his more boisterous sayings, has been unjustly accused of indifference to morality,[1] had to denounce an early associate of his, Johannes Agricola, for his antinomianism.   The Anabaptists were for the most part men of simple and austere morality, but, as the grim tragedy of Münster reminds us, some of them lapsed into antinomianism.   Antinomianism was found among some of the Calvinist sectaries of the Commonwealth period ;[2]   later it infected even some of the followers of John Wesley and at his direction was formally condemned at the first annual Methodist Conference.[3]   In modern times, some, who would repudiate the name, have ignored the sombre warnings of the Bible, and, by speaking as if God's love has in it no severity, have so sentimentalized the Christian message as to deprive it of its moral content.   Yet not antinomianism but nomism has been the commoner perversion of the Christian Gospel, and this legalism goes back to the very beginnings of Christianity.

In the Graeco-Oriental world in which Christianity won its

[1] Cp. Maritain's attack on Luther in his *Three Reformers* which, owing much to Denflie and Grisar, quotes Luther's less guarded words and especially his extravagant, though half humorous, letter to Melanchthon, with its notorious *Pecca fortiter*.   For the defence of Luther see P. S. Watson, *Let God be God*, pp. 152–60.

[2] Thus Richard Baxter writing in 1653 in his Preface addressed " to the Poor in Spirit " of his book on *The Right Method for a Settled Peace of Conscience and Spiritual Comfort*, refers to " the Antinomians' common confident obtrusions of their anti-evangelical doctrines and methods for comforting troubled souls " and speaks of them as " the most notorious mountebanks in this art, the highest pretenders, and most unhappy performers, that most of the reformed churches ever knew ".   *The Practical Works of the Rev. Richard Baxter*, 1830 edit., vol. IX. p. xvi.

[3] In 1744 ;   for the relevant Minute see Maximin Piette, *John Wesley and the Evolution of Protestantism*, p. 425.

first victories there were philosophies which presented high ethical ideals and mystery cults which spoke of purification, but, as Holl has shown, Christianity differed from all these in that it, and it alone, proclaimed forgiveness of sins and had a message for the sinful.[1] But this proclamation of a God who welcomes back the prodigal, and of a salvation which comes from God's grace and not from man's desert, was as difficult for converts from paganism to understand as it was for Jewish Christians. Christianity was strange and new. It was hard to believe in God's grace; it was easier to think of Christianity as a teaching to be learned and a law to be obeyed.[2]

Thus in the earliest Christian writings outside the new Testament Canon, the writings of the so-called Apostolic Fathers, we find an almost complete failure to realize God's grace. To the Church at Rome St. Paul had written his fullest exposition of a salvation given by God's grace and incapable of being earned by works. St. Clement of Rome, writing as the responsible leader of the Roman Church to the Church at Corinth, though he reminds the Corinthians of the Epistle sent them by " the blessed Paul the Apostle ", shows very little understanding of St. Paul's meaning, whilst Hermas, an earnest " prophet " of the Church at Rome, speaks of Christianity in a purely legal way, and this was so congenial to many in the early Church that his book *The Shepherd* came to be regarded by some as part of the New Testament. In it we find already the conception of supererogatory works. " If you do anything good, beyond the commandment of God, you will gain for yourself greater glory, and shall be more honourable with God than you were destined to be ". Especially is fasting praised. If Hermas will fast on bread and water, and give to the needy the money thus saved " this fast shall be written down to your credit ".[3]

[1] *Urchristentum und Religionsgeschichte. Gesammelte Aufsätze zur Kirchengeschichte*, II. 1–32.

[2] When the writer in his early years as a missionary in India was beginning a course on Christian Theology with a class for Indian evangelists, he began by asking " What is Christianity ? " Student after student replied (in Tamil), " It is a doctrine to be learned and a law to be obeyed ".

[3] *Sim.* V. 3. E.T. by Kirsopp Lake in the Loeb edition of *The Apostolic Fathers.*

The Shepherd contains long lists of virtues and of vices. There is a similar codification in the very early document, " The Two Ways ", found at the beginning of *The Teaching of the Twelve* and at the end of *The Epistle of Barnabas*. *The Teaching of the Twelve* goes on to say, " Let not your fasts be with the hypocrites, for they fast on Mondays and Thursdays, but do you fast on Wednesdays and Fridays ".[1] By the " hypocrites ", the Jews are meant, but, anti-Jewish as is this book, it reflects a legalism like that of the Judaizers whom St. Paul had attacked. Almsgiving is described as a " ransom for sins ", for God is " the good Paymaster of the reward ".[2] The legalism, found thus early in the Church, was developed by Tertullian whose pages bristle with legal and commercial terms, like " satisfaction " and " merit ", and who taught that it was by painful penance that God could be appeased.

With legalism goes the uncertainty of salvation. It was St. Augustine's great service to the Church that he revived the conception of God's grace and was not only the great teacher of the Western Church but the reformer of Christian piety. As Harnack said, " He preached the sincere humility which blossoms only on ruins—the ruins of self-righteousness ; but he recognized in this very humility the charter of the soul ". " He preached to Christendom the words, ' Blessed is the man whose strength Thou art ; in whose heart are Thy ways ' ".[3] He knew too well his own heart to believe that anything could save him except God Himself. Western Christendom owes him an immeasurable debt, yet, although he reasserted the primacy of grace, he misconceived its meaning. Not only does his teaching oscillate between the " Catholic " conception of grace as something " infused " through the Sacraments, and the evangelical conception of grace as freely given, but in his development of this evangelical conception of grace, he spoke of grace as if it were the arbitrary operation of an omnipotent God who dealt with men, not as with persons but as with things, electing some to blessedness and leaving others to damnation. St. Thomas Aquinas sought to unify these two conceptions of grace—the grace operative in the Sacraments and the grace which elects

[1] VIII. i.   [2] IV. 6 f.   [3] *History of Dogma*, E.T.V. p. 65 f.

to salvation.   Accepting St. Augustine's principle that, " when God crowns our merits, it is nothing but our gifts that He crowns ", St. Thomas taught that merits are required for blessedness, but taught also that there are no merits without grace.   No medieval theologian sought more eagerly to acknowledge the place of grace in man's salvation, but the conceptions of grace and of merit cannot really be reconciled, unless grace be given a different meaning than it has in the New Testament.[1]

The Reformation had its beginning in Luther's protest against the sale of Indulgences in which the conception of merit found its crude expression, for salvation was treated not merely as something to be earned by the living but as something that could be bought for the dead.   At times Luther spoke, as had St. Augustine, of the grace of God as if it were an omnipotent force, but the impulse of the Reformation lay not here but in its discovery of a gracious God who in Christ has taken the initiative for our salvation.   All thought of human merit was abandoned for it is from God alone that our salvation comes. In his *Liberty of the Christian Man* Luther proclaimed a liberty which has no need of law, for, though faith makes free, love brings with it obligation, and makes the Christian the most dutiful servant of all.   Luther's discovery of Christian liberty was the discovery of one whose attempt to earn salvation by monasticism had brought not peace but despair.   But he found, as St. Paul had done, that liberty could be turned into licence. Anabaptists, and later the Pietists, sought to purify Christian life by more rigorous austerity.   Calvin's reliance on God's sole grace was accompanied by the resolute attempt in all things to secure the doing of His will by the maintenance of a discipline more rigorous than that of Rome, because it was impartial in its incidence, and immunity from it could not be secured by money payments.   Yet Calvin, like Luther, proclaimed anew that salvation came from God alone, and by him, too, all conception of human merit was abandoned.   It was on God's grace received in faith that the Reformers relied.   They knew what St. Paul had taught, " If righteousness comes by law, then Christ died in vain ".[2]

---

[1] Cp. the writer's *The Christian Estimate of Man*, pp. 108–18.
[2] Gal. ii. 21.

Extremes meet, and the conception of Christianity as obedience to law was revived by Faustus Socinus, the founder of modern Unitarianism, and is continued in the modern endeavour to identify Christianity with the Sermon on the Mount interpreted as a new and harder law.

Now, as in the pagan world in which Christianity was first preached, the distinctiveness of the Christian message lies in its proclamation of God's free forgiveness. Grace is the great word of the Gospel, for the Gospel speaks of a gracious God, the God who in Christ's Life and Death and Resurrection has taken the initiative in our salvation. Law, in the sense of legalism, has lost its authority, and yet we live in a world where acts go on to their effects, where what men sow, they reap. The stern warnings of the Old Testament are confirmed by the New, and yet all is of God's free gift. The words of St. Augustine, *Dilige, et quod vis fac*, " Love and do what you will ",[1] are true in the sense in which St. Augustine meant them, that " from the root of love good alone can come ", but, taken out of their context, they do not speak to our condition, for our love is not yet perfected. We have to seek to do not what we wish but what God wills. Knowing in Christ the grace of God, we find the impulse to the Christian life not in any attempt to earn God's favour but in the gratitude which God's grace inspires.[2]

Christianity is both gift and demand. But even to begin to meet the demand we must first receive the gift. A religion which speaks first of demand, drives the earnest few to despair, and leads the insensitive many to complacency. We think, *e.g.*, of a sensitive and serious-minded youth driven to nervous breakdown through the teaching of a robust and pugnacious preacher who presented Christianity merely as a demand—a

[1] *In Epistolam Johannis, Tractatus*, VII. 8. (Migne XXXV. col. 2034.)

[2] So the *Heidelberg Catechism*, the lovely little Catechism written by two of Calvin's younger disciples and published a year before Calvin's death, deals with the whole sphere of Christian Ethics under this one head of Gratitude.

demand which cannot be even partly fulfilled except in relation to the gift. But, for the many, legalism leads to self-complacency. A schoolmaster of the writer's youth used often to quote a line from some play, " She turned upon him with the wicked smile of a good woman ". We have all seen that " wicked smile " of " good " men and women—that smile of self-complacency at others' failure. They think their own goodness entitled to some reward and do not like to have the prodigal forgiven. Dr. Underwood tells us that shortly before his death T. R. Glover told him that " the only memorial he would like would be a small tablet with the words, ' T.R.G. *etiam cucurrit* ' ".[1] *Also ran*—that is the most that any can claim who realize the tremendous gulf which separates the profane from the holy, and their own indebtedness to the grace of God. As we remember the Cross of Christ, wherein that grace has been revealed, it is the prayer of the " publican ", not of the Pharisee, which rises to our lips, " God, be merciful to me a sinner ". It is because of what God has done for us in Christ that we are impelled to seek to do what He would have us do, for God's grace evokes our gratitude.

(2) FAITH AND WORKS

The problem of the relation of Faith and Works is closely related to the relation of Law and Grace. Where Grace is preached, Faith is emphasized ; where Law, Good Works.

As we have seen, our Lord began His mission with the proclamation that the Kingdom of God was at hand ; let men repent and believe in the Good News. He called men to " enter into " or " receive " the Kingdom of God, to respond by their faith to God's redemptive work, and the Gospels give many an instance of the transforming influence of His message on those who trusted in Him. It was not enough to call Him, Lord, Lord ; those who thus speak must do the will of His heavenly Father if they would enter into the Kingdom. Yet, as the Parable of the Prodigal Son reminds us, forgiveness may precede even the beginning of good works.

[1] A. B. Underwood, *A History of the English Baptists*, p. 258.

The Parable of the Prodigal Son has often been used to contrast " the simple teaching of Jesus " with the " sophistications " of St. Paul. But the forgiveness of which the parable speaks has in it an element of paradox, and cannot be regarded as if it were a matter of course. The parable, as St. Luke tells us, was spoken to rebuke the murmurings of the Pharisees and the scribes that Jesus " receiveth sinners and eateth with them ". It would have been easy for listeners to retort that in actual life a wiser father would have put his wastrel son upon probation before he received him back again to the home he had not only left but had disgraced.[1] Yet the forgiveness which our Lord proclaimed was not mere condonation. This Man who received sinners did not make sin seem unimportant, and the Gospels, which enshrine His teaching, find their climax in the story of the crucifixion in which the sinfulness of sin received full exposure.

The message of God's free forgiveness sounded so strange to pagan and to Jew that it is not surprising that even within the New Testament itself there is an apparent difference of opinion on the relation of faith and works—a difference which continues until this day. Once more, it has been on St. Paul's Epistles that the argument has been based.

In the most elaborate of his writings, the Epistle to the Romans, St. Paul sets forth at length the new way of faith. In the Gospel which is " the power of God unto salvation to every one that believeth " there is " revealed a righteousness of God by faith unto faith ". By the way of law no one is " justified ", for all have sinned. Yet we may be " justified " freely by God's grace " through the redemption that is in Christ Jesus whom God set forth to be a propitiation, through faith, by his blood, to show his righteousness " " that he might himself be just and the justifier of him that hath faith in Jesus ". The passage, as the Revised Version thus gives it, is full of difficulty. The word translated " propitiation ", as we have seen, is probably an adjective, not a noun, and is used not in the pagan sense of classical Greek of " placating " but

[1] See earlier, p. 48, for Nygren's comments on this parable in contrast to Jülicher's interpretation of it.

in the Biblical sense of " expiatory ", the means of " covering "
or removing guilt.   Sacrifices were a witness to man's sense of
estrangement from God.   Now God had taken the initiative in
reconciliation and in Christ crucified had Himself provided the
means by which we may be reconciled to Him.   From our side,
faith is required, faith which is the response to God's gracious
act.   Thus God may be " just and the justifier ", a God who
forgives with a forgiveness which is not mere condonation.
" Righteousness ", " justified ", " just " and " justifier " all
come in Greek from the same root.   " Justifying " is a legal
term and means to " acquit ", and yet it is not used in a merely
legal sense.   A God who " justifies the ungodly ", *i.e.*, acquits
the guilty, is acting as no judge may do.   St. Paul's doctrine of
" Justification by Faith " expresses the teaching our Lord gave
in the Parable of the Prodigal Son, but with this difference :
there was now the Cross of Christ to which to direct men's gaze
so that none might think that sin was unimportant, or that God's
free forgiveness was the condonation of weak indulgence or
indifference.[1]

In St. Paul's view, this new way of salvation was thus
" apart from works ", and yet it was productive of good works.
In this vehement attack on the Judaizers whom his converts at
Galatia were tempted to follow, in the very passage in which he
declared that " by the works of the law " no man is justified,
he declared that the faith in which he lived was " faith in the
Son of God who loved me and gave himself for me ".[2]   The
freedom won through Christ was meant to be so used that
Christians might " through love be servants one to another "
and in love of the neighbour the whole law is fulfilled.   Walking
by the Spirit, they would show the fruit of the Spirit, and
bearing one another's burdens " fulfil the law of Christ ".   Yet
" boasting " is excluded.   Only in this would Paul glory " in
the cross of our Lord Jesus Christ, through which the world
had been crucified " unto him and he unto the world.[3]   And
in the Epistle to the Romans St. Paul speaks of the joy of
receiving " the spirit of adoption, whereby we say ' Abba,

---

[1] Rom. iii. 19–28 ;   iv. 5.   For these passages see earlier, p. 75.
[2] Gal. ii. 16–21.   [3] v. 13 f., 16 ;   vi. 2, 14.

Father ' " ;   we are " children of God ", " joint-heirs with
Christ ", we are meant to be " more than conquerors through
him that loved us ", confident that nothing need separate us
from the love of God in Him.[1]   Nor was this salvation solitary.
Christians are one body in Christ, called to serve in the Church
in any way they can.[2]

St. Paul could not understand how any could imagine that
the way of faith was not the way of obedience and of service.
Works do not earn forgiveness.   That is received on the response
of faith, but faith, as Paul understood it, leads inevitably to love,
and love, such as that Christ showed, is the highest of all God's
good gifts.   Many of St. Paul's converts could not grasp his
meaning.   Since forgiveness did not come from " works ",
they thought that there could be a faith which did not issue in
Christian character.   " Justification by faith " is a phrase that
can easily be misunderstood.   In Ephesians St. Paul speaks
with more precision.   " By grace are ye saved through faith ".[3]
It is not our faith which saves ; it is the gracious God.   But the
grace of God is received through faith, through our personal
response to the gracious initiative of God in Christ's Life and
Death and Resurrection.   Faith which is personal response to
the gracious God cannot be " without works ".   But a faith
which is merely assent to some statement about God may, as
St. James warns us, be " barren ".   " Thou believest that God
is one ; thou doest well ; the devils also believe and shudder ".
Such faith is " dead ", but that dead faith is not the faith of
which St. Paul wrote.

The conception of faith in the Latin Church was nearer to
that of St. James than to that of St. Paul.   Thus to St. Thomas
Aquinas the objects of faith were the Articles of the Creed.   If
to meet new needs a new edition of the Creed was required, that
could be published only on " the sole authority of the Sovereign
Pontiff ".[4]   Faith is defined as " thinking with assent ".   The
" form " of faith is " charity in so far as the act of faith is
perfected and formed by charity ".   " Faith is a perfection of
the intellect " ; it is charity which pertains to the will, and

---

[1] Rom. viii. 15 ff., 37 ff.   [2] Rom. xii.
[3] Eph. ii. 8.   [4] *Summa Theologica*, II. ii. i. 9 and 10.

which makes faith " living " instead of " lifeless ".[1]   It was
Luther who revived St. Paul's conception of faith, and made
" Justification by Faith " once more an alternative to the
attempt to earn salvation by the way of " works ", and his
teaching came to be as much misunderstood and misinterpreted
as had been the teaching of St. Paul.

Luther's conversion, like that of St. Paul, was the conversion of a devout and zealous man who had been eager to earn
God's favour.   Brought up in a harsh home, against his father's
wish he had abandoned the study of law and entered a monastery, hoping thus to avert God's anger.   Later he could claim
that he had been a zealous monk, and that, if peace could have
been earned by austerities, peace would have been his.   For
long he took the words " righteousness of God " (*iustitia dei*)
of Rom. i. 17 in its active, punitive sense, and believed that
this was the common interpretation of " all doctors except
Augustine ".[2]   Although Luther was wrong in this, yet in the
Roman Church even those who, like St. Thomas, emphasized
God's grace, spoke also of human merit.   In his Lectures on the
Psalms given in 1513–15, Luther already proclaimed his discovery that God's grace was identical with His forgiveness,
received by the response of faith.   " God's grace accepted is
justification ".[3]   As he declared in his lectures on Hebrews in
1517, " Nothing takes away the consciousness of sin except faith
in Christ because victory is given us in Jesus Christ ".[4]

In 1517 Luther posted on the door of the University Church
at Wittenberg his famous Ninety-five Theses.   Against the
conception of merits which could be marketed, Luther declared,
" The true treasure of the Church is the most holy Gospel of the
glory and grace of God ".[5]   That glory and grace he had discovered in Jesus Christ, and it gave him a confidence which
before he had lacked.   In the lectures given in 1531, which

---

[1] *Op. cit.* II. ii. ii. 1 ; iv. 3 f.

[2] Wrongly as Denifle, the great Dominican scholar, has shown. *Die
abendländlichen Schriftausleger bis Luther über Justitia Dei (Luther und
Luthertum,* I. ii).

[3] On Ps. iv (*W.A.* III. p. 47. *Gratia dei accepta est iustitia*).

[4] F. Loofs, *Leitfaden der Dogmengeschichte* [4], p. 710.

[5] The 20th Thesis.

form his longer *Commentary on Galatians* compiled in 1535, he wrote, " Because of that pestilential doctrine and opinion that Christ was a lawgiver ", which " I had imbibed from my boyhood, I used to be terrified and tremble at the name of Christ, because I believed Him to be a judge ".   Now he knew Him to be " a justifier and saviour ".[1]   Time after time in his works, Luther refers to the grace of Christ which he now knew to be the grace of the God he had so much feared.   Emphasis on faith may lead to a subjectivity which makes the believer dependent for his confidence upon his moods.   But, Luther's confidence came not from his moods, but from his abiding certainty in Christ of God's forgiveness.   God's forgiveness is not a solitary act.   " Just as the sun shines and illuminates none the less brightly when I close my eyes, so this throne of grace, or this forgiveness of sins, is always there, even though I fall.   And just as I see the sun again when I re-open my eyes, so also I have forgiveness of sins once more when I look up and come back to Christ ".[2]

What of the relation of faith and works ?   Paul, having in mind the teaching of the Judaizers, had spoken of a way of faith " apart from works ".   Luther re-echoed his words in reference to " works " regarded as meritorious, and thus conceived as earning salvation.   His views are well expressed in his curt Propositions of 1520.

" Faith, unless it is without even the smallest works, does not justify, indeed, is not faith ".

" It is impossible for faith to exist without assiduous, many and great works ".

" Neither faith nor justification comes from works, but works come from faith and justification ".[3]

In this same year, the year of his excommunication and final breach with Rome, Luther wrote not only his three *Primary Works* but his less famous *Treatise on Good Works*.   In it to show that a Christian " enlightened and strengthened by faith "

[1] *W.A.* XL. i. p. 298 (on Gal. ii. 20).
[2] Cp. W. Herrmann, *Communion of the Christian with God*, E.T.[2], p. 249.
[3] *Propositiones a Martino Luthero disputatae*, 3, 4, 20 (*W.A.* VII. p. 231).

does not need " a teacher of good works ", Luther uses the illustration of a man and wife living together in complete mutual trust. Such "make no difference in works" but do whatever is necessary whether great or small, " with joyful, peaceful, confident hearts ". Faith is like health without which our limbs cannot fulfil their function. " When some say good works are forbidden when we preach faith alone, it is as if I said to a sick man : ' If you had health, you would have the use of all your limbs ; but without health, the works of all your limbs are nothing ' ; and he wanted to infer that I had forbidden the works of all his limbs ; whereas, on the contrary, I meant that he must first have health, which will work all the works of all the members. So faith also must be in all works the master-workman and captain, or they are nothing at all ".[1] And Luther dealt in this Treatise with all the Ten Commandments from this point of view.

In his great Treatise on *Christian Liberty*, written in the same year, Luther asserted not only the liberty of faith but the bondage of love. The Christian " ought to think : ' Though I am an unworthy and condemned man, my God hath given me in Christ all the riches of righteousness and salvation without any merit on my part, out of pure free mercy, so that henceforth I need nothing whatever except faith which believes that this is true. Why should I not therefore freely, joyfully, with all my heart, and with an eager will, do all things, which I know are pleasing and acceptable to such a Father, who has overwhelmed me with His inestimable riches. I will therefore give myself as a Christ to my neighbour, just as Christ offered Himself to me : I will do nothing in this life except what I see is necessary, profitable and salutary to my neighbour, since through faith I have an abundance of all good things in Christ '. Lo, thus from faith flow forth love and joy in the Lord, and from love a joyful, willing and free mind that serves one's neighbour willingly and takes no account of gratitude or ingratitude, of praise or blame, of gain or loss. . . . Therefore, if we recognize the great and precious things that are given us, as St. Paul

---

[1] *Works of Martin Luther*, E.T. edited by H. E. Jacobs, I. pp. 191, 199.

says, there will be shed abroad in our hearts by the Holy Ghost
the love which makes us free, joyful, almighty workers and
conquerors over all tribulations, servants of our neighbours and
yet lords of all ".[1] Through love we learn to imitate our Lord,
and yet " it is not our imitation which has made us sons, it is
our being sons which has made us imitators ".[2]

Forgiveness to Luther was primary. Repentance is not
" to be reached by merely meditating upon sin and its consequences ". " True contrition " comes as we " look into the
wounds of Christ, and see in them His love towards us and our
ingratitude towards Him, and thus, with heartfelt affection to
Christ and detestation of self, to meditate upon our sin ".[3]
The Roman conception of penance was thus abandoned. As
Luther puts it in his *Little Catechism*, " Where there is forgiveness of sins, there is also life and blessedness ".

Luther had translated Rom. iii. 28 " justified by faith
alone ".[4] His addition of the word " alone " was much condemned, and his teaching characterized as " solifidianism ".
In his *Preface* to the Epistle to the Romans of 1522, Luther
makes clear how inevitably faith, as he conceived it, leads to
works. Faith " changes us and makes us to be born anew of
God ; it kills the old Adam, and makes us altogether different
men, in heart and spirit, and mind and powers, and it brings
with it the Holy Ghost. O, it is a living, busy, active, mighty
thing, this faith ; and so it is impossible for it not to do good
works incessantly. It does not ask whether there are good
works to do but before the question rises, it has already done
them, and is always at the doing of them. . . . Faith is a
living, daring confidence in God's grace, so sure and certain
that a man would stake his life on it a thousand times. This
confidence in God's grace and knowledge of it makes men glad
and bold and happy in dealing with God and with all His
creatures ; and this is the work of the Holy Ghost in faith.

[1] *Op. cit.* II. pp. 337 f.

[2] *W.A.* II. p. 518 (on Gal. iii. 13, from the *Commentary on Galatians*,
of 1519).

[3] *Works of Martin Luther*, III. p. 47.

[4] For Luther's defence of this translation, as required by German
idiom, see his *On Translating. An Open Letter, op. cit.* V. pp. 10–23.

Hence a man is ready, and glad, without compulsion, to do good
to everyone, to serve everyone, to suffer everything, in love
and praise of God, who has shown him this grace ; and thus it
is impossible to separate works from faith, quite as impossible
as to separate heat and light from fire ".[1]

In his passionate attacks on the Roman conception of
meritorious works, Luther employed at times expressions which,
taken out of their context, can be used by those who hate the
Reformation to prove his indifference to good works. But his
real teaching is unmistakable. With St. Paul he asserted that
God's forgiveness is received by the response of faith and yet,
like St. James, he taught that a faith which does not lead to
" works " is dead. Talking about faith and love and repeating
doctrines and formulae are not enough. " God does not want
hearers and repeaters of words, but doers and followers who
exercise themselves in the faith that worketh by love. For a
faith without love is not enough—rather it is not faith at all,
but a counterfeit of faith, just as a face seen in a mirror is not
a real face, but merely the reflection of a face ".[2] So Luther
warned his fellow-townspeople at Wittenberg in 1522. But the
excitement at Wittenberg, which caused Luther, at the peril of
his life, to leave the retirement into which he had gone for
safety after the Diet of Worms, illustrates the turbulence of the
age in which he lived. In such an age it was almost inevitable
that his teaching on the sufficiency of faith should be misunderstood, and his proclamation of liberty made a pretext for licence.

The development in view of Luther's friend Melanchthon is
of interest. In the first edition of his *Loci Communes* published
in 1521, a year after Luther's breach with Rome, he describes
faith as " not a mere opinion, the uncertain, inconstant and
changing thought of the mind on the Word of God ". Instead,
it is " nothing else than trust (*fiducia*) in the mercy of God
promised in Christ Jesus. This faith in the benevolence or
mercy of God first brings peace to the heart and then enkindles
gratitude to God so that we freely and gladly fulfil the law ".[3]
In the greatly enlarged third, and final, edition of his book

[1] *Op. cit.* VI. pp. 451 f.   [2] *Op. cit.* II. p. 392.
[3] pp. 160 and 163 of Plitt-Kolde's edition of 1900.

published in 1545, Melanchthon was no longer content to define faith as trust.   With trust (*fiducia*) there had to be also know-ledge (*notitia*) and assent (*assensus*).   " When we speak of assent to the promise ", he writes, " we include knowledge of all the articles " ; though he adds " all the other articles of the Creed are referred to thus : I believe in the forgiveness of sins, I believe in eternal life.   This is, indeed, the sum and end of the promises to which the other articles refer ".   Faith, which is man's response to the grace of God in the Cross of Christ, leads to a life of obedience to God and love to men.   But faith which is merely assent to orthodoxy, may be a faith " without works ", and Melanchthon had now to emphasize that those reconciled to God needed " the righteousness (*iustitia*) of a good con-science ".[1]   Melanchthon's careful teaching on the place of good works in the Christian life was attacked by some who regarded themselves as the Genuine-Lutherans (Gnesio-Lutherans).   As Harnack says, " The Lutheran Church had to pay dearly for turning away from ' legal righteousness '. . . . Through having the resolute wish to go back to *religion*, and to it alone, it neglected far too much the moral problem, the ' Be ye holy, for I am holy ' ".[2]

The Thirty-Nine Articles of the Church of England of 1562 rightly declared " that we are justified by Faith only is a most wholesome Doctrine, and very full of comfort ", and affirmed that " Good Works, which are the fruits of Faith, and follow after Justification . . . do spring out necessarily of a true and lively Faith ; inasmuch as by them a lively Faith may be as evidently known as a tree discerned by the fruit ".[3]   But unless the doctrine of " Justification by Faith only " be associated with the grateful realization of God's grace in Christ's Cross, then the doctrine may be to some unwholesome. It is a false comfort which believes :

> A lively faith will bear aloft the mind
> And leave the luggage of good works behind.[4]

---

[1] *Corpus Reformatorum*, XXI. cols. 751 and 780.   Cp. the writer's *The Christian Estimate of Man*, pp. 141 f.

[2] *History of Dogma*, E.T. VII. p. 267.   [3] Articles XI and XII.

[4] J. Dryden, *The Hind and the Panther*, iii.

That has always been the peril of Evangelicalism, but this peril is no disproof of its truth.

John Wesley, who owed to his Moravian friends his vivid realization of the doctrine of Justification by Faith, was soon repelled by what he called their *solifidianism* and strongly condemned Luther's *Commentary on Galatians* which earlier he had praised.[1] In his *Plain Account of Christian Perfection*, completed in 1777, he wrote, " Once more, beware of Solifidianism ; crying nothing but ' Believe, believe ', and condemning those as ignorant or legal who speak in a more scriptural way ". Instead, he bade his Preachers preach " perfection to believers constantly, strongly, and explicitly ; and all believers should mind this one thing and continually agonize for it ".[2] Wesley's doctrine of Christian Perfection is not without its difficulties, but his endeavour " to spread Scriptural Holiness throughout the land " remains as a salutary challenge to any conception of Christianity which, rightly emphasizing the primacy of faith, so interprets faith as to allow the believer to be content with his failure perfectly to respond to the grace of God in Christ.

In one of his *Short Studies on Great Subjects*, J. A. Froude speaks in strong condemnation of a hymn he heard sung at an " Evangelical prayer-meeting " :

> Nothing either great or small,
> Nothing, sinners, no ;
> Jesus did it—did it all,
> Long, long ago.

> It is finished, yes, indeed,
> Finished every jot ;
> Sinners, this is all you need,
> Tell me, Is it not ?

> When He from His lofty throne
> Stooped to do and die,
> Everything was fully done ;
> Hearken to His cry,—

---

[1] In his *Journal* of June 15th, 1741.
[2] *The Works of the Rev. John Wesley* [5], XI. pp. 431 and 443 ; see later, p. 165.

Weary, weary, burdened one,
   Wherefore toil you so ?
Cease your doing, all was done
   Long, long ago.

Till to Jesus' work you cling
   By a simple faith,
Doing is a deadly thing,
   Doing ends in death.

Caste your deadly doing down,
   Down at Jesus' feet,
Stand in Him, in Him alone,
   Gloriously complete.

Froude comments, " And this we said to ourselves is Protestantism, to do our duty is a deadly thing. This is what, after three centuries, the creed of Luther, of Coligny and Gustavus Adolphus has come to ". " How has a creed which once sounded the spiritual reveille like the blast of an archangel's trumpet now come to proclaim in passionate childishness the ' deadliness ' of human duty ? [1]

Froude's criticism shows how easily the Evangelical doctrine may be misunderstood. These doggerel lines, which we have not found in any modern hymnbook, were intended to bring to troubled consciences the great truth of the perfect adequacy of what Christ has done for men. We cannot earn God's forgiveness by any " doing " of our own. So St. Paul and Luther found ; so many have found who have sought to win the confidence of God's forgiveness by a scrupulous obedience to some external law. But teaching thus crudely expressed could lead to complacency and spiritual indolence. Henry Drummond once remarked, " The sin of Evangelicalism is laziness ". A degenerate Evangelicalism may lead some so to rely on what Christ has done as to feel that there is nothing they themselves need do. They have " faith ", what need of " works " ? Like St. Paul's converts at Corinth, such act as if the Kingdom were already perfected, as if they could share its blessings and evade its struggle.[2] For St. Paul, faith brought new zeal and new energy. His conversion turned his gaze from his own achieve-

---

[1] *Short Studies in Great Subjects*, 1872, edit., II. pp. 150 f., 153.
[2] 1 Cor. iv. 8.

ments and failures to the contemplation of Christ, his crucified and risen Lord, and, seeing Christ, he saw the needs of men and sought to serve them by his abundant labours.   The leaders of the Reformation were likewise men who gained from their faith the impulse to an amazing activity.   It was those who thought not of their " works " but of God's grace in Christ who later helped to free the slave, and to rid our land of some of its gravest social evils, whilst the mission field provides many an instance of the devoted energy which faith can inspire.

Every truth can be perverted.   Faith can degenerate into a mere assent to correct opinion ; liberty can lead to lassitude ; noble professions can become a substitute for humble and devoted service.   It is useless to say, Lord, Lord, if we do not seek to do the things which He commanded.   What men are determines what they do, but it is by their fruits that men are judged.   It is perilous to rely only on an initial response of faith.   Our forgetful minds and wayward wills need to be controlled.   The world for which Christ died is still a world of sin and sorrow, and we cannot serve Him in it if we refuse to exercise self-discipline.   God's forgiveness is received on the response of faith, and yet there is need of what may be called an evangelical asceticism.

(3) EVANGELICAL ASCETICISM

Asceticism had in the pagan environment of early Christianity a double significance.   It was an attempt to win self-redemption ;   it was a means employed to avert the anger of some god or goddess.   Like the Indian *sadhu*, the ascetic might be good or bad, but his asceticism was held to give him mysterious potency, and, since matter was regarded as evil, asceticism was esteemed as a means of liberation, even although the ascetic had neither faith in God nor love to men.   And where gods were feared, asceticism was used to avert calamity.   Who that has seen it, can forget his first sight of a vast crowd of low-caste Indians gathered in the honour of a cruel goddess, not only making to her sacrifices of blood, but seeking by their own austerities to avert her anger ?   I remember seeing a little child led round and round a shrine at one such festival, crying piteously, as was natural, for his back was pierced with an iron wire.   And yet his parents were acting not from cruelty but from love.   Their child had been ill, and, believing that his illness came from this goddess, they had vowed that if only she would spare their child's life they would carry him from their distant home to the place of her festival and march him round her shrine with his back thus pierced.

If asceticism be given these pagan meanings, then Evangelical Asceticism would be a contradiction in terms.   The Gospel knows nothing of self-redemption achieved by austerities, and is concerned not with liberation from the material, but with salvation from sin, whilst the God of whom it speaks is not a God who needs to be appeased by self-inflicted suffering, but the God of grace who requires from us the response of faith, and a repentance which is a " change of mind " and not a painful penance.   But, in spite of the accretions from pagan belief and practice which have influenced the meaning of the word, *askesis*, asceticism, has, for its prime meaning, training, like that which every athlete must undergo, and such training, such self-discipline, is a necessary part of the Christian life.

In the New Testament the verb connected with the noun *askesis* occurs only once : in Acts xxiv. 16, where St. Paul says " I exercise myself ", *i.e.* " I put myself in training ", in order to have " a conscience void of offence toward God and men ". It is significant that it was the great Apostle of Christian liberty who thus spoke of a Christian asceticism.   Elsewhere, although he employs different words to express his meaning, he uses the strongest terms to describe his own self-discipline.   Competitors at the Isthmian games at Corinth had to go into rigorous training, and did so for a prize which was only a garland which would soon wither away.   For the higher prize—the prize of sharing in the work of the Gospel—St. Paul bruised his body and brought it into bondage, lest he, who summoned others to race, should be himself disqualified.[1]   But he condemned those who subjected

---

[1] 1 Cor. ix. 24–7. Cp. 1 Tim. iv. 7. " Exercise thyself unto godliness " or, as Moffatt translates, " Train for the religious life ". The word translated " exercise ", or " train ", is the verbal form of the noun transliterated into English as " gymnast ".

themselves to external ordinances : " Touch not, taste not, handle not ". Such " severity to the body " was " not of any value against the indulgence of the flesh ".[1]

Much of the asceticism of the Church has been derived from ideas more pagan than Christian, for early Christianity not only influenced its pagan environment but was influenced by it. Against the pagan belief that matter was evil, the Church affirmed that the Word had become flesh but, although it resisted in the sphere of belief the excesses of Gnosticism, in the sphere of ethics this pagan belief that matter was evil led to the view that virginity was the supreme Christian virtue. And asceticism was prized not only as a means of suppressing bodily desires but as a means of winning God's favour. For-giveness was associated with Baptism, but there was from very early times grave uncertainty about the possibility of winning forgiveness for sins committed after Baptism. It was easier to believe that His favour had to be won by renunciation and austerities so that eternal punishment could be averted by temporal afflictions. As Tertullian put it, " the less you spare yourself, the more God will spare you ". Repentance, $\mu\epsilon\tau\alpha\nuo\iota\alpha$, a change of mind, was interpreted as penance—" an affliction of the flesh " by which God could be " appeased ".[2] The New Testament speaks much of joy—a joy in which even the perse-cuted could share. How different from this joy was the sour fanaticism of the learned St. Jerome. We think, for instance, of his praise of Paula, because, although a mother, " she mourned and fasted, she was squalid with dirt and her eyes were dim with weeping. For whole nights she would pray to the Lord for mercy, and often the rising of the sun found her still at her prayers ".[3]

So long as Christianity was a proscribed religion, the call to heroism had been answered by readiness to endure martyrdom. But, when through Constantine's patronage of Christianity the Empire became nominally Christian, the Church increased in numbers and in worldliness, and, in reaction from that

---

[1] Col. ii. 21, 23.
[2] Tertullian, *On Repentance*, IX ; *On Patience*, XII. Cp. the writer's *The Christian Estimate of Man*, pp. 70 f.   [3] Epistle XLV.

worldliness, monasticism had an enormous vogue. *The Life of St. Anthony*, ascribed to St. Athanasius, provided for many the ideal of the Christian life, and in Egypt vast numbers of monks sought to find peace in the desert, whether in solitude or in communities. Their quest for ever-greater deprivation was not always marked by humility. How illuminating, for instance, is Palladius's story of Macarius of Alexandria who sought to outbid all others in his asceticism. At length, hearing of the rigour of the rule observed in a certain monastery, disguising himself as a workman, he asked its archimandrite, Pachomius, to let him become a monk. He was told he was too old to endure the hard labours of the brethren, but at last he obtained the permission he sought, and soon surpassed all the fourteen hundred brethren by his austerities. Angry at this, they went to Pachomius and said, " Where did you get this fleshless man from, to condemn us ? Either drive him out, or know that we all are going ". Pachomius, discovering that the stranger was the famous ascetic Macarius, brought him into the house of prayer and said to him " Here, good old man, you are Macarius and you hid it from me. . . . I thank you for letting my children feel your fist, lest they should be proud of their ascetic achievements. Now go away to your own place, for you have edified us sufficiently. And pray for us ". And he went away.[1] Yet although some, like this Macarius, and the still more famous St. Simeon Stylites, practised their austerities as if they were athletes seeking to beat a world record, others were humble and gentle men, who sought in the desert a way of perfection which they felt they could not attain in the busy haunts of men.

The energy and earnestness of monasticism were controlled and directed to less self-regarding ends by St. Basil in the East who associated work with worship, and made monasteries centres of Christian education. In the West, monasticism gained in the sixth century stability and usefulness through the Rule of St. Benedict, and the Benedictine Abbeys, in Italy, in France, and in England, became centres of useful work as well

---

[1] *The Lausiac History* of Palladius, E.T. pp. 81 f. by W. K. Lowther Clarke. For an attractive account of these Egyptian monks, see Miss Helen Waddell, *The Desert Fathers*.

as of devotion.   In the thirteenth century there arose the great
Mendicant Orders of Dominicans, Franciscans and Carmelites,
and Europe owed much to these Preaching Friars, whilst after
the Reformation the Roman Church found new shock-troops
in the Jesuit Order whose members were trained to absolute
obedience, the complete surrender of private judgment, and
willingness to endure any hardship in the service of the Church.

Christian asceticism, in its ancient or its modern Roman form,
though marred at times by pride, or masochism, or by pagan views
of God or man, has yet been an impressive witness to the zeal with
which some have sought to fulfil, as they believed, the will of God.

A legal conception of man's relationship with God led at a
very early stage in Christian history to the division of works
into the supererogatory and the obligatory.[1]   This distinction
merged into the distinction of the " Counsels " and the " Precepts ".   The Precepts were for every Christian ; the Counsels
for those who sought Perfection by obedience, poverty and
chastity, and by chastity was meant the purity not of the married man or woman but of the celibate.   It has been suggested
that this distinction corresponds to a Pass and Honours standard
in Christianity, with only the few expected to take Honours.
But as Canon Lindsay Dewar says, " This way of putting the
question is somewhat repulsive to the Christian conscience,
conflicting as it does with our Lord's explicit call to perfection,
when He said ; ' Be ye perfect, even as your Father in heaven
is perfect '.   The solution of the difficulty seems to be in a consideration of the word ' perfect '.   It is plainly a relative term ;
it only means ' complete '.   If I have it in me to be only a
twenty-five-per-cent man, my attainments will obviously be
less than if I am a seventy-five-per-cent man, even if I am
' perfect ' ".[2]   This suggestion is an interesting one, but it is
perilous to assume that those who live what is called the
" religious " life have reached a higher standard than those in
the ordinary avocations of the world.   We remember what
Father Giles, a companion of St. Francis said, " I would rather
have a little of the grace of God as a Religious in the Order

[1] Cp. earlier, p. 129, on *The Shepherd of Hermas*.
[2] *Christian Morals*, p. 195.

than have many of the graces of God while living in the world :
for in the world there be many more dangers and hindrances,
and much less healing remedy and help than in the religious
life ".[1]   The employer or trade union leader, the statesman
or the soldier, may need not less courage but more to live the
Christian life than those do who, as set aside for the service of
the Church, are expected to be what men call " good ".   What
matters is that we should seek to do what God would have us
do, living in humble dependence on His grace, trusting in Him
to give us strength to bear such special burdens as our calling
or our circumstances may put upon us.

The conception of " calling " or " vocation " received at the
Reformation a wider meaning.   In place of the tendency to
restrict the conception to the " religious " life, Luther proclaimed that the mother, or the maid-servant in the home had
as truly a Christian calling as any monk or nun.   Christians
were not called to flee from the world, but to be Christians in
their ordinary callings.   The priesthood of all believers became
one of the great watchwords of the Reformation.

As often, the rediscovery of a great truth was not without
its danger.   In asserting the sacredness of the secular it is easy
to secularize the sacred.   Those words of Christ on which the
" Catholic " doctrine of Perfection had been based, were, indeed,
addressed to individuals, and are to be interpreted by the
concrete circumstances in which they were uttered.   Not all
were called to be " eunuchs for the Kingdom of heaven's sake ",
to sell all that they had to give to the poor, to take up the cross.[2]
Yet these sayings are a reminder that some are called to special
tasks which may involve special privations.

It is significant that those branches of the Church, which
emphasize most the priesthood of all believers, lay great stress
on the necessity of a call or vocation for the ministry, and will
not knowingly ordain, or even accept for ministerial training,
any but those to whom, as it is believed, God's call has come.
Where such seek missionary work, there is the still greater need
to be sure of the reality of their vocation, for such work means

[1] *The Little Flowers of St. Francis*, E.T. by T. W. Arnold, Temple
edition, p. 308.   [2] On these sayings see earlier, pp. 57 f.

not only loneliness and privation but may mean apparent failure and even peril. The writer thinks with pride of two of his own former students. One of them, Alfred Sadd, was a man of abounding cheerfulness and vitality. He entered College to train for missionary service, and, when his course with us at Cambridge ended, went to the lonely Gilbert Islands and showed there amazing patience and fortitude. He would have ridiculed the notion that his life was one of self-sacrifice. He would have said that he had the job he wanted and that was that. When the Japanese drew near, he refused to leave his work, and, when they landed and decided to kill their British captives, he remained cheerful to the end and stood in front of the others so that he should be the first to die. As a Gilbertese Pastor later wrote, " There came a Jap and struck him with the sword and all the Europeans clapped their hands and were happy and unafraid, when they saw the courage of Mr. Sadd ". The other, R. J. B. Moore, his contemporary at Cheshunt College, went to do pioneer work in the Copper Belt in Africa, and, after years of hard, and apparently unrewarding, work, died when only thirty-three, his last year being one of torturing pain which he endured with unfailing courage.[1] Neither man was an " ascetic ", if by asceticism is meant the pursuit of deprivation and suffering as ends in themselves. Both were " ascetics ", in the other and earlier sense, for they had trained themselves, as athletes train, to endure hardness. They did not speak, or think, of their self-sacrifice, but faced with cheerfulness loneliness, drudgery and difficulty, as the necessary accompaniments of their vocation, and when that vocation led them to early death, they met it with courage and without complaint.

No man can do effective work without self-discipline, and in this world where many are in want, and where hard tasks have to be done, pleasant things, good in themselves, have to be renounced, and our lives lived with a diligence which excludes all self-indulgence. Yet life's simple pleasures are not to be shunned because they are pleasant. As even Calvin reminds us, the " gifts of Providence " were created " for our good ",

---

[1] There are short memoirs of both these men : *Alfred Sadd of the Gilberts*, by Nelson Bitton, and *Moore of the Copper Belt*, by H. Theobald.

and God " consulted not only for our necessity, but also for our enjoyment and delight ".   " Has the Lord adorned flowers with all the beauty which spontaneously presents itself to the eye and the sweet fragrance which delights the sense of smell, and shall it be unlawful for us to enjoy that beauty and this fragrance ? "[1]   The splendour of the starlit sky, the loveliness of valleys and of hills, the charm of little children, the joys of pure wedded-love, the consolations of friendship, the delights that come from great literature and art—all these are God's good gifts, and, as such, to be received with gratitude.   There is, as a Baptist scholar has said, a Protestant asceticism which " gives the ' world ' the impression that Christianity is inseparable from narrow-mindedness, bigotry and gloom ".[2]   That is a misrepresentation of the Gospel.   Our Lord called some to renounce home, and, if need be, life itself.   And yet it was Good News He preached.   Renunciation there must be in every Christian life, and yet renunciation is not to be sought as if it had value in itself, instead of in the end it serves.   We remember Dr. John Oman's wise and weighty words :   " As an arranged scheme of self-deliverance from evil, self-sacrifice is apt to be only an arranged scheme of self-exaltation.   The only denial of self worth anything is from the challenge of following the highest ;   and this never calls itself self-sacrifice and much less self-immolation ".[3]   As Christians we have to ask ourselves not, How may I deny myself, but how, in obedience to God's will for me, may I be faithful in my vocation and thus show my gratitude to God for the good gifts He has given us in Creation, and for the still greater gift of His redeeming love ?

Different men have different tasks, and these tasks differ much in their scope and cost.   But from all believing men and women one demand is made—fidelity.   It is in regard to faithfulness in vocation that we may speak of the Imitation of Christ as the Christian ideal.   If by the Imitation of Christ is meant that Christ is our exemplar whose every act we have to seek to copy, then the Imitation of Christ, as Thomas à Kempis'

[1] *Institutes*, III. x. 2.
[2] L. H. Marshall, *The Challenge of Christian Ethics*, p. 183.
[3] *The Natural and the Supernatural*, p. 500.

lovely book reminds us, is a monastic ideal, relevant only to those freed from common human ties and tasks. Our Lord had but one vocation—to be the agent of God's saving work for men. It was a vocation universal in its significance which precluded any private vocation. We have our private vocations, are husbands, it may be, and fathers, and have our professional or business responsibilities. We have to seek to be faithful in our callings as He was faithful in His, but we may not copy His acts as if our vocations were identical with His. The question, " What would Jesus do ? "—the sub-title of that once famous religious best-seller, *In His Steps*—is not a guide for Christian conduct. Jesus would not be where we are ; He had not those private callings in the context of which we have to live our Christian lives. But it is no less necessary to emphasize that in our callings we have to seek to live the Christian life. We have to endeavour to fulfil efficiently the duties of our station, but we may not act as if our secular vocation could be abstracted from the control of God, or as if it were sufficient to do on week-days as others do, leaving to Sundays the recognition of God's rule. We may not say, as F. H. Bradley did, " There is nothing better than my station and its duties, nor anything higher or more truly beautiful ". That is the kind of teaching that leads to the claim : " business is business ", and " politics are politics " ; so they are, but in these spheres, too, we have to seek to be obedient to God's will. Bradley wrote as a disciple of Hegel and quoted with approval Hegel's words that " wisdom and virtue consist in living according to the Ethos of one's own people ".[1] That is certainly the easiest way to live, but it is not to this easy way that Christ summons His disciples. If that were all He desired from men, no one would have troubled to have Him crucified. There is no sphere of life, and so no vocation, of which we may say, " With this God has nothing to do ". Whatever be our calling, in it we have to seek to live as God would have us live ; Christ's vocation was unique and inimitable, but we are called in our private callings to be faithful as He was.

[1] *My Station and its Duties* (*Ethical Studies*, 1935 reprint, pp. 201 and 187).

But if we are in this sense to imitate our Lord, there is need of evangelical asceticism. Traditional asceticism, as we have seen, was based in part on the pagan belief that matter was evil, and the body a " tomb ", from which the spirit must win deliverance. The self-indulgent are impressed by such asceticism, but that kind of mortification of the body does not meet the spirit's needs. Hitler increased his prestige by his vegetarianism and his celibacy, but that did not make him less an influence for evil ; it would have been better had he been a debauchee and a glutton, for he would then have had less power to torment the world. Nor does Protestant asceticism, with its avoidance of the so-called *adiaphora*, the things indifferent, suffice. We need, indeed, what some of the Puritans called " weaned affections ", that we may use simple pleasures as a means and not an end, but it is possible to live a life of austere self-denial, and yet to be hard and loveless. Zeal, and what men call self-sacrifice, if we have not love, profit us nothing. As Dr. Temple wrote, " It is the spirit that is evil ; it is reason which is perverted ; it is aspiration itself which is corrupt ".[1] How is our spirit to be freed from evil, our reason from perversion, our aspiration from corruption ? Rules, such as those which the Moral Theology of Roman, and of some Anglo-Catholic, theologians provide, do not suffice, nor do the prohibitions of some Protestant pietists meet our need. We are called to the Christian liberty of the children of God, but that liberty, as many an ancient and modern instance shows, is a perilous delusion unless it be accompanied by the continuous remembrance of what we owe to God and so to men.

Evangelical Christianity finds its characteristic expression in the doctrine of Justification by Faith, but faith may become " dead ", unless it be the present experience of God's mercy. Christian character springs from Christian gratitude, and gratitude may be lost through forgetfulness.

> But each day brings its petty dust
> Our soon choked souls to fill,
> And we forget because we must
> And not because we will.[2]

---

[1] *Nature, Man and God*, p. 368.   [2] Matthew Arnold, *Absence*.

Even human friendships need to be kept in repair, and neglect leads to indifference. As a Scandinavian proverb says, " Go often to the house of thy friend for thorns block up the unused path ". The initial experience of God's mercy will not secure a life-long allegiance, unless it be renewed through all our years. We cannot serve God as we ought, unless our service be based upon our worship, and worship means gratitude and recollection, a realization of God's mercy which belongs not to the past alone but to the present.

Christian life becomes vital and personal for many in their youth, when, in the years of decision, they make their response to the challenge of the Gospel. The Church has no more urgent, and no more rewarding, task than thus to lead the young to personal allegiance, whilst, without the enthusiasm of youth, Churches would lose much of their strength and most of their attractiveness.

" O Jesus, I have promised to serve Thee to the end ". With that promise many begin their conscious Christian life, although they, in many cases, owe more than they realize to the Christian nurture of Church and home. But " confirmation ", or " joining the Church " in youth, though it means very much, is not in itself sufficient. The heroism of youth is not without its self-deception. The first acceptance of Christ as Master, the first promise to serve Him to the end, are inadequate, unless they be confirmed by growing and continuous experience. How many there are without the Church who once were in its communion ; how many within the Church who have become complacent or indifferent because they have sought to live their lives on the experience of their youth and who, in consequence, have lost not only zeal but joy.

> Where is the blessedness I knew
> When first I saw the Lord ?
> Where is the soul-refreshing view
> Of Jesus and His word ?

How is that " soul-refreshing view " to be preserved ? It will not be, if the first view, the initial experience, be regarded as sufficient. What we do not increase we lose, and the Christian life cannot be worthily maintained on the first response of youth. If we know no more of Christ at sixty than at sixteen, then our knowledge of Him will have ceased to inspire us to zeal and service.

That great Evangelical, Dr. R. W. Dale, in his weighty, little book, *The Old Evangelicalism and the New*, points out that Evangelical congregations once " assumed that what they called mere moral teaching was unnecessary to spiritual people. They were apt to say : ' Make the tree good and the fruit will be good as a matter of course '. They forgot that grapes under culture are very much better than grapes which are left to grow wild ".[1] We need that " culture ", that self-discipline, that evangelical asceticism, which speaks not only of love but of duty. In its reaction from the legalism of Roman Catholicism, Protestantism has, at times, too lightly assumed that faith goes always on to love. True faith does, but it is easy to grow forgetful of God, so that faith becomes too weak to pass into love. There is truth in Professor Emil Brunner's words : " Duty and genuine goodness are mutually exclusive. Obedience due to a sense of unwilling constraint is bondage, and, indeed, the bondage of sin. If I feel I *ought* to do right, it is a sign that I cannot do it. If I could really do it, there would be no question of ' ought ' about it at all. The sense of ' ought ' shows me the Good at an infinite impassable distance from my will. Willing obedience is never the fruit of an ' ought ' but only of love ".[2] Brunner is attacking the legalism which leads to self-righteousness, and thus isolates the legalist from his fellows. But the exclusion of the conception of duty from the Christian life is not without its dangers. Were we better men than we are, love might be our only obligation. But it is perilous to assume that our love is such that it leads always to obedience. There are times when inclination would cause us to shun the unpleasant interview and the tedious task, which yet, we know, are in the way of our duty. If we were better than we are, the love which springs from faith might be all we need to maintain

---

[1] p. 29.

[2] *The Divine Imperative*, p. 74. For a criticism of Brunner's position here, see Reinhold Niebuhr, *The Nature and Destiny of Man*, **II.** p. 196 ff.

our fidelity.   But, being what we are, we need the self-discipline, the *askesis*, the evangelical asceticism of obligation ; otherwise love may become mere sentimentality, for it does not express itself in action.

Yet a Christian life, based only on obligation, would lack that joy which is one of the keynotes of the New Testament. God does not need our prayers, except as a mother desires the confidence of her little child, but we need to pray, even when we do not feel like praying.   The Christian life requires the regular moments of private prayer, the recollection of God's mercy, the meditation on the words of Jesus, the participation in the experience of the writers of the New Testament.   God knows our weakness.   He has given us, in Calvin's phrase " helps in accommodation to our infirmity "—the public worship of the Church and its proclamation of the Word, and the Sacrament in which Christ meets with His people, and gives Himself to them, renewing in them the joy of their forgiveness. How can we live as we ought to live except with the remembrance of God's grace in Him, how forgive except as we know ourselves forgiven, how be saved from weakness and failure, except by conscious dependence on His Spirit ?   St. Paul wrote his greatest affirmations of Christian truth in connexion with the ordinary obligations of the Christian life.   We, too, need to live in humble recollection of God's mercy.   In Richard Baxter's words, " Let Thankfulness to God thy Creator, Redeemer and Regenerator, be the very temperament of thy soul, and faithfully expressed by thy tongue and life ".[1]   That cannot be except as we keep fresh the remembrance of God's grace, nor can we live the Christian life on earth except already we know in part the resources of the unseen and the eternal.

(4) THE RELEVANCE OF THE ETERNAL

F. W. H. Myers reports that he once asked a Churchwarden what he thought would happen to him at death.   The Churchwarden replied, " I shall immediately depart unto everlasting

---

[1] *A Christian Directory*, I. iii.   *Grand Direction* XIV.   In 1830 edit., vol. II. p. 421.

felicity but I wish you wouldn't talk about such unpleasant subjects ". That Victorian Churchwarden is not without his representatives to-day. Such do not renounce the traditional Christian belief that there is a future life, and yet the thought of the life beyond the grave is merely an " unpleasant subject ". *Memento mori* is not, indeed, a Christian motto. It is life, not death, which is our immediate concern, but the Christian message is unintelligible, except it be related to the Eternal, whilst to reduce it to an ethic concerned only with action in this world is to make it not a Gospel but a demand which, if taken seriously, would drive us to despair.

Thoreau, the New England Transcendentalist, complained of Jesus, " He taught mankind but imperfectly how to live. His thoughts were all directed towards another world ". That is not what we learn from the Gospels. They depict Jesus as concerned with men's present needs, their sins, their sorrows and their sicknesses. And yet He called them to live their present life as those sure of their heavenly Father's care. Only so could they be free from the distraction of anxiety, and, fearing God, fear no one else. The kingdom to which He summoned men was not merely a future realm. It was the reign of God whose redemptive power they could already in part experience. When asked about life beyond the grave, our Lord based His certainty of that life on this : that God was the God of the living and would not allow a communion with Him begun on earth to lapse at death.[1]

The resurrection of Jesus from the dead made the unseen world a present reality to His disciples. The " Age to Come " had broken through into this present age and its redemptive powers were already in part realized. This new experience found in St. Paul its great interpreter. Influenced by Luther's controversy with the Roman Church, Protestant scholars have often spoken as if the Christianity of St. Paul could be explained as the substitution of Gospel for Law, of Faith for Works. But that is an undue simplification. As Julius Kaftan, himself a Lutheran, reminds us, the Judaism of Paul's time had two *foci* : the Law and the Messianic hope. The first concerned

[1] See earlier, pp. 39 f.

" righteousness before God " ; the second, a redemption from the world associated with the irruption into this age of " the Age to Come ". At his conversion, St. Paul found both these aspirations fulfilled. Not only did he gain a new power and joy through his response of faith to God's grace in Christ ; he also felt himself already in part possessed of the spiritual resources of " the Age to Come ", the unseen and the eternal. As Kaftan points out, Protestantism has paid a heavy price for this one-sidedness. The Roman Church had in monasticism a symbol of Christian unworldliness, but it was an unworldliness available only for the monk. At the Reformation monasticism was abandoned, but " Protestantism had nothing to put in its place ". Its hymn-writers did, in part, fill up the gap, but its theologians failed to make clear that a Christian is meant to find in the eternal his present.[1]

There is an otherworldliness which is unchristian, for it robs our present life of its significance by dwelling only on the life to come, and this other worldliness may lead to an acquiescence in social injustice and to an indifference to other's needs, through failure to relate the Christian message to the present life of men. Yet there is an unworldliness which is integral to the Christian Gospel. Already in time we may know in part the resources of the eternal. As we have seen, St. Paul expressed this Christian experience from three aspects : he was adopted into sonship, for God who was the Father of our Lord Jesus Christ was his Father, a " Father of mercies, a God of all consolation "; he was " in Christ Jesus "—Christ was, as it were, the very atmosphere he breathed, the life in which he shared ; he had already the partial experience of the Spirit's power, an experience which was like a first instalment, guaranteeing that full posses-sion which would eventually be his. Thus the future salvation was already present, and yet remained future, for its completion lay in the life beyond the grave.[2]

The same experience is found in other New Testament writers, although expressed in different words. St. Peter,

---

[1] In his essay on *The Significance of Christ's Death for Paul*, *Zur Dogmatik*, pp. 271, 297, 299.

[2] See earlier, pp. 75 f.

addressing simple folk expecting persecution, reminds them of " the living hope " which was theirs through Christ's resurrection, " whom not having seen ye love ; on whom, though now ye see him not, yet believing, ye rejoice greatly with joy unspeakable and full of glory ". The writer " to the Hebrews " speaks of Christ as the pioneer of salvation, the High priest who knows His people's needs ; insignificant as the Church then seemed, Christians had " come into Mount Zion ", " to God, the Judge of all, and to the spirits of just men made perfect ". The Book of Revelation summons to courage Christians expecting extermination by reminding them of the realities of the unseen world : of the God who still reigns undefeated, of the Lamb that was slain, and of the redeemed who already sing their song of victory.

In St. John's Gospel and First Epistle this experience of eternal life finds its consummate expression. Our Lord is presented not only as the Way and the Truth but as the Life. His words are the words of eternal life. As death drew near, He promised His disciples, He would not leave them " orphaned ". He bids them abide in Him that He may abide with them, and compares their relationship with Him to that of branches to the vine from which the branches derive their life and can bear their fruit, and apart from which they die. To know God and Him whom He has sent, is eternal life, and the Gospel was written that its readers, believing in Jesus as the Christ, the Son of God, may have Life in His name. The First Epistle of St. John was written with the same purpose : that those who believe in the Son of God may know they have eternal life. It is a life which manifests itself in a love which is the response to the love of God. Christianity means fellowship with God, and this fellowship is eternal life. He who has eternal life may stand firm amid the flux of time, and for him the world has lost its glamour. The selfishness, ostentation and vainglory, the overprizing of material success,[1] which are the marks of the world's life, do not belong to the Father, and can no longer allure those who have learned to love Him. " The world passeth away and the

[1] " the lust of the flesh, the lust of the eyes, the vainglory of life ", ii. 16. On this see earlier, p. 92.

lust thereof ; but he that doeth the will of God abideth for ever ".
Already God in His love made us His children.   Not yet is our
full salvation but " we know that when He shall be manifested,
we shall be like Him for we shall see Him as He is ".   " The
mere contemplation of Christ ", as Dr. Arnold said in his last
Rugby sermon, " shall transform us into His likeness ".   But
at once comes the ethical demand, " And every one that hath
this hope in him, purifieth himself even as he is pure ".

This is not an otherworldliness which finds in the thought
of the world to come an escape from life's duties and life's
sorrows.   The hope of the future is made sure by the experience
of the present, and our present struggle becomes possible through
the certainty that the communion with God we already have
will be perfected at death.

It is natural that in times of difficulty and trouble some
should turn from their experience of present sorrow to the
thought of the joy that will one day be theirs,

> Jerusalem, my happy home
> Would God I were in thee !
> Would God my woes were at an end,
> Thy joys that I might see !

Yet there is a note of weariness in that sixteenth-century hymn
which is not found in the New Testament.   When a prisoner,
awaiting execution, St. Paul did, indeed, speak for a moment
of his desire that death might come that he might be with Christ
" which is better far ", but, at once, he returns to the thought
of his converts' needs, and remembers that " to abide in the
flesh is more needful " for their sake.   To this man, worn out
as he was by his labours, since life already meant for him Christ,
death could be only gain.   But we misrepresent New Testament
Christianity if we speak as if the only true life lay beyond the
grave, and, if we so speak we ought not to complain if only the
aged find meaning in our words.   As Dr. John Oman wisely
wrote, " Young and generous souls are, and ought to be,
intensely conscious of life. Nothing could convince them,
nothing should convince them, that life is not their immediate
concern. . . .   Weakness, captivity and old age have a right to
be weary of life ; youth and vigour under the open sky have not.

Even in Paul, the aged, the mood is only of nature, and not of grace. The true religious note is his triumph over that natural impulse, the glorious assurance that this life, to its last dregs, would have meaning and value. . . .   The only truly religious hope of immortality so lives with God now as to know that God is not the God of the dead but of the living. It does not say, Let us live for the life to come, but, Now have we eternal life. Instead of having us miserable now to be happy hereafter, it would give us present possession of a blessedness of such a quality that we know it cannot end ".[1]

The belief in a life beyond the grave has often been regarded as an expression of a prudential morality which seeks goodness only for its reward, and shuns the bad only because of its penalties and St. Paul's words in 1 Cor. xv have been thus interpreted. In it St. Paul had to fight on a double front, for his teaching on the life to come was opposed to that of Gentile converts who, although they may have believed in some dim sort of after life, yet denied the resurrection, and so the continuance and perfection of personal life beyond the grave. At the same time, his teaching was opposed to that of converts from Judaism who held a view of the future life which seemed to him unduly material. Against the view of the Jewish converts, he protested that " flesh and blood cannot inherit the kingdom of God ". The life beyond the grave is not material, and yet personal identity is not lost. Since he had no word to express personality, he speaks of " a spiritual body "—a phrase which to his readers must have sounded strange and even self-contradictory. But it was the denial of the resurrection by converts from paganism which aroused his greatest indignation. The resurrection of Christ was part of the universal proclamation of the Church. To say that there was no resurrection was to say that Christ had not risen. Were that true, then both Paul's proclamation and his converts' faith were "empty", devoid of meaning, for a dead Christ could not save. " If in this life only we have hoped in Christ, we are of all men most pitiable ". His own life was one of frequent peril. What profit was there in such a life ? " If the dead are not raised, let us eat and drink, for to-morrow we die ".[2]

---

[1] *Grace and Personality* [2], pp. 288 f.   [2] vv. 14, 19, 32.

These words have been much condemned. We remember, for instance, T. H. Huxley's words after the death of his much-loved child : " As I stood behind the coffin of my little son the other day, with my mind bent on anything but dissipation, the officiating minister read, as a part of his duty, the words, ' If the dead rise not again, let us eat and drink for to-morrow we die '. I cannot tell you how inexpressibly they shocked me. Paul had neither wife nor child, or he must have known that his alternative involved a blasphemy against all that was best and noblest in human nature. I could have laughed with scorn. What ! because I am face to face with irreparable loss . . . I am to renounce my manhood, and, howling, grovel in bestiality ? Why the very apes know better, and, if you shoot their young, the poor brutes grieve their grief out and do not immediately seek distraction in a gorge ".[1] But Professor Huxley misunderstood St. Paul. St. Paul's " alternative " was not " dissipation ". Before his conversion, he had not been a debauchee but a strict Jew, held in high honour by other Jews, as a gifted and zealous young leader of his nation. At his conversion he believed that the Jesus whose followers he had persecuted was the Messiah of Jewish hope and his risen Lord. Because of that belief, he had incurred the bitter hatred of his friends and had lived the hard life of an itinerant missionary. If there was no resurrection, then how could he claim that Christ had risen ? If Christ had not risen, then his life as a Christian was based on a tragic error. Not only were his own hardships useless but he had called others to face persecution for the sake of a proclamation which was false. In that case he would have been of all men most " pitiable ". " Dissipation " would still have had for him no attraction ; yet it would have been better had he remained the honoured leader of his nation, instead of the despised preacher of a message which, if Christ had not risen, was only a delusion.

Professor Huxley's condemnation of St. Paul was without foundation. Yet, it may be, St. Paul would have understood that condemnation better than he would have done the flimsy

[1] From a letter to Charles Kingsley, *Life and Letters of Thomas Henry Huxley*, by Leonard Huxley, I. p. 220.

faith of those who see in Christianity an attractive embellishment of life, to be prized as such, whether it is true or not. Christianity, such say, has purified our homes, and brings to us comfort. Even if, after all, there is no life beyond the grave, Christianity would still be useful, for it provides us noble ideals and much needed consolation. Paul's life was not based on that kind of compromise. Christianity was not for him merely a graceful addition to a rich and harmonious life. It was not with the rewards of virtue that he was concerned, but with the reality of his experience and the truth of his proclamation.

Christianity has, at times, been commended on prudential grounds as a means of securing safety in this life and profit in the next. We remember Pepys's commendation of " a good sermon of Mr. Gifford's at our church upon ' Seek ye first the kingdom of Heaven and its righteousness, and all things shall be added to you '. A very excellent, persuasive, good and moral sermon. He showed, like a wise man, that righteousness is a surer moral way of being rich, than sin and villainy ".[1] Such prudential morality may lead some to the avoidance of wrongdoing, not because it is evil, but because they desire to escape penalties and secure rewards in the life after death if such there be. In such thoughts St. Paul had no interest. His concern was with the truth of the Gospel and the validity of his missionary work. The chapter ends with thanksgiving to God who " giveth us the victory through our Lord Jesus Christ ", and an appeal to his readers " to be steadfast, immovable, always abounding in the work of the Lord, forasmuch as ye know that your labour is not vain in the Lord ".

It is here that we have the relevance of the Eternal for Christian Ethics. We are not called only to obedience ; we are called to the present, if partial, experience of a communion with God which death will not interrupt but make complete. We live in an age in which we cannot count on the obvious victory of good on earth. We do not yet know whether the discovery of nuclear energy will be used for human welfare, or whether, in the words from 2 Peter which the President of the British Association, Sir Richard Gregory, quoted in his Presidential

[1] *Diary* of Aug. 23rd, 1668.

address in 1945, through the clever folly of men, " the elements shall melt with fervent heat, and the earth also, and the works that are therein shall be burned up ".   Yet we may know that our struggle is not in vain, for already we have an experience of God which nothing can destroy. If our gaze be limited to the seen and the present, then it would be easy to falter.   It is from the unseen that we may gain strength and confidence for service in the seen. As Troeltsch said, " The life beyond the world is, in very deed, the inspiration of the life that now is ".[1]

Christian hope looks to the future, but it finds its confirmation in the experience of the present.   And yet in the present there is not only possession but failure and frustration.   Why is it that the Christian, confronted by the grace of God in Christ, and reinvigorated by the power of the Spirit, fails to reach that perfect love which would be his one adequate response to the grace of God ?   It is easy, indeed, to minimize the claim of love upon us, or to make excuses for our daily failure.   That way leads to complacency, and removes the tension of the Christian life by allowing our soul to live

> With ghastly smooth life, dead at heart
> Tame in earth's paddock as her prize.

Greek moralists bade us avoid the " too-much ".   But $\mu\eta\delta\grave{\epsilon}\nu$ $\mathring{\alpha}\gamma\alpha\nu$ " nothing too much ", is no motto for the Christian, for the God he worships is the God who has met his need in the hyperbole of the Cross.   In the New Testament, and in many Christian teachings of later times, there comes the demand for what John Wesley called " Christian Perfection ", " Entire Sanctification ", " Scriptural Holiness ", or " Perfect Love ". Yet somehow the road winds " up-hill all the way ".   In our life on earth temptation changes its form but its power remains. St. Paul, even when awaiting death, counted himself not to have " attained ", and, although the teaching of Christian Perfection has been a distinguishing characteristic of Methodist teaching, John Wesley made no claim that he himself was perfect, and, at times, spoke as if this perfection was not sinless.   We are told that no section of the Methodist Hymnbook has been

[1] *The Social Teaching of the Christian Churches*, II. p. 1006.

more prized than that entitled "For Believers seeking Full
Redemption ".[1]

This Perfectionist teaching is a necessary rebuke to all
contentment with partial failure. Perfect love may be as far
beyond our earthly reach as perfect knowledge and yet there is
what Professor Niebuhr calls, "The Relevance of an Impossible
Ethical Ideal ".[2] As George Herbert put it long ago :

> Sink not in spirit : who aimeth at the sky
> Shoots higher much than he that means a tree.
> A grain of glory mixed with humbleness
> Cures both a fever and lethargicness.

It is in the present possession of an eternal life, which will reach
its fullness only after death, that we may be saved from the
"fever" of fantasies, and the "lethargicness" of satisfaction
with the attainment of small aims. Yet, as Dr. Forsyth has
said, "Penitence, faith, sanctification always co-exist ; they do
not destroy and succeed each other ; they are phases of the one
process of God in the soul ". "It is better to trust God in
humiliated repentance than to revel in the sense of sinlessness ".[3]
Our most necessary prayer is the prayer for pardon, and yet
that prayer for pardon should lead to the resolve, so far as in
us lies, to be freed from our servitude to sin. Yet the only
holiness which may be ours on earth is the holiness of faith, our
penitent response to the holy love of God. We are *viatores* not
comprehensores ; pilgrims not those who have attained. But, as
we stumble on along our pilgrim way on earth, we may do so
as those who know that the journey ends in the Father's home,
where faith and hope will have their full fruition and love be
perfected. Yet the great experience of God's mercy which the
New Testament variously describes as receiving the Kingdom of
God—the resources of God's gracious rule—as Adoption into
Sonship, Life in Christ, the Possession of the Spirit, and as
Eternal Life, belongs not to the future only but to the present.

[1] See R. Newton Flew, *The Idea of Perfection in Christian Theology*,
pp. 313–41, and John Wesley's *Plain Account of Christian Perfection* and
his *Brief Thoughts on Christian Perfection Works* ⁵, vol. XI, pp. 366–446.

[2] *An Interpretation of Christian Ethics*, chap. iv.

[3] *Christian Perfection*, pp. 8 and 135.

When we have " attained ", this experience will be made complete, and we shall worship God with a worship unmarred by sin and failure. As with the sense of our own failure we seek to do God's will on earth, we may be cheered and strengthened by our Christian hope of that consummation, when penitence shall be merged into praise, and the vision of God bring us at last to perfect love. The Gospel speaks not only of a present task, and of hope in a life beyond the grave. It gives us the present, if partial, experience of a communion with God which death will not interrupt but make complete.

It is hard to live the Christian life in those social relations, those "Orders of Creation ", which we know only as they are perverted by that sin in which we share. Yet the Christian life is not all demand and struggle ; there is the relevance of the Eternal. We gain strength for our task as we participate already in the life which is eternal.

PART III

LIFE IN COMMUNITY

CHAPTER VII

THE ORDERS OF CREATION

IN words which have become famous, St. Augustine declared, " God and the soul I desire to know. Anything else ? No nothing whatever ".[1] So spoke the Neo-Platonist, freed from sensuality through his conversion to Christianity, but not yet led into the large places of service and responsibility. Religion has to do with man's relation to God, but the God who confronts us in Christ is not the dim Absolute with whom the mystic seeks identity. He is the Creator and Redeemer, and the Christian's relation to God brings him at once into relation with his neighbour. We have to live our Christian lives not as Robinson Crusoes, isolated from other men, but in communities. The Christian religion is not merely concerned with " what the individual does with his own solitariness ".[2] Our lives are lived not in solitariness, but in the communities of Marriage, Industry and the State. In these communities we are called to strive to do God's will, whilst as Christians we are given a new community in which to live, the community of the Church.

Some choices we can make, but we did not choose the family into which we were born, the economic order of our time and place, nor the nature of the State to which we owe allegiance. These communities belong to the " givenness " of life. They are anterior to our own power of choice ; we do not begin as individuals, and then become the voluntary members of communities. We belong to a family and nation before we have any individual life, and our personalities develop in environments which are not of our making. We are born not " man ", but

---

[1] *Soliloquies*, I. 7.
[2] A. N. Whitehead's famous description of religion, *Religion in the Making*, p. 16.

either male or female. The race owes its continuance to the difference and the coition of the sexes ; to live, we have to eat, and our food comes from the labour of many ; we belong to a society ruled by a particular type of government. Such statements are so obvious that we are almost ashamed to make them. And yet the interpretation of these truisms has led to bitter controversy not in the past only but in the present, whilst the solutions offered have profoundly influenced the course of European history, and some of them account, in part, for the estrangement from the Churches of many who feel that Christianity is necessarily identified with the social and economic oppression from which they are struggling to be free.

In this connexion Luther's teaching of the " Orders " or " Ordinances of Creation " has had very great importance. It enabled him to assert the possibility of fulfilling God's will as truly in the Family, in Industry and in the service of the State, as in the so-called religious vocations of monk, or nun, or priest. Luther had an intense and gloomy sense of the power of sin, and his pessimism made him emphasize the more the duty of recognizing in the authority of the State an ordinance of God to which submission must be made.[1] This doctrine of the Orders of Creation was used to perpetuate a patriarchal conception of the Family, a static view of Industry, and an authoritarian conception of the State. Although Luther himself had no illusions about the goodness or wisdom of princes, later Lutheranism in Germany adopted readily the romantic view of the State, and, until the downfall of the Hohenzollerns, was unduly eager to support all that its imperial patron and supreme bishop willed. When the Nazis came to power, German Christians used the conception of the Orders of Creation to justify the Nazi emphasis on the supreme importance of Blood and Soil. This may in part account for the fierceness with which Barth attacked Brunner for his retention of this conception of the Orders of Creation.[2] Brunner has guarded carefully his words, and cannot rightly be accused of using this conception

[1] See later, pp. 243 f.
[2] Cp. Barth's *Nein*, E.T. in *Natural Theology*, edited by John Baillie, pp. 85 ff.

of the Orders of Creation to justify acquiescence in things as they are ; he regards these Orders as the spheres in which we have to seek to obey, as best we may, the one command, to love God and man. Barth's attack on Brunner ignored Brunner's explicit teaching that we know the Orders of Creation, not as God would have them be, but as they have been perverted by sin. The acceptance of this conception need not lead us to a static conservatism, whilst its rejection may lead to a self-centred piety which neglects the urgent moral problems of industry and politics. It is not enough to emphasize the need of Christians to live their personal lives in accordance with the will of Christ. Lives are lived in community, and in community we have to seek to do God's will. The conception of the Orders, or Ordinances, of Creation may be saved from error, if it be combined with Calvin's emphasis that Marriage, Industry and the State must all alike be subordinated to the will of God, and that there is no sphere outside God's just rule. We have not only to live in the Orders of Creation ; we have to seek to make Industry and the State less in opposition to God's will. There is danger of self-deception here. It is all too easy to claim for social programmes and political panaceas a higher moral value than they possess, and to cloak our own self-interest with the language of Christian love. Yet hard and perilous as is the endeavour, the Church has to seek not only to convert individuals but to moralize the industrial and political Orders. Even so ardent, and politically conservative, a Lutheran as Reinhold Seeberg, though he had much to say about English " cant ", and about the unconscious hypocrisy of what he called " Anglo-Calvinism ",[1] yet admitted that the Lutheran restriction of religion to the sphere of individual lives brings with it the danger that besets " the Lutheran type of the indifference of public life to Christian morality, and of the weak and uncritical subordination of individual persons to the forms and ordinances of the State ".[2]

The command to love concerns in the first instance personal relationships. Confronted by the love of God, we have to seek

---

[1] *Lehrbuch der Dogmengeschichte* [3], IV. pp. 641 ff.
[2] *System der Ethik* [2], p. 123.

to love our neighbour as we are loved of God. Our Lord gave this command to men and women who were living in an agricultural community, and who had no responsibility for the decisions of their government. The neighbour, whom they were summoned to love, was the neighbour whom they themselves could help. In a modern democracy Christians may not be indifferent to the actions of the Government, whether national or local, for that Government acts as the representative of all citizens. The Industrial Order and the modern State are too vast to be interpreted in terms of personal relationships. Yet these spheres are subject to the sovereignty of God, though in them love has to take the form of justice. It is very hard to relate the Christian message to these immense spheres of collective, and so inevitably, to an extent, impersonal, relationships. But we may not evade the difficulty by retreating from public obligations, or by removing the sense of tension by speaking of these relationships as if they were unrelated to God's just rule. We may not live in isolation from the world or be indifferent to social needs or public events, whilst, if we are loyal to the Gospel, we cannot be so at home in the world as to accept without demur in the spheres of Industry and the State principles of conduct which are in clear contradiction to our professed belief in a God of righteousness and love.

Dr. R. W. Church, in a famous sermon preached before the University of Oxford in 1867 on *Christ's Words and Christian Society*, after speaking of the separateness of the Christian Society in early times, went on to say, " And now Christianity claims to have possession of society. Not only is the Church no longer opposed as it then was to society, but we find a difficulty in discovering the line between them. It seems impossible to conceive three things more opposed at first sight to the Sermon on the Mount than War, Law and Trade ; yet Christian society has long since made up its mind about them, and we all accept them as among the necessities or occupations of human society ". " Even war and riches, even the Babel life of our great cities, even the high places of ambition and earthly honour, have been touched by His spirit, have found how to be Christian ". " The Tempter offered all the kingdoms of the world to Christ, and He refused them, and chose poverty instead.   And yet they have become His, with all the glory of them, with all their incidents ".[1]   This claim is the more notable because made by one of the wisest teachers of the Church of England in the Victorian age.   It is not possible for modern Christians to share in the complacency of this Victorian compromise.   The society in which we live has, indeed, been permeated with Christian ideals but, if we " find a difficulty in discovering the line " between the Church and society, that is due less to the Christianizing of society than to the secularization of the Church.   We may not seek to remove, or to conceal, that tension which exists between Christian Ethics and the common practices of the world.   The Words of Jesus give us, indeed, no direct guidance on the problems of Industry and the State, and yet we are not called merely to lives of personal self-dedication.   We have to try to bring not only the Family but Industry and the State into closer conformity with divine Justice.   The " Orders of Creation " are known to us only as they have been perverted by collective sin.   We have to live and work within the Orders and, at the same time, to seek to purge them of their injustice.

[1] *The Gifts of Civilization and other Sermons and Lectures*, pp. 40 f., 48.

CHAPTER VIII

THE COMMUNITY OF MARRIAGE

(1) THE NEW MORALITY

IN the Victorian age no institution was so unquestioned as that of marriage. The Divorce Act of 1857 had for the first time in England made divorce in the full sense available for all, and not merely to those wealthy enough to obtain a Dispensation of Parliament, but, although a husband could divorce his wife for adultery, and a wife her husband for adultery and cruelty, divorces were rare, and incurred much social inconvenience and stigma. The standards of sexual morality were rigidly observed by the many and, where they were disregarded, vice paid its homage to morality by the hypocrisy of concealment. The " fallen woman " was regarded with contempt by many Christians who somehow forgot our Lord's condemnation of the Scribes and Pharisees for their harshness to the woman taken in adultery.[1] It was impossible to walk at night in London without being aware of the vast army of professional prostitutes and yet there was a curious veil of secrecy about their activities, and those who, like Mrs. Josephine Butler, sought their redemption were regarded by some as " improper " or " unwomanly ". The typical Victorian novel spoke of romantic love ending with wedding-bells and was not concerned with " problems of sex ". Anthony Trollope, that most decorous of novelists, even felt it necessary to apologize in his preface to *The Vicar of Bullhampton* for introducing " the character of a girl whom I will call,—for want of a truer word that shall not in its truth be offensive,—a castaway ". Those who speak of the

---

[1] John vii. 53–viii. 11 is found only in D among the Uncials. The Ferrar group puts it after Luke xxi. 38. Synoptic, and not Johannine in style, it is a part of the tradition the evangelists did not care to record.

degeneracy of modern morals would do well to remember the awful cruelty of the White Slave traffic, and the harshness of the treatment often meted out to young and ignorant girls seduced by men who thought that money had the right to buy anything. The casualness of modern " affairs " between young people of the same " set " is degrading and deplorable, but it lacks the deliberate cruelty of the seduction of foolish girls by men who would not so have behaved to those whom they regarded as belonging to their own class, and thus as potential wives.

Much as we may regret the moral laxity of our time, at least we can rejoice that professional prostitution is less common than it was, and that fewer girls are forced, through the harshness of those who should have helped them, to pass into a life of degradation from a first sexual sin, or even from a seduction for which they had little responsibility. We hear to-day many a sad story of illicit relations and of broken marriages, but we do not often hear to-day a story such as the writer heard in his youth. A young doctor died too soon to make adequate provision for his wife and two daughters. The younger girl came to London and became an assistant in a West End Store. There she met often one of the customers, a middle-aged woman, who, after she had gained the girl's confidence, invited her to spend the week-end at her house in a suburb then notorious for its expensive vice. The girl in her ignorance did so, was drugged, and, while drugged, raped. The " Madam " sent her out into the streets. She met there a prostitute who was " working " on her own, who, seeing she was ill, had pity on her and took her to her room. A letter was sent to her mother, who wrote back, " What you have done, you have done. You are no longer my daughter ". As the girl was very ill, the prostitute, who had taken her in, asked if she had any friend, and getting from her the name of her Sunday School teacher in her home town, sent for her, and she came at once and arrived in time to be with the girl before she died of shock and exposure. That Sunday School teacher henceforth gave up her life to work of rescue, and it was through her that the story reached the writer. The ignorance of the innocent girl sent unwarned to live amid the perils of a great city, the wickedness of the White Slave traffic, the callousness of the " Christian " mother—these things, we trust, belong to conditions which in England have, for the most part, ceased to exist.

Marriage for the great bulk of the population was not thought of as a problem. It was assumed that marriage was woman's destiny, and marriage was regarded as permanent and final. It is significant that Dr. Newman Smyth, in his manual on *Christian Ethics* published in 1892 in the well-known *International Theological Library*, devoted only ten of his five hundred pages to Duties in the Family, Marriage and Divorce. The unmarried girl was protected by careful chaperonage and, where religion had little influence, fear of pregnancy for the woman, and of venereal disease for the man, were powerful aids to self-restraint. Whatever other institution might be questioned, that of marriage seemed secure. Immorality there was, as there has always been, but not " New Morality ". Some men might be wicked, and some women silly, but the existence of sin and folly was not regarded as invalidating the obligations of a strict sexual morality.

The First World War marked the end of that old stability, It was preceded by the Edwardian revolt against the reticence and prudery of Victorianism. The Victorian social system assumed that every woman existed only for the home. The Feminist movement, with its just demand that women should be free to develop their gifts, even although these were not those of domesticity, and the Suffragist demand for political equality, were alike indications that the Victorian compromise had become insecure, and that the cruel Victorian jests at " old maids ", as we get them in W. S. Gilbert's operas, were no longer to be tolerated. That women have the same right as men to the development of their capabilities, is congruous with the Christian belief that in Christ Jesus there is neither male nor female. But the union of two equal persons, though it has in it possibilities of greater happiness than a union where the wife is subordinate to the husband, and in economic dependence on him, is a union harder to achieve. As Mr. Walter Lippmann wrote, " It takes two persons to make a successful marriage in the modern world, and that fact more than doubles its difficulty ".[1]

[1] *Preface to Morals*, p. 311.

Tendencies implicit in the early years of the twentieth century found full expression after the First World War. Neither the nation nor the Churches was prepared for that long apocalypse of cruelty which seemed for many to reduce the Liberal trust in reason and hope of progress to a bitter jest. The separation of husbands from their wives, the tedium and the suffering of trench-warfare, the slaughter of so many of the nation's best youth, the disillusionment and weariness which succeeded the first exultant idealism, the resentment of the young against the misery they assigned to the folly of the old— all these contributed to the widespread revolt against traditional morality and religion. The New Psychology of Freud came to many as a new revelation ; it seemed to substitute impulse for reason, and to provide a scientific justification for self-indulgence. The writer lived in Cambridge in those years, in close touch with undergraduate life, and noticed how readily young men and women used the Freudian phrases, although it would have been an excess of charity to suppose that many of them had read much of his writings. The books, which it was the proper thing to read, were those on marriage by Bertrand and Dora Russell, whilst the early novels of Mr. Aldous Huxley were very popular in which he depicted men and women who were obsessed with sex, and whose sex-adventures had no more significance or dignity than that of cockerels in a poultry-yard.[1] At other levels of society the false romanticism of the films had a dissolvent effect. No working wife or mother can be as glamorous as film-stars, and, if love be something over which there can be no control, then love is unstable and loyalty insecure.

Much of the revolt against traditional standards was more in words than deeds. Broadcasting in 1932, Sir William Beveridge gave the result of an investigation based on particulars received from 18,000 families. He reported that most who had

[1] Of *Antic Hay*, published in 1923, Dr. B. Ifor Evans (*English Literature between the Wars*, p. 59) remarks, " The mood of the novel was implied by the quotation from Marlowe on the title page :

My men like satyrs grazing on the lawns
Shall with their goat-feet dance the antic hay."

filled in the forms were " obviously normal people with happy family lives ", and that the impression got from these replies is " that there have not been any very great changes in family life in the last generation, but what changes there are, are on the whole an improvement ". " The resultant better companionship of husband and wife comes out again and again in every class ".[1] At the Universities in this country, and in the United States, as I learnt when lecturing there shortly before the Second World War, the mood of levity which marked the nineteen-twenties changed into a mood of greater seriousness. " The philosophy of meaninglessness ", which, as Mr. Aldous Huxley was later to admit, had been used to justify not only political but " erotic revolt ",[2] ceased to attract.

On this generation, recovering from the moral and spiritual wounds of the First World War and eager for peace, came the Second, and still longer and more devastating World War. In this war women, for the first time in our country's history, were mobilized as well as men, so that girls, as well as men, were thrust from the security of their families into moral, as well as physical, dangers. We have reason to be proud of the way so many men and women maintained their loyalties, and resisted temptation. Homes were broken up, husbands were abroad on active service, wives were dispersed with their children to safer areas where they lacked the protection and support of their familiar environment. On anti-aircraft gun-sites and in civil defence, men and women, strangers before, worked together night after night. It is not surprising that many marriages came to an end. Yet how many women there were who kept firm their loyalty, how many men who carried with them the purifying love of wife and children whose photographs they proudly showed to those who won their confidence. We hear a great deal about the moral débâcle of our time. The other side ought not to be forgotten. When we remember how many men returned after long years of absence to wives who, like

[1] From the Report given in the *Listener* of April 13th, 1932, quoted on p. 45 of *The New Morality*, by G. E. Newsom, at that time the Master of Selwyn College, Cambridge.

[2] *Ends and Means*, 1938, p. 273—the book which marks Mr. Aldous Huxley's new interest in religion, though not in Christianity.

themselves, had been much changed by the cost of the struggle, it is not strange that many marriages became insecure. It would have been difficult in any circumstances to restore these interrupted marriages. It was immensely more difficult because in many cases the shortage of houses meant that long-separated husbands and wives had to live with relatives without that privacy a home requires. But the enormous increase in divorces is not only found where husbands and wives have been long separated through the War. As a recent writer has pointed out, " In Sweden and Denmark, countries scarcely affected by the War, there is an increase of broken marriages which indicates that the moral problem of monogamy is universal ".[1] The stability of marriage can no longer be assumed.

Some gains the years have brought. The old reticence allowed some young men and many more young women to enter marriage with little knowledge of its physical expression. We no longer have to deal, as did city ministers of an earlier generation, with the tragedy of the young bride who, through her ignorance of sex, was shocked by her husband's first approaches, nor are marriages so often marred, as once they were, by the false belief that a " pure " woman must be frigid, submitting to her husband's embraces, but not prepared to be awakened, to the glad response of love to love. Statistics are in the nature of things unobtainable, but some of us who have the confidence of many young couples get the impression that, although some marriages end in open failure, there are many very happy marriages, of those who are bound together not by duty only, or by the dictates of society, but by love, which, on the wife's side as well as on the husband's, is unashamed, and where a true union is achieved, a union both of body and of spirit. It is well that there are now many books, some by ministers of religion, some, and these among the best, by women doctors, from which bride and bridegroom may get before their marriage the knowledge of each other that they need, knowledge which

<hr>

[1] *The Disintegration of Matrimony*, by Elmer G. Homrighausen. *Theology To-day*, October 1947, p. 407.

many of an earlier generation could only gain by much fumbling and blundering. Yet the very multiplicity of these books shows that marriage has become for many a problem; not all these books give advice which is wise or even moral, and divorces still increase in number. Some of those who have achieved a happy marriage feel that they have won this best of all their earthly joys, not because of, but in spite of Christian teaching, whilst others, to whom sex is a perplexing problem, believe that Christian Ethics can give them no help, and turn for advice not to the representatives of religion but to psychiatrists.

(2) FALSE ASCETICISM

It has to be admitted that much teaching which has professed to be Christian has been perverted by a false asceticism which found it hard to believe that the union in marriage of man and woman is an Order of Creation, designed by the Creator not only for the continuance of the race but for mutual comfort and common happiness. Some have tried in Titius's words to be " wiser than the nature God created ",[1] and have so praised virginity as to make marriage appear as a concession to human weakness, permitted to the many, but to be shunned by those who would aim at Christian perfection. Too often the saint has agreed with the debauchee that the only difference between married love and lust is that one is allowed and the other is not, and, in consequence, it has been assumed that the unmarried alone are truly chaste.

Even in the New Testament there is reference to those who forbid marriage, and the warning had to be given that marriage is to be had in honour among all.[2] Later, when Christianity was preached by converts from paganism, the tendency to depreciate marriage became inevitably more strong. For this there were two reasons : one speculative, one practical. Graeco-Orientalism regarded matter as evil. The Church resisted the corollary of this in the realm of thought, and maintained the reality of the Incarnation against all attempts to deny that One truly divine became for our sakes truly man, but it was less

---

[1] *Natur und Gott*, p. 829.   [2] 1 Tim. iv. 3; Heb. xiii. 4.

successful in resisting the ethical implicates of Graeco-Orientalism. If matter was evil, how could marriage be pure ? But
there was another, and more weighty reason, why virginity
should be prized. In a world of licentiousness, virginity seemed
the supreme expression of moral power. Adultery was condemned by paganism as an infringement of the husband's rights,
but fornication was regarded as degrading, indeed, but as natural
as the indulgence of any other appetite ; marriage was generally
unrelated to romantic love, and men held the friendship of men
as nobler than the love of women. Continence, by its very
rarity, seemed a wonderful achievement. Thus St. Athanasius
in his book *On the Incarnation*, written when Christianity had
won at last immunity from persecution, gave as the supreme
instance of the power of Christianity that what was thought
impossible had been achieved ; not only those of adult years but
even children had taken vows to maintain " that virginity which
lies beyond the law ",[1] and this great leader of the Church was
famous not only for his writings on theology but for *The Life
of St. Anthony*, which depicts the trials and glory of the monastic
life. So wise and gifted a teacher as St. Ambrose, in his book
Concerning Virgins, though he formally condemned heretics
who discouraged marriage, yet spoke in glowing words of
virginity as the supreme Christian virtue, and urged parents to
bring their daughters up to attain this, the highest, honour.
In the New Testament the supreme command is to love ; by
this time not love but virginity had come to be regarded as
the noblest achievement of Christian character.

In some of the Christian writers of the West we find not
only this overprizing of virginity but a morbid horror of sex.
Thus Tertullian (writing to his wife !) speaks of marriage as a
" voluptuous disgrace ", " frivolous and impure ". Marriage
was to him " good " only in the sense that it was " better to
marry than to burn ".[2] In denouncing the marriage of Christians with unbelievers, he does, indeed, refer to the community
in praise and prayer, in fastings and almsgiving, which Christian
husbands and wives may enjoy,[3] but he rejects with scorn the

[1] § 51.   [2] *To his Wife*, I. i, iii.
[3] *Op. cit.* II. viii.

suggestion that marriage should be prized because of offspring.[1] In another book, he definitely asserts that marriage differs from fornication only in being legalized, " The principal sanctity is that of the virgin, because it is free from affinity to fornication ".[2] The same low view of marriage is found in the writings of the learned St. Jerome.   " I praise wedlock ", he writes, " I praise marriage, but it is because they give me virgins ".   Why should a mother object to her daughter choosing virginity since in this way she makes her mother " the mother-in-law of God " ?[3] With perverse ingenuity, he points out that in the story of Creation the words, " God saw that it was good ", was not inserted after the second day, and deduces that " there is something not good in the number two separating us as it does from unity, and prefiguring the marriage-tie ". Besides, in the account of Noah's ark, " the animals that enter by two are unclean, but those of which an uneven number is taken are clean ".   In this way he sought to prove that " virginity was cleaner than wedlock ".[4]   He denied that in this he was condemning marriage, but to him, too, marriage, though permissible, seemed impure.

The Church owes to St. Augustine an immeasurable debt, and it is lamentable that this great teacher of the Western Church gave his immense authority to an inadequate view of marriage.   This was doubtless due in part to his own experience. In his *Confessions* he records with shame that, in his sixteenth year the " madness of lust " " held complete sway " over him. He entered into an illicit union which lasted for fourteen years with a woman who was his faithful companion and who bore him a son.   At length, through his mother Monica's influence, he put her away and arranged to marry.   The bride chosen was too young to become his wife at once, and since he could not endure the two years' delay, he took another woman, though not as a wife, being, as he says, " not so much a lover of marriage as a slave of lust ".   At his conversion, Augustine learnt to repress his sexual nature but not to think of marriage in a worthy way.   Although he wrote on *The Good of Marriage*, he,

[1] *Op. cit.* I. v.   [2] *On Exhortation to Chastity*, ix.
[3] *To Eustochium*, 20.   [4] *To Pammachius*, 19.

too, spoke of desire in marriage as if it differed from fornication only in that it was allowed for the purpose of procreation.[1] Before his conversion he had been for long a Manichean, and it is not surprising that Julian accused him of still holding the Manichean heresy that marriage was essentially impure. The last book of this great teacher of the Church, his *Unfinished Work against Julian*, written when he was over seventy years of age, makes, as Mr. J. Burnaby has said, " melancholy reading ".[2] In it he sought to defend himself from Julian's attacks, but in his dreary discussions on marriage he shows no comprehension of the possibility of pure married love in which body and spirit have alike their part to play.[3]

Monasticism was at first a laymen's movement, and arose at a time when even some bishops were married. At the Councils of Nicaea in A.D. 325 the attempt to compel married bishops to abandon their wives failed through the opposition of Paphnutius, an Egyptian bishop in high repute for his own asceticism. Gregory of Nazianzus's father was a bishop ; Synesius announced that, if he was made a bishop, he would keep his wife and have children by her. Justinian I. forbade a married man to be made a bishop and the Trullan Council, usually assigned to A.D. 692, confirmed this prohibition, but, in opposition to the rule of the Roman Church, decreed that those in holy orders as priests or deacons, if married before their ordination, should continue to live with their wives.[4]

In the Western Church the attempt was made to enforce

---

[1] For a poignant modern parallel, see *The Diary of Tolstoy's Wife 1860–91*, E.T. by Alexander Werth, in which is depicted her sorrow at her discovery, after she had borne him many children, that his dissolute youth has led him to think of love as mere sensuality and later to teach asceticism for all, *e.g.* p. 235 (Dec. 14th, 1887), " I copied Lyova's (Tolstoi's) diaries up to where he says, ' There is no love, there is only a physical craving for intercourse and the rational need of a life-companion ' ", and p. 262 (Jan. 18th, 1891), " I simply cannot reconcile the idea of woman's marriage and man's debauchery ".

[2] *Amor Dei*, p. 239.

[3] Cp. the writer's *The Christian Estimate of Man*, pp. 85–99.

[4] Canons XII and XIII (*The Seven Oecumenical Councils, Nicene and Post Nicene Library*, pp. 370 f.). This rule is still the custom of the Eastern Churches. Bishops are appointed as unmarried men ; priests may be ordained as married men but not marry after their ordination.

celibacy on all the clergy. This attempt naturally had the support of Jerome, Ambrose and Augustine, but there was very strong opposition, and the attempt was unsuccessful. At length Hildebrand, who, as Gregory VII, was Pope from A.D. 1073 to 1085, insisted on the deposition of all married priests, and, soon after his death, the celibacy not only of priests but of deacons and subdeacons was enjoined by Canon Law.[1] It was easier to prevent the clergy from marrying than it was to secure their continence, and, until the purification of the Latin Church by the Counter-Reformation, there were many abuses. The Council of Trent, the great Council of the Counter-Reformation, anathematized those who said that clerics might marry, or who said " that the conjugal state is to be preferred before that of virginity or celibacy, and that it is not better and more blessed to remain in virginity or in celibacy than to be joined in matrimony ".[2]

No action of Luther's has been more condemned by Roman Catholic writers than his rejection of his monastic vow and his marriage with an escaped nun. Denifle, in his immense and very learned book, *Luther und Luthertum*, even explained his revolt from Rome by his desire to violate his vow of chastity without incurring a sense of guilt. To this it is a sufficient answer that the Pope of Luther's youth was the Borgia Alexander VI, one of the most profligate of men. In 1521, when he had as yet no thought of marrying, Luther had written a Latin treatise *On Monastic Vows*,[3] in which he had denounced such vows as an attempt to earn salvation by works. In the following year he wrote in German his so-called Sermon, *On Married Life*,[4] which has become well known because of the many references to it in the writings of his modern detractors. As its editor in the Weimar Edition points out, it is far too long to be a Sermon, though it may be based upon a Sermon. Its outspoken references to sexual matters could scarcely, even in that age,

[1] Cp. E. Vacandard, *Dictionnaire de Théologie Catholique*, II. col. 2068–88.   [2] Session XXIV of Nov. 1563. Canons IX and X.

[3] *Weimar Ausgabe*, VIII, pp. 573–669. For a summary, see J. Mackinnon, *Luther and the Reformation*, III. pp. 22–34.

[4] *W.A.* X. ii. pp. 267–304. For summary, J. Mackinnon, *op. cit.* III. pp. 133–7.

have been made in a Sermon, and even in a controversial Tract could with advantage have been more restrained. Here, as sometimes in his private letters, Luther wrote indelicately, and laid too exclusive an emphasis on the physical side of marriage. His own marriage in A.D. 1525 to an ex-nun was a notable breach with the monastic ideal. No one who remembers his playful references in his letters to his *Domina Kethe*, his " Lady Cathy ", and his tender references to his children, can doubt the sincerity with which his wife at his death, in her letter to her sister, mourned the loss of " so noble a man as my dear lord ". Luther's happy parsonage became the prototype of many a happy vicarage and manse, from which have gone forth children to serve in Church and State, and in which have been illustrated the possibilities of Christian marriage.

In its exaltation of marriage, Protestantism has sometimes forgotten what our Lord taught when He spoke of those who were " eunuchs for the kingdom of heaven's sake ". There are those called to be celibate because the requirements of God's Kingdom come first and must be met at any cost. We think of St. Francis of Assisi who took " Lady Poverty " as his bride, and did a work for his generation which no married man could have done. There are still tasks in the mission-field or in city slums which are best done by the unmarried, and those that do them are to be honoured for their readiness to accept the call to work that is hard and lonely. And for others, training for the ministry or mission-field may mean postponement of marriage till that training is completed.[1] But Protestantism

---

[1] Any Principal of a Theological College, troubled by the pressure of fiancées on his students to marry before the completion of their course, can sympathize with Kierkegaard's words, " It may be, as Don Juan says to Zerline, that only in the soft arms of a blameless wife does true felicity reside, and possibly it is true, as both poets and prose writers have affirmed, that in these soft arms one forgets the world's alarms ; but the question is whether there is not also something else one can only too easily forget in these soft arms—namely, what Christianity is ". " The twaddle into which Christianity has sunk " "is due in part to the fact that these soft arms have come to interfere a little too much, so that, for the sake of Christianity, one might require the respective proprietors of these soft arms to retire a little more into the background ". *Attack upon Christendom*, p. 145.

has gained much by its abolition of the compulsory celibacy
of the clergy.   Marriage is not a concession to human weakness,
and married life is not less " pure " or " spiritual " than the
unmarried.   Marriage is an Order of Creation, and in Christian
marriage *eros* may pass into *agape*, natural love into that love
which has learnt from Christ's love how to forgive, and which
partakes already of the love which is eternal.

(3) MARRIAGE AS AN ORDER OF CREATION

To our Lord, as we have seen, marriage was an Order of
Creation.[1] When the Pharisees asked Him whether it was
lawful for a man to put away his wife, He did not base His
answer, as did the Jewish teachers of His time, on the interpretation of that " unseemly thing " in a wife which, according
to Deut. xxiv. 1, justified a husband in divorcing his wife.
Instead, He referred them to God's creative act. Moses, for
the hardness of men's heart, had allowed divorce but that was
contrary to the divine intention.   " From the beginning of the
creation ", God had made man " male and female ".   " For
this cause shall a man leave his father and mother and shall
cleave to his wife and the twain shall be one flesh : so that
they are no more twain but one flesh.   Whom, therefore, God
hath joined let no man put asunder ".[2]   Our Lord thus reminded
His hearers of the story in Genesis in which the creation of man
is depicted as the result of a divine resolve, and the man created
in God's image is described not as a solitary individual but as
" male and female ".   Karl Barth in his immense *Treatise on
Creation* explains these words, " Let us make man in our
image ", as " a speech of God with Himself, a taking counsel
with other divine Councillors ".   " Certainly ", he adds, " the
first account of creation is naïve enough, or knowing enough,
to think of God as capable of a speech with Himself expressly
related in plural form ".   " *The tertium comparationis*, the
analogy between God and man, lies simply in the existence of
the I–thou relationship.   That relationship is constitutive for

[1] See earlier, pp.
[2] Mark x. 2–9 (= Matt. xix. 3–9), quoting Gen. i. 27 and ii. 24.

God ; it is constitutive also for man created by God ".[1]   That
seems better theology than exegesis, but Barth does well to
remind us that in the Genesis story the creation of man is
represented as incomplete until woman was created.   The man
in the image of God is not an individual, but a society of two,
a potential family, whilst in the later Christian revelation God
is depicted not as a solitary individual but as One in whom
are real distinctions and so the possibility of mutual love.

Our Lord used the fact that God created man, male and
female, as the reason why a man should cleave to his wife for
man and wife were meant to be no longer two but one.   He
warned men that some might, for the sake of God's Kingdom,
have to renounce marriage, but He did not speak as if marriage
was a questionable relationship unsuited to those called to a
higher life.   Whereas Tertullian and Jerome speak as if children
were a bitter burden, our Lord called children to Him, and
declared that " of such is the kingdom of God ".   Marriage was
for Him an Order of Creation.   Man and wife were intended
to live in indissoluble unity.   That is God's will ; that the
demand of divine justice.   And our Lord's own life and death
gave to love new possibilities and opened up the way to distinctively Christian marriage.

In this respect also St. Paul became the great interpreter
of His Lord.   Whether St. Paul had been married before his
conversion, we do not know.   If he had, his wife must have
died before he became a Christian for it was as a celibate that
he did his work.   Absorbed as he was in his work, he had himself
no wish to marry although, as he reminded his converts, he
had as much right to travel about with a wife as had Peter
and the other apostles, and the brethren of the Lord.[2]   As we
have seen, St. Paul's earlier references to marriage were made
in reference to his converts' needs.[3]   The pagan world in which
they lived was marked by the common characteristics of a

---

[1] *Die kirchliche Dogmatik*, III.   *Die Lehre von der Schöpfung*, I.
pp. 204, 207 (cp. pp. 214–32).

[2] 1 Cor. ix. 5.   In view of the Roman demand for the celibacy of the
clergy, it is interesting to note that Peter, the Apostle, most prized in the
Roman Church, was married.

[3] See earlier, pp. 81 f.

licentious society : indulgence in sexual sin, and the belief that a married life, like one of vice, was incompatible with higher spirituality. In what was probably the earliest of his extant Epistles, St. Paul had to warn his converts against fornication. Let each man live with his own wife in " sanctification and honour ", remembering that God has called us not " to uncleanness but in sanctification ".[1] At Corinth St. Paul had to rebuke his converts for their condonation of a case of incest such as even pagans condemned, and yet it was in Corinth that many thought that marriage should neither be entered into, nor, if already existing, be maintained, and St. Paul was asked to give his decision on this. He did so with obvious reluctance and, before doing so, warned his readers against fornication. How can a Christian thus defile his body which is meant to be the sanctuary of the Holy Spirit ? Christians are not their own; they are bought with a price, the price of Christ's Cross, and they must glorify God in their body and in their spirit.[2] When St. Paul wrote this letter he still thought that the end of the world was very near. For himself marriage had no attraction, but he knew too well the temptations of his converts to suppose that what he regarded as his gift was theirs. He advises that men and women should be married and maintain normal relationships. Yet if the unmarried can so remain, they will be better able to serve the Lord. The reason St. Paul gives is significant. It is because of the " present distress ",[3] that " impending Tribulation ", which, as a Jew, he believed would precede that coming of the Messiah which at this time he thought was imminent. The time was short ; why then, change their estate ?

St. Paul's treatment of marriage in his Epistles has naturally been used to support the view that marriage is a concession to weakness, and inferior to virginity. It is important to remember that St. Paul bases his argument not on the view that marriage was in itself impure, but on his belief that the Tribulation would come so soon that it was not worth while to enter into marriages which would only increase the difficulties

[1] 1 Thess. iv. 3–7.　　　　　　　　[2] 1 Cor. vi. 15–20.
[3] 1 Cor. vii. 26.　See earlier, p. 82.

of a cruel time. Later, his expectation of the speedy return of Christ, and so of the still more imminent Tribulation, grew less intense, and his letters show a new appreciation of the significance of marriage and the family. From his prison in Rome, he wrote those admonitions on marriage which most clearly express how the natural order of marriage may be so transformed, through faith in the great Christian facts, that marriage may become distinctively Christian. The relation of husband to wife is compared to the relation which to St. Paul was the most sacred and intimate of all : the relation of Christ to the Church. Husbands are called to love their wives even as Christ loved the Church and gave Himself for it. They are to love them as their own bodies so that a man in loving his wife will be loving himself, and St. Paul repeats the words from Genesis our Lord had quoted, " They two shall be one flesh ", and adds " This mystery is great : but I speak in regard of Christ and of the Church ".[1]

The Vulgate translated " mystery " (μυστήριον) by *sacramentum*, and in the Roman Church marriage is defined as one of the Seven Sacraments. The Reformers strongly opposed this description of marriage. Thus Calvin wrote, " All admit it to be an institution of God ", but " no man ever saw it to be a sacrament until the time of Gregory ". Calvin points out that the only Scriptural argument that could be adduced for this was based on a misunderstanding. The " mystery " concerns Christ and the Church, not man and wife ; to translate *mysterion* by sacrament showed linguistic ignorance, and he not unnaturally added that, if marriage be a sacrament, it is " absurd to debar priests from it." To Calvin to call marriage a sacrament seemed no small error, for it enabled the Roman Church to claim control of all matrimonial causes, and, on the grounds of affinity and spiritual kindred, to place unwarrantable restrictions upon marriage.[2] If, in the words of the Church of England Catechism, a sacrament is " an outward and visible sign of an inward and spiritual grace given unto us, ordained by Christ Himself ", then there are only two sacraments : Baptism and

[1] Eph. v. 22–32. See earlier, p. 83.
[2] *Institutes*, IV. xix. 34–7.

the Lord's Supper. Our Lord gave to marriage a new sanctity but He did not ordain it for it was already in existence.

Marriage belongs, in the first instance, to the Order of Creation not to the Order of Redemption. For Christians, as for non-Christians, it consists in the pledge of man and woman to live together as man and wife, and in the fulfilment of that promise. Marriage may exist where there is only the promise and its fulfilment. Thus in India, in conservative Hindu families, the bridegroom may see his wife for the first time when he unveils her face after marriage, for marriage is arranged by the parents of the bridal couple.[1] If the bridegroom is kind, such marriages may have a measure of success, for the girl bride has been taught from childhood that her destiny is wifehood, and that a wife's duty is one of perfect obedience ; natural desire comes after marriage and may be so ratified by the birth of children as to bring about true unity. There have been instances in the mission-field, especially in German missionary societies, where lonely men have had wives sent out to them by their home society, and sometimes, where the wife has shared to the full the husband's interests, such marriages have been successful. With the growth of personality, which is itself a product of Christianity, marriage should be the culmination of mutual attraction, and ought not normally be entered into except there be already mutual love. Any marriage based merely on calculation of convenience will, in a society where women have attained to full personality, be a marriage unsatisfying, and so insecure. Yet natural love alone is not enough. It may suffice for a honeymoon, or for a few untroubled years of married life, but not for the stress and strain that the years may later bring. The stability of marriage depends not only on the natural love with which it should begin, but on the loyalty by which it can be maintained. Natural love, *eros*, may be cruel and, at its worst, may be indistinguishable from lust, if it seeks only its own pleasure, without regard to the well-

---

[1] Even in simpler Christian homes, the same custom obtains. The writer was asked by a theological student of his to officiate at his marriage. He replied, " Yes, but whom are you marrying ? " and got the answer, " That is not yet arranged ".

being of the object of its passion. That is the love of which
Blake wrote,

> Love seeketh only self to please,
>   To bind another to its delight,
> Joys in another's loss of ease.
> And builds a Hell in Heaven's despite.

But there is another love which Blake has thus described :

> Love seeketh not itself to please,
>   Nor for itself hath any care,
> But for another gives its ease,
> And builds a Heaven in Hell's despair.[1]

Passion there should be in the love of all young married couples,
but passion alone is not enough. Love to endure needs tenderness and common interests such as the coming of children brings.
Sexual love may help to make firmer the ties of affection and
of attraction, and without this love, although a marriage may
survive through loyalty, it has in it little joy. Yet love alone
is not enough unless with love is loyalty.

Love and loyalty in marriage are not restricted to the
Christian sphere. There are many couples who live in life-long
union not only because that is best for their children, or because
of their desire to stand well with their neighbours, but because
they are thus united by love and loyalty, by mutual consideration and by regard for each other's needs. Yet Christian
marriage has motives and sanctions peculiar to itself. The
mere fact that bride and bridegroom are baptized, or that they
have been married in Church, does not, indeed, secure that their
marriage will be truly Christian. No " infused grace " is given
to make their marriage immune from peril. But if Christians
marry " in the Lord ", if husband and wife are united in common
devotion to their Saviour, then their marriage is secure, and
St. Paul's words to which we have referred become true in their
experience. The " great mystery " of Christ's love to the
Church inspires each to love the other, with a love which can
bear and forgive in a way that natural love alone does not do.
A man and wife, who live themselves by the divine forgiveness,
can forgive each other as need arises ; they can learn through

[1] *Songs of Experience. The Clod and the Pebble.*

their experience of the love of Christ to curb resentment, and, because they know His love, they can take with confidence the tremendous vow of life-long devotion, not because they ignore the solemnity of its words but because they live in dependence on that divine grace which found its full expression in Christ's Cross. If children are given them, then they will feel that they are sharing in God's creative work, and, in their love for their children, they will learn new lessons of how God forgives us our ingratitude and folly; if children are denied them, they may find in common service interests which bind them the closer to each other. "For better for worse", "in sickness and in health", a Christian marriage can be maintained, for the resources of the Gospel are sufficient for this and for much more. To husbands and wives thus united in Christian faith, marriage ceases to be a problem. Instead, it is a great enrichment of life, and the Christian home, for all its earthly imperfection, becomes a means of blessing not only to its own members but to others. When husbands and wives are both living by the divine forgiveness, marriage is stable, and divorce is inadmissible. The two are "one flesh", linked together in indissoluble unity, worshipping one God and seeking to do His will.

Where husbands and wives are Christians, homes are stable but they are not always happy. It is terribly easy for the earnest to become the censorious, and for parents, who are deeply concerned with their children's character, to be unduly restrictive, relying too much on law and too little on love, and seeking to demand obedience from those who have passed from childhood into the adolescent age when it is natural for the young to be self-assertive, and critical of the traditions in which they have been reared. And there are Christian homes which lack the attractiveness of joy because the union of the parents, though made firm by loyalty, yet has lost the glow of natural love. Marriage has for one of its main ends the procreation of children, and healthy-minded couples would not have it otherwise, for love finds its fulfilment in increase, and, although children mean many a care, they may bring with them many a joy. But married love is not to be interpreted only as a means for procreation. We have seen how early in the history of the

Church the current belief that matter was evil, and the reaction from pagan licentiousness, caused many to regard sexual intercourse as shameful, as something to be tolerated only as necessary for the prolongation of the race. That view has lingered on till quite recent times. In consequence, married love has often been robbed of its joy. Prudery has been mistaken for purity, and women have been brought up to believe that a woman's part in married intercourse should be purely passive ; a " pure " woman endured, but did not desire, her husband's approach, and endured it because she was so bound in wifely duty, and because, by the strange design of God or nature, that was the only way in which children could be conceived. In this way married love often lost the glow of joy ; wives seemed frigid, whilst husbands failed to satisfy their wives because they did not know how to meet those unrealized desires of which their wives would have been ashamed to speak. Ignorance is not a protection to marriage but a peril, and the frankness of modern young couples is a gain and not a loss. One of the problems these have to face to-day is what is commonly called birth control, but should be called control of conception.[1]

(4) RESPONSIBLE PARENTHOOD

Means of evading conception are not new ; Juvenal referred to them, and St. Augustine denounced them, but it is only in relatively recent years that science has made available for general use mechanical and chemical contraceptives. This Neo-Malthusianism received its " first national advertisement " in the prosecution in 1877 of Bradlaugh and Mrs. Besant for publishing an illustrated pamphlet giving methods of birth control. By the 'nineties it had become " evident that a reduction was beginning in the size of families, in the first instance in those of the professional and middle class, charged with heavy public-school fees, and among the better to do artizans struggling to keep up a high standard of life ".[2] It is

---

[1] Birth-control would naturally mean abortion—that vile crime.
[2] G. M. Trevelyan, *English Social History*, p. 563.

not surprising that the use of such methods was at first generally condemned by Christian people. Contraceptives were often displayed in shop windows side by side with pornographic books, and the traditional association of such goods with prostitution was thus maintained. A Committee of Anglican Bishops in 1913 issued a report which " condemns entirely the use of mechanical and chemical means to prevent conception, but admits that there may be cases in which a married pair may legitimately desire to limit the family. In these cases the Committee does not condemn those who reduce their marital relations to those parts of the month in which conception is less likely to take place ". Even in regard to this concession the Committee was divided. A Committee of the National Free Church Council likewise condemned the use of contraceptives.[1] The Lambeth Conference of 1920 uttered " an emphatic warning against the use of unnatural means for the avoidance of conception ".[2] The Report of its Committee on " the Problem of Marriage and Sexual Morality " was equally emphatic in its condemnation, although it was " aware that many persons of undoubted sincerity whose opinions are entitled to respect, do not share this view, considering the whole matter as chiefly a question of expediency to be determined on medical, financial and social grounds ".[3]

The C.O.P.E.C. Conference held at Birmingham in 1924 was unable to come to any decision on this matter, but the Report of the Commission on " The Relation of the Sexes " gave an admirably objective statement of the view-point of those who approved, as well as of those who condemned, the use of contraceptives in marriage.[4] The Lambeth Conference of 1930, by a majority of nearly three to one, adopted the following Resolution : " Where there is a clearly felt obligation to limit or avoid parenthood, the method must be decided on Christian principles. The primary and obvious method is complete abstinence from intercourse (as far as may be necessary) in a life of discipline and self-control lived in the power of the Holy Spirit. Nevertheless

---

[1] See A. E. Garvie, *The Christian Ideal for Human Society*, pp. 322 f.
[2] Resolution 68.   [3] *Report*, p. 112.
[4] See C.O.P.E.C. Commission Report, vol. iv. pp. 150–62.

in those cases where there is such a clearly-felt obligation to limit or avoid parenthood, and where there is a morally sound reason for avoiding complete abstinence, the Conference agrees that other methods may be used, provided that this is done in the light of the same Christian principles. The Conference records its strong condemnation of the use of any methods of conception-control from motives of selfishness, luxury, or mere convenience ".[1]

The Roman Church condemns all use of contraceptives. Thus the Encyclical *Casti Connubii* given at Rome in 1930 by Pope Pius XI says, " No reason, however grave, may be put forward by which anything intrinsically against nature may become conformable to nature and morally good ".[2] There are many Christians outside the Roman Church who hold this view, and the repugnance which they feel to such usages has naturally been increased by the extravagance of some of their advocates. Modern contraceptives do not constitute a gospel, and their use is not a panacea for married unhappiness. Nor does their discovery make morality obsolete. Some exponents of the " New Morality " have claimed that, since sexual relations could

[1] Resolution 15. For the relevant part of the Report of the Committee on *Marriage and Sex*, see pp. 89–92.

[2] It is truer to say that the Roman Church forbids any use of contraceptives than to say it excludes all birth control. The Encyclical contains the significant words : " Nor are those considered as acting against nature who in the married state use their right in the proper manner although on account of natural reasons either of time or of certain defects, new life cannot be brought forth. For in matrimony as well as in the use of the matrimonial rights there are also secondary ends such as mutual aid, the cultivating of mutual love, and the quieting of concupiscence, which husband and wife are not forbidden to consider so long as they are subordinated to the primary end, and so long as the intrinsic nature of the act is preserved ". *Christian Marriage* p. 28. On the paper cover of the part of the *Dictionnaire de Théologie Catholique*, issued in 1941, we notice a whole-page advertisement of a French translation (from the German book published in Czechoslovakia with the *imprimatur* of the Archbishop of Vienna), entitled *Vie Conjugale, Fécondité et Agénèse, Nouvel Exposé de la Méthode du Docteur Smulders*. The advertisement states that " the ideal to aim at is not that of a family unhappy because it has too many members but rather of a reasonable number of children who can be brought up as men and Christians ", and that the book provides tables indicating for each month the days of continence corresponding to the different forms of the cycle.

be severed from procreation, casual " affairs " should no longer be condemned, and the fidelity of man and wife was no longer important. So to speak is to degrade love into mere sexuality. Love, which means life-long union, is one thing ; lust, which is merely the titillation of a nerve, is another. True love says, in the words of that glorious poem of pure and monogamous love, *The Song of Songs,* " I am my beloved's and my beloved is mine ".[1]

Contraceptives, like many other discoveries of science, can be used for base ends, and, in consequence, some Christians feel they ought not to employ means that may increase temptation for the unmarried by removing the fear of pregnancy, in the same way as many are teetotallers, not because they think it wrong to drink a glass of wine or beer, but because they feel that they ought not to countenance what for many in this country leads to abuse. Others object on aesthetic grounds to contraceptives, and are able so to sublimate their desires in common interests as to live happily even through many years of married celibacy. But there is always the risk of sublimation being incomplete ; in that case, there is likely to be nervous strain which may lead to irritation and a measure of estrangement. Of the many pamphlets now available on marriage, none is more authoritative than that written jointly by Dr. F. R. Barry, the Bishop of Southwell who is the author of one of the most influential books on Christian Ethics, by Mr. Claude Mullins who, as a Metropolitan Magistrate, speaks with long knowledge of broken marriages, and by Dr. Douglas White, a Christian Physician. It states, " Deliberate prevention of conception is necessary in the normal marriage. It follows that to deny to married couples the use of contraceptives must result either in the conception of children in wrong circumstances or in the risks that follow indefinite abstention from sexual intercourse ".[2] With that judgment Protestant Christians increasingly agree. As is well known, couples differ immensely in fertility. Every marriage that can be should be fruitful, but does that mean that it must be unlimitedly fruitful ?

The command, " Be fruitful and multiply ", was given in

[1] vi. 3.   [2] *Christian Marriage,* p. 24.

Genesis in the context of an uninhabited earth, not in a land of dense population. The time of large families was a time of a great death rate. As Brunner points out, " About the year 1800 the population of Europe was reckoned to be about 160 millions, whereas to-day its total population has risen to about 460 millions. Infant mortality used to be so great that, on the average, only a third of the children survived, so that a mother needed to bear six children in order to preserve the race. To-day, three births per mother are considered adequate for this purpose ".[1] Where there were maids, mothers might have large families without imperilling their health, but how many mothers died in early middle age from overwork and strain. Brunner uses the phrase of a German woman, " responsible mother-hood ".[2] Responsible motherhood means that there are no " unwanted children " ; that every child is a child desired.

Some pronouncements of ecclesiastics on this subject seem strangely remote from the actualities of life. A man and woman who marry, say, at twenty-five may have three children by the time they are thirty. If they feel they ought not to have more, what is to be their married life after that time ? To live as celibates is one thing ; to live as married celibates another. It is strange that such married celibacy should be extolled as the " Christian " way, for St. Paul, as we have seen, explicitly warned married Christians against so living for more than a short period.[3] It would be different if there were no other way to save the wife from overstrain. In that case a husband who loved his wife with tenderness could abstain from intercourse in the same way as he would do if some illness of his wife made complete abstinence desirable. These means can be abused by those who use them to thwart one of the purposes of marriage by seeking thus to evade parenthood, although only the foolish and the ignorant will assume that every childless marriage is so because of the use of such means. There are many couples to whom their childlessness is the great disappointment of their lives, and it ought in justice to be remembered that the medical science which has provided means by which conception may be

[1] *The Divine Imperative*, p. 654.
[2] *Op. cit.* p. 371.   [3] See earlier, p. 82.

prevented and births thus spaced out, has also provided the means by which some marriages, which otherwise would be sterile, may become fruitful. To-day many marriages end in divorce, but there are also many very happy marriages where husbands and wives love each other without fear or prudery, where children are desired, and in which no child comes as an " unwanted " child.

(5) THE PROBLEM OF DIVORCE

Where husbands and wives are both Christians, marriage may present difficulties, but these difficulties can be solved by understanding and forgiving love. The immense majority in our land live their lives without conscious experience of God's grace. We have to recognize that the Churches seem to many to be more quick to condemn the sinner than to help him or her back to better ways, whilst traditional Christian teaching appears inadequate and, indeed, misleading.

There are many who attend Church for weddings who are rarely there at other times. It is unfortunate that the language of the 1662 Prayer Book conveys the impression that marriage is a concession to " such as have not the gift of continency ". Natural love is not something of which to be ashamed, and marriage is not rightly regarded as a " concession " ; it is the opportunity of lifelong partnership issuing in the establishment of a home and the nurture and education of children. Here, as nowhere else, it is given to men and women to co-operate with God in His creative work.

What of the permanency of marriage ? As we have seen, when our Lord was asked whether divorce was permissible, He did not refer His hearers to the Law in Deut. xxiv. 1, which permitted the husband to divorce his wife for an " unseemly thing ", but, instead, went back to those words in Genesis which speak of God creating men, male and female, so that a husband " shall cleave to his wife ; and the twain shall be one flesh ". When asked why, if that were so, did Moses command to give a bill of divorcement and to put her away, our Lord replied : " Moses for your hardness of heart suffered you to put away your wives ; but from the beginning it hath not been so. And I say unto you, whosoever shall put away his wife and marry another committeth adultery ". In St. Matthew's version here, and in a similar passage in the Sermon on the Mount, divorce is permitted in the case of fornication. It is hard to believe that the words " except for fornication " are original. It was not our Lord's way to give detailed laws. He expressed the divine ideal for man of indissoluble marriage, and it is probable that the exception of fornication in Matthew reflects the transition from an ideal into the law of that Jewish Christianity which that Gospel reflects.[1]

" Hardness of heart " does not belong only to the time of " Moses ", and it is useless for positive laws to go far beyond the recognized requirements of secular morality. The absence of any provision for divorce and remarriage merely results in a larger number of transitory unions from which still greater evils arise. The Divorce Act of 1857 restricted the grounds of divorce to adultery in the wife, or adultery and cruelty in the husband, and this led to the sorry farce of the hotel visit. The Matrimonial Causes Act of 1937 permits divorce not only for cruelty and incurable insanity, but for three years' desertion. A law of the State has to represent not the highest but the average morality of its citizens, and this Act probably represents as strict a law of marriage as the hardness of men's heart allows. The vow taken at the Register Office does not in itself make clear that civil marriage means the intention to enter into a lifelong union. " Lawfully wedded wife ", as the Archbishop of Canterbury pointed out in his speech in the House of Lords in November 1947, may be understood to mean merely " legally registered and therefore mine ". " In Halsbury's *Laws of England*, it is stated : ' The only kind of marriage which the English Law recognizes is one which is essentially the voluntary union for life of one man and one woman to the exclusion of all others '. Lawful means that in the English law, and nothing else, although that lifelong union may be put an end to for some misdemeanour which cancels it ". " It seems to me ", he added, " quite intolerable that we should allow the use of a

[1] Matt. xix. 1–9. See earlier, pp. 62 f.

form of words to go on which admittedly vast numbers of people misunderstand ". That misunderstanding ought no longer to persist for, since the Archbishop's speech, Superintendent Registrars are asked before the marriage vows are taken not only to declare their " solemn and binding character " but also to state : " Marriage according to the law of this country is the union of one man with one woman, voluntarily entered into for life, to the exclusion of all others ".

Where both parties to marriage are Christians, divorce is not thought of even as a possibility, for they have resources of spiritual power sufficient to keep their vow " to love, honour and serve " each other until " death them do part ". But if only one party is Christian, the problem is more complex. Ought the Church to recognize a marriage when one of the parties has a divorced partner still living ? The Roman Church forbids divorce in the sense of freedom to remarry, although the severity of the prohibition is mitigated by declarations of nullity of marriage, and by the recognition of the " Pauline privilege ".[1] Some Anglicans likewise refuse to admit that the parties in a valid and consummated marriage can ever be released from their bond except by death. " Whatever the law of the State may be, neither of them can be married again in Church while the other lives ". " If either of them so marries elsewhere, the Church will not regard it as a marriage and as long as it continues will not allow them to come to the Altar ".[2] Certainly divorce is a very grave matter. Where there are children of the marriage, its dissolution inflicts on them a cruel wrong, for it deprives them of that sense of security which is a child's first requirement, and even where a marriage is childless, divorce is still contrary to the divine ideal of the indissolubility of marriage. No one ought to be married by Christian rites unless he or she means lifelong marriage.

But it takes two to make a marriage, and in our time the two are equal personalities. What if the marriage is broken by

[1] For the Roman teaching on the " Pauline Privilege " (1 Cor. vii. 12 ff.), see H. Davis, *Moral and Pastoral Theology*, IV. pp. 223–7.

[2] T. A. Lacey, *Marriage in Church and State*, revised by R. C. Mortimer, 1947, p. 210.

the action of one against the wish of the other ? The writer thinks of a young couple who married during the last war. The husband had soon after his marriage to go overseas. His wife took as lover a close friend of his who stayed in civilian employ. When the husband returned on leave, he did his best to win his wife back, acting not in censoriousness, but in forgiving love. She refused, saying she preferred the other man, and asked him to divorce her to let her marry her paramour, which he did. Some years later, this young man became engaged to be married to a woman who genuinely shared his Christian faith. Was he to be condemned ? Should this young man have been all his life cut off either from the comfort of a home, or from the full fellowship of the Church ? Some of us would not thus judge. If bride and bridegroom desire to be married in church, and one of them has had a marriage dissolved, it is the more necessary to make sure that they seek a Christian service, not because the bride wants, as one divorced woman told the writer, a " white wedding ", but because they desire God's blessing on their union, and care should obviously be taken that they understand that the solemn vows made in a Christian service are those of lifelong fidelity. Even an " innocent " partner of a broken marriage may well feel his or her share of responsibility for its failure. The Christian ideal of marriage is that of indissoluble unity. But we all alike need the divine forgiveness, and it is difficult to see on what ground failure in marriage should be treated as if it was the one failure for which the penitent cannot be forgiven.

No one who realizes the terrible consequences of broken homes can read without concern the present statistics of divorce. And yet, as Bishop Hensley Henson said, " Divorce statistics have of themselves little value as evidences of social morality ".[1] There was no divorce in Western Europe in the Middle Ages, and yet there was much vice. In England the period most notorious for the profligacy of the ruling classes and the

[1] From his wise and weighty paper on *Marriage and Divorce, Bishoprick Papers,* p. 12.

licentiousness of the stage, was one in which a dispensation to marry after divorce could be obtained only by an Act of Parliament procurable by the rich alone.   The narrow facilities for divorce provided in the Divorce Bill of 1857, and the wider facilities of The Matrimonial Causes Act of 1937, have made divorce possible for many, but the frequency with which these facilities are utilized is not the cause but the symptom of moral decadence.   The New Morality, which makes light of marriage vows, is not really new ; it is the old immorality, seeking to justify itself by pretentious phrases.   When love is thought of only as passion, then such love, which might be called by another name, lacks the permanency of loyalty, whilst a false romanticism makes marriage insecure.

The Christian view of marriage would be more readily commended had not much Christian teaching been vitiated by a false asceticism.   Purity need not be prudery, and marriage should be accepted as an Order of Creation, designed by the Creator, not only for the purpose of procreation, but for the solace and happiness of husband and wife.   To concentrate on its physical aspect is to rob love of its tenderness and permanency, and yet to despise that aspect is to deprive love of its joy, and may lead to an estrangement which is more easily repressed than removed.   It is unfair to bride and bride-groom to allow them to enter marriage in an ignorance which may lead to impatience with each other through misunder-standing of each other's needs, and proper instruction should be part of the preparation for marriage.[1]   Many a marriage which is in jeopardy may be saved by the help given by Marriage Guidance Councils, or by the wise and frank advice of older and more experienced friends.   Marriage may become, and is, indeed, for very many, the best of earthly joys.   Yet a " happy marriage " may be merely double egoism, and, enriching as is the care of children, even the family is not an end in itself. " The father of the family ", as the French saying goes, " is capable of anything " ; devotion to wife and children has made many a man avaricious and even dishonest.   The loyalties of

[1] Admirable pamphlets and books may be obtained from The Alliance of Honour.

the family have to be subordinated to loyalty to God, and in that subordination these loyalties gain new strength and meaning.

Where husband and wife are united in a living Christian faith, then the divine ideal of indissolubility of marriage will be realized, for the resources of the Gospel are sufficient to secure fidelity, understanding and forgiving love. In the Churches best known to the writer, divorces are very rare, and, where they occur, are usually the result of the abnormal strain imposed by war. It is well that the old prudery is gone, and that fewer marriages are marred by ignorance and repression. Men and women are endowed with sex, and may so use that endowment as to win from it joy and comfort. Yet we are not merely creatures of sex and sex belongs to this life alone. The best preparation for marriage is the common possession of that faith in Christ which is adequate to every need, and enables men and women to fulfil their vows of lifelong loyalty. Marriage, then, becomes a sphere not only of joy but of responsibility, and the home presents many an opportunity of shared service. The marriage of men and women is always a union of two imperfect, sinful creatures. But those who live by the divine forgiveness need fear no permanent estrangement, for marriage, which is an Order of Creation, has become for them Christian marriage, in which human love is sanctified and made strong through the experience of that love of God made known to us in Christ's Life and Death and Resurrection.

CHAPTER IX

THE COMMUNITY OF INDUSTRY

(1) THE CRISIS OF INDUSTRY

HUMAN life is so constituted that to live a man must eat, and the food he eats is obtained not by his unaided efforts but by co-operative labour. Seed-time and harvest, rain and sun, provide the possibilities of daily bread, but that bread is not obtained except through human toil. Labour is thus an Order of Creation ; it is the will of the Creator that men should work. In the symbolic presentation of man's creation and estate the sin of our first parents is described as leading to their expulsion from Eden so that to toil was added sorrow, but work is not depicted as the result of sin ; even in Eden man had to " dress " the garden and to " keep it ".[1] Only by work can the race continue and, since food is the most obvious of human needs, the relation of work to welfare is most clearly visible in a simple agricultural community. In such communities, the necessity of work and the dependence of the workers on a divine power, or powers, are readily recognized.

Industrial science and capitalist organization have made possible provision for the ever-increasing populations of our own and many other lands, but the vaster and more complex the organization, the harder is it for many to discern any purpose in their work beyond the provision of their own needs, so that work becomes something to be endured and minimized, and the industrial order a sphere not of co-operation but of strife and frustration. In his novel, *Two on a Tower*, Thomas Hardy depicts a young astronomer who, as he gazes at the starry sky, exclaims, " There is a size at which dignity begins. Further on, there is a size at which solemnity begins ; further on, a size at

[1] Gen. ii. 15.

which awfulness begins ; further on, a size at which ghastliness begins ". Modern industry seems to have reached that size, Work once brought a sense of " dignity " or even of " solemnity ", but it is hard for one who finds himself reduced to a mere cog in a vast machine so to regard the industrial order of which he feels himself an insignificant fragment. Books, like Samuel Smiles' *Self Help*, so admired by our Victorian forefathers, appear to many ridiculous because of their complacency. There is joy, if strain, in all creative work, but few are craftsmen to-day. Instead, men tend machines, and the division of labour, which makes possible mass production, often induces in the worker the sense that he, too, is merely an unimportant part of a machine.

During the war those engaged in the construction of " Mulberries " could not be told the full significance of those parts of them which they made. But they knew they were engaged in work of grave importance, and that gave their work a meaning. It is that sense of significance which is often lacking in modern industry. Mr. Maurice Reckitt tells the story of a welfare worker who asked an operator in the Ford factory at Detroit, " What are you making ? " and received the answer, " C. 429 ". " What is C. 429 ? " " I don't know ". " What becomes of C. 429 when it leaves you ? " " I don't know ". " How long have you been making C. 429 ? " " Nine years ", was the reply. This represents, as Mr. Reckitt says, almost " the nadir of depersonalizing mechanization ".[1] It is not the use of machinery that is at fault. The machine relieves the worker of much heavy and painful toil, and alone makes possible provision for the needs of the dense populations of the modern West, but, where men are treated as robots, all talk of the dignity of work becomes to them a cruel jest.

The immense complexity of commerce makes the prosperity of one country dependent on the actions of another, and the industrial order reaches " the size at which ghastliness begins ". I remember vividly a conversation I had in the early nineteen-thirties with a man from a Lancashire cotton town, who had been sent by his Church to a Conference for Sunday School

[1] *Faith and Society*, pp. 351 f.

Teachers at which I was lecturing. That man had been out of work for several years. He had kept his Christian faith and maintained his Christian service. More painful than the privations of his poverty was his sense of not being wanted. That was no fault of his ; the specialized manufacture for which his town was famous had ceased to be in demand in foreign markets. There was the absurdity of what was called over-production but which should have been called under-consumption. This book is written at a time of under-production, when war has led to the scarcity of goods, and when more exports are required if necessary imports are to be purchased. Clamant as is this need, it is not strange that those who suffered from unemployment should be slow to respond to the appeal for more production. There is the bitter memory of the time when to work harder seemed to result in there being fewer workers. Modern industry is so vast and complex, so interrelated with world events, that it appears to subjugate men to its vagaries ; to many it seems an enclave, incapable of moralization and governed by laws as impersonal as the law of gravitation, whilst some have even claimed that these laws are ordained by the Creator. " The laws of commerce ", wrote Edmund Burke, " are the laws of Nature and therefore the laws of God ". In business, we are told, self-interest must be the sole consideration, and the political economy, for long dominant in the West, taught that if each sought his own good, the common good would be secured. As Edmund Burke wrote, " The benign and wise disposer of all things obliges men, whether they will or not, in pursuing their own selfish interests to connect the general good with their own individual successes ".[1] Or, as Henry Ford Senior has put it in our own day, " We now know that anything which is economically right is also morally right ; there can be no conflict between good economics and good morals ".[2]

Few things have contributed more to the growth of secularism in our land than the acquiescence of many Christians in such teaching. Whereas some, like Lord Shaftesbury, and many a social reformer since, have found in the Christian proclamation

[1] See C. E. Raven, *Christian Socialism*, pp. 32 and 34.
[2] Quoted by C. E. Hudson, *Christian Morals*, p. 209.

of God's concern for every soul of man and the significance of the life beyond the grave, a motive for the removal of those social wrongs which imperil not only the happiness but the character of the dispossessed, others have restricted Christianity to the sphere of individual life, and they have made it " not a standard by which to judge the institutions of society, but a reason for accepting them ".[1] Christianity, they have said, can help to make men honest and truthful ; it can inspire to the philanthropy which seeks to alleviate distress ; it can bring to the poor the consolation of religion, and the hope of a better life beyond the grave, and patience to bear their lot, but it has no responsibility for changing the conditions from which poverty originates. This acquiescence in unjust social conditions has made Christianity appear to many irrelevant to the needs of modern men, whilst to some it appears not only irrelevant, but mischievous ; its talk about God and the life to come is regarded as a convenient device of the possessing classes to distract attention from man and his immediate needs. A spirituality, which ignores material needs, evokes a materialism to which the spiritual is unreal. When the comforts of religion are offered as a substitute for the necessities of earthly life, not only is religion rejected, but the suspicion is created that the promise of blessings beyond the grave is merely an evasion of the demands for justice in this present life. As Felix Holt, the Radical, put it in George Eliot's novel, " We'll give them back some of their heaven and take it out in something for us and our children in this world."

It is the old story, " The fathers have eaten sour grapes and the children's teeth are set on edge." The Christian Church which, in many of its branches, has in this century been deeply conscious of social needs, finds its approach rejected because of its identification in the minds of many with a social order which seems to them unjust and oppressive.

(2) THE INDICTMENT OF THE CHURCHES

From the time when the Church, instead of being persecuted, won the patronage of the Emperor, Christianity has been so

[1] J. L. and B. Hammond, *The Town Labourer*, p. 225.

interwoven with European civilization that it is easy to hold it responsible for all the social evils from which that civilization has suffered. The medieval church put avarice among the seven deadly sins, and honoured those who, abandoning the world, gave themselves as monks to contemplation and to service. But order after order, beginning in simplicity, became corrupted by wealth, and even the Friars, who began as preachers to the poor, gave way to avarice. St. Thomas Aquinas made no distinction between interest and usury, and condemned as a sin the taking of usury for money lent,[1] but the Fuggers, the great moneylenders at the eve of the Reformation, were regarded as pious Catholics, and it was partly to repay a loan owed to them by an Archbishop that the Papal Court arranged for that sale of a Jubilee Indulgence which was the immediate occasion of Luther's breach with Rome.[2] Luther emphasized the sanctity of common life and affirmed that God could be as well served in life's ordinary tasks as by any priest or nun. But his movement became identified with the secular interests of the powerful. The liberty he preached was restricted to the sphere of religion, and the poor were estranged through his violent intervention in the Peasants' Revolt when he bade the Princes, " Stab, smite and slay ", those who were seeking by force of arms to secure some measure of social justice.[3] And in our country also the Reformation was not at first distinguished by sympathy with the poor.

In recent years, many of the intelligentsia who dislike Calvin, whose writings they have not studied, and the Free Churches

---

[1] *Summa Theologica*, II. ii. lxxviii. 1.

[2] For the sordid story see the writer's *The Christian Estimate of Man*, p. 128. Albrecht, Prince of Brandenburg, already Archbishop of Magdeburg and acting Bishop of Halberstadt, at the age of twenty-two, obtained the Electoral archbishopric of Maintz. For these offences against Canon Law, he had to pay an enormous sum to get a papal dispensation and did this through a loan from the Fuggers. It was arranged that half the amount obtained from the Indulgence by his territories was to be retained by him to repay this loan.

[3] *Against the Robbing and Murdering Hordes of Peasants*, W.A. XVIII. p. 361. (*Works of Martin Luther*, E.T. edited by H. E. Jacobs, IV. p. 253 ; on Luther's conception of the Two Kingdoms, see later, pp. 243 f.)

whose life they have not shared, have spoken as if it were a proved fact of historical research that the teaching of Calvin, or of the Puritans, was responsible for the Capitalism they also dislike. This view usually claims to be based on Max Weber's *The Protestant Ethic and the Spirit of Capitalism*, which, written in German in 1904 and 1905, was published in English in 1930, and became widely known in England through the references to it in Professor Tawney's famous and fascinating book, *Religion and the Rise of Capitalism*.[1] The view has been subjected to severe and damaging criticism by Dr. H. M. Robertson in his *Aspects of the Rise of Economic Individualism*. He quotes a characteristic sentence by Mr. Aldous Huxley, " The Reformers read their Old Testament, and trying to imitate the Jews, became those detestable Puritans to whom we owe, not merely Grundyism and Podsnappery, but also (as Weber and Tawney have shown) all that was and still is vilest, cruellest, most anti-human in the modern capitalist system ". Dr. Robertson comments, " To follow this modern way of connecting capitalism with the religion founded by Calvin is to follow a mere will-of-the-wisp. Too much attention has been paid to certain aspects of Puritanism, and too little to what was happening outside the Puritan world ".[2] Weber himself described as " foolish and doctrinaire " the thesis that " capitalism as an economic system is a creation of the Reformation ", and denied that it was his " aim to substitute for a one-sided materialistic an equally one-sided spiritualistic causal interpretation of culture and of history ".[3]

It is significant that Weber illustrates the Spirit of Capitalism from Benjamin Franklin who, as he admits, was " a colourless Deist ",[4] one who had renounced not only Calvinism but

---

[1] Weber's view was in part anticipated by H. R. Percival, who in the Preface to the *Seven Oecumenical Councils* (*Nicene and Post-Nicene Fathers*), 1900, p. 37, wrote, " The glory of inventing the new moral code on the subject by which that which before was looked upon as mortal sin has been transfigured into innocence, if not virtue, belongs to John Calvin. He made the modern distinction between ' interest ' and ' usury ' and was the first to write in defence of this then newfangled refinement of casuistry ".   [2] p. 208.

[3] *The Protestant Ethic and the Spirit of Capitalism*, pp. 91, 183.

[4] *Op. cit.* pp. 52 f.

Christianity. Professor Tawney, in his Foreword to the English Translation of Weber's book suggests important modifications of his theory, and, in his *Religion and the Rise of Capitalism*, mentions several points on which Weber's arguments appear, " one-sided and over-strained ",[1] and remarks that " the picture of Calvin, the organizer and disciplinarian, as a parent of laxity in economic matters is a legend ".[2] And Professor Robertson concludes, " The decline of the Churches in England as witness to the Christian code of social ethics was not due to a Puritan belief that ' the Lorde was with Joseph, and he was a luckie felowe '. It was due to the unwillingness of a rising bourgeoisie to be bound by what it considered anti-quated rules ",[3] and in this judgment Professor Clapham concurs.[4]

Neither Calvin nor the Puritans can be held responsible for the rise of Capitalism nor for its abuses. The real indictment of the Churches lies in the acquiescence of many Christians, Anglicans as well as Dissenters, in the social injustices which accompanied the Industrial Revolution. Like others, they accepted the false philosophy of *laissez-faire*, which some Dissenters found the more attractive in that their distrust of any interference of the State in the sphere of religion blinded them to the need of that action of the State in the sphere of industry by which alone abuses could be checked. The worst of these abuses was the apprenticeship of little children from the workhouses of London and other great cities to manufacturers in the industrial towns. The long quotations which Karl Marx gives from Fielden's description of the cruelty inflicted on these children makes very painful reading, and makes intelligible his

[1] *Pelican Edition*, pp. 247 f.

[2] *Op cit.*, p. 91. Much has been made of Calvin's recognition of interest and especially of his letter to a correspondent, *De Usuris, Corpus Reformatorum*, XXXVII. col. 245–9. There are good discussions of this in Dr. Robertson's book, pp. 115–20, and by Albert Hyma, *Christianity, Capitalism and Communism*, pp. 66–90, who expounds also Calvin's references to usury in his Commentaries.

[3] *Op. cit.* p. 211.

[4] In his " Editor's Preface " to Dr. Robertson's book, " We see at close quarters the Puritan spirit not begetting capitalism but coming to terms with it. Christian makes agreement with Mr. Worldly Wiseman ".

comment that " capital comes dripping from head to foot from every pore, with blood and dirt ".[1]

The evils of that time are familiar to many in our country through the sombre but fascinating books of Dr. and Mrs. Hammond, and, in consequence, their quotation from William Wilberforce is widely known in which this great Evangelical, the brave leader in the emancipation of the slaves, with a strange complacency, reminded the poor that " their more lowly paths had been allotted to them by the hand of God ; that it is their part faithfully to discharge its duties, and contentedly to bear its inconveniences : that the present state of things is very short ; that the objects about which worldly men conflict so eagerly are not worth the contest ; that the peace of mind which Religion offers indiscriminately to all ranks affords more true satisfaction than all the expensive pleasures which are beyond the poor man's reach ; that in this view the poor have the advantage ; that if their superiors enjoy more abundant comforts they are also exposed to many temptations from which the inferior classes are happily exempted ; that, ' having food and raiment they should be therewith content ', since their situation in life, with all its evils, is better than they deserved at the hand of God ; and finally, that all human distinctions will soon be done away, and the true followers of Christ will all, as children of the same Father, be alike admitted to the possession of the same heavenly inheritance.   Such are the blessed effects of Christianity on the temporal well-being of political communities ".[2]

A workman, faced with the alternative of low wages or starvation, was powerless alone.   Only by union could workmen win strength.   But the Combination Acts of 1799 and 1800 forbade that union, and allowed magistrates to send to prison any workman who associated with others in seeking to secure any increase of pay or decrease in the time of work.[3]   It is lamentable that, in his fear of revolution, Wilberforce should have given these Acts his support and thereby earned the hatred

[1] *Capital I*, XXXI.   *Handbook of Marxism*, pp. 399 ff.
[2] *The Town Labourer*, pp. 231 f.
[3] The 1799 Act required only one magistrate—the amended Act of 1800, two.   In no instances were these Acts used to prevent joint action by employers.

of some of the working-class leaders.   But it ought in fairness
to be remembered that it was he who secured the appointment
of a Parliamentary Commission on Children's Employment, and
took a leading part in seeking to secure the prohibition of the
cruelties connected with the employment of boys as chimney-
sweeps.   His often-repeated quotation from *The Practical View
of the System of Christianity* needs to be supplemented by such
other words from it as those in which he taught his readers to
regard others ' as members of the same family entitled not only
to the debts of justice, but to the less definite and more liberal
claims of fraternal kindness ".[1]   And Wilberforce had a right
to speak of " fraternal kindness " for he impoverished himself
by his generosity.   But his much publicized reference to the
advantages of a " lowly path " may warn us of the danger of
unimaginative complacency.   We all tend to be blinded by our
prejudices and our self-interest.   How else, when Shaftesbury
strove for the passing of the Ten Hours Bill, should he have
found his " most malignant of opponents " in John Bright, the
devoted advocate of Peace and the honoured member of the
Society of Friends ?

The memory of those ancient wrongs still remains, and
accounts for much of the estrangement from religion of many
who seek social justice.   If religion seems only " pie in the sky,
when you die ", then it is naturally regarded as a " lie ".

There is the other side.   The element of truth in Karl Marx's
description of religion as the " opium of the people " was
recognized by Charles Kingsley [2] who in 1848, the year of the
Communist Manifesto and the failure of the Chartists, in his
letter to the Chartists wrote, " it is mainly the fault of us parsons
who have never told you that the true ' Reformer's Guide ', the
true poor man's book, the true voice of God against tyrants,
idlers and humbugs was the Bible ".   The Bible " was the poor
man's comfort and the rich man's warning ".   " It is our fault.

---

[1] G. C. Binyon, *The Christian Socialistic Movement*, p. 223.

[2] It is often said that Kingsley was the first to speak of religion as
" opium ".   Dr. W. E. Sangster points out, in his letter to the *Spectator*
of December 17th, 1948, that Marx in his critique of Hegelianism
published in the *Deutsch-Französische Yahrbücher* of 1844 had already
spoken of religion as " the opium of the people ".

We have used the Bible as if it were the special constable's book— an opium dose for keeping beasts of burden patient while they were being overloaded,—a mere book to keep the poor in order ". The Christian Socialist Movement, founded by Maurice, Ludlow, Hughes and Kingsley, led in the Church of England to a fresh emphasis on the social implications of Christianity, which later found notable expression in the work and writings of great Christian leaders like Bishop Gore and Archbishop Temple.[1]

Even the Roman Catholic Church, for all its conservatism, has shown itself at times sensitive to social needs. Thus Cardinal Manning played an honourable part in the Dock Labourers' Strike in 1889, and his influence is thought to have been at work in the notable Encyclical of Leo XIII, *Rerum Novarum*, published in 1891, in which it was taught that " there is a dictate of natural justice more imperious and ancient than any bargain between man and man, namely, that wages ought not to be insufficient to support a frugal and well-behaved wage-earner. If through necessity or fear of a worse evil the workman accepts harder conditions because an employer or contractor will afford him no better, he is made the victim of force and injustice ". This teaching was reaffirmed forty years later by Pius XI in his Encyclical, *Quadragesimo Anno*, " Labour . . . is not a mere chattel : the human dignity of the working-man must be recognized in it, and consequently it cannot be bought and sold like any piece of merchandise ".[2]

The attitude of the Free Churches to social questions has naturally been influenced by the fact that they themselves have known oppression. Whereas the founders of Christian Socialism in the Church of England belonged to the privileged classes, and thought of industrial problems as those who themselves had not faced them, the ministers of the Free Churches were excluded from the ancient Universities, and were not drawn from one social class. The Dissenting Academies, in which lay as well as

---

[1] The movement is well described by C. E. Raven, *Christian Socialism*, 1848–54 ; by G. C. Binyon, *The Christian Socialist Movement in England*, and by M. C. Reckitt, *Maurice to Temple*.
[2] M. Oakeshott, *The Social and Political Doctrines of Contemporary Europe*, Basis Book Edition, pp. 69 and 58.

ministerial students were educated, were distinguished both by sound learning and by great simplicity of life.[1] In the early years of the Industrial Revolution, as Dr. Trevelyan has said, " The mass of unregarded humanity in the factories and mines " had " no one but the Nonconformist minister " as " their friend ". " They had no interest or hope in life but Evangelical religion or Radical politics. Sometimes the two went together, for many Nonconformist preachers themselves imbibed and imparted Radical doctrines ".[2] Nonconformity became very strong in the industrial areas. With their hereditary distrust of State interference in religion, some Dissenters, too, readily accepted the doctrine of *laissez-faire*. But employers and employees were often found as members of the same congregation, sharing in the common interests of the Church, and many a labour leader gained not only his inspiration to social service, but his first experience of public speaking and organization in the fellowship of a chapel. As Mr. Jack Lawson, M.P., who held office in the first Labour Government, has written, " The most powerful force for the mental and moral elevation of the workers during the industrial era has been this contemptuously called ' Little Bethel ' ". " The so-called intellectuals ", he continues, " speak of these as ' reactionary '. In truth, the gentlemen who speak so know as much about the real living history of the people of this land, as pigs know of aeroplanes ".[3] " Our unhappy divisions ", regrettable as they now are, have prevented the identification of Christianity with a State Church having all the advantage and disadvantage of social prestige and the patronage of the powerful. In some of the Free Churches the interest in social reform became dominant. No hymn was sung with more fervour than that written by Ebenezer Elliott,

[1] The account books of Dr. Philip Doddridge, preserved in the Library of New College, London, provide interesting evidence of this.

[2] *English Social History*, pp. 476 f.

[3] *A Man's Life*, p. 66. Cp. J. W. Bready, *England : Before and After Wesley*, p. 396. R. C. K. Ensor, *England* 1870–1914, pp. 528 f., speaking of the years before the First World War, remarks, " The rising labour movement owed an immense debt to nonconformity. Broadly it was due to nonconformity that socialism in England never acquired the anti-religious bias prevalent on the Continent ".

the Corn Law rhymer, " When wilt Thou save the people ? "
with its passionate prayer :

> Shall crime bring crime for ever,
>   Strength aiding still the strong ?
> Is it thy will, O Father,
>   That man should toil for wrong ?

The temptation of these Churches was not to other-worldliness,
but to a too facile identification of the Kingdom of God with that
devout democracy for which they strove, and an undue reliance
on the belief that " the voice of the people " would be " the
voice of God ".

The days have long since passed when the Church of England
could be described as the " Conservative Party at prayer " or
the Free Churches, as an Anglican scholar put it to me, as " the
Liberal Party on its hind-legs ! "   Interest in the social welfare
of the people is not confined to any section of the Church nor
to any political party ; yet the Church's social efforts to-day
would be more effective if it were not for the failures of the past.
No Christian can accept the Communist rejection of any moral
law, and the identification of morality with the convenience of
class interests.   Yet, remembering the errors of the past, as we
turn to the social teaching of the New Testament and its application to modern needs, we shall do well to remember how easy it
is to allow our views to be coloured by prejudice and selfishness.

(3) NEW TESTAMENT TEACHING

Our Lord's teaching does not provide us with a " Social
Gospel ", and yet it does not permit us to be indifferent to the
needs of others nor to acquiesce in those injustices which it has
been the aim of the " Social Gospel " to remove.   Like the
prophets before Him, our Lord denounced the combination of
worship and social injustice.   He drove the money-changers
from the temple, and spoke in words of strong condemnation of
those who " devour widows' houses ", who oppress the poor and
the defenceless, and yet claim to be religious men.   He knew
how imperative were life's common needs, and bade His disciples
pray not only for forgiveness and for guidance, but for the bread

they needed for the coming day. His teaching was occasional and, to be understood, has to be studied in relation to the concrete needs of those whom He addressed. Thus the parable which speaks of labourers in the vineyard, receiving equal pay for unequal work, is not a commendation of equalitarian socialism but a presentation of the strange paradox of God's grace which gives men more than they deserve. The rich young man was bidden to sell all that he might follow Jesus, for only one unencumbered by wealth would be able to follow Jesus up to Jerusalem, there to face danger and, it might be, death. But that was a special and not a general command. Not all were summoned to homelessness and poverty. Lazarus and Mary and Martha retained their home in Bethany, and most whom He addressed were not called to abandon their livelihoods. He bade men give to those who asked for help, and, at the same time, told His disciples not to cast their pearls before swine. Gautama the Buddha forbade his monks to have any money; all they needed was a begging-bowl to hold the food they received as alms. Jesus and the Twelve had that bag of money which Judas held. To the poor Jesus spoke of the menace of anxiety, and He who, as the eldest son of a widowed mother, had known the cares which poverty can bring, spoke of the need of trust in a heavenly Father's care, and bade men be content to face each day's trouble as it came. Mr. Bernard Shaw informed his " intelligent woman " that Jesus " tells you to take no thought for to-morrow's dinner or dress." " To take no thought for to-morrow, as we now are, is to become a tramp; and nobody can persuade a really intelligent woman that the problems of civilization can be solved by tramps ".[1] If the woman be " intelligent " enough to have read the Gospels, she would realize the absurdity of Mr. Shaw's remark. It is not the way of tramps to provide for their parents. Jesus sternly condemned those who used religion as a pretext to evade this obligation.[2] A " really intelligent woman " might remember that the Authorized Version was made some centuries ago, and that words sometimes change their meaning. If, with this in mind, she

[1] *The Intelligent Woman's Guide to Socialism and Capitalism*, p. 98.
[2] Mark vii. 11.

turned to the Revised Version, she would find instead of, " Take no thought ", " Be not anxious ". It is not forethought, but distracting anxiety which is condemned. Not only is such anxiety useless ; it is also a sign of lack of faith in the God, who knows His children's needs.

Our Lord summed up His teaching in the double command : Thou shalt love the Lord thy God with all thy heart, and with all thy soul, and with all thy strength ; and thy neighbour as thyself. When the lawyer asked Him, " Who is my neighbour ? " He told the Parable of the Good Samaritan. Like that lawyer we have not to ask, " Who is my neighbour ? " ; we have to be a neighbour to anyone in need whom we can help.[1] In another parable, He speaks of the rich man condemned to punishment in Hades, not because he had been cruel to Lazarus at his gate, but because he had ignored his needs, and left his poverty unrelieved. In the parable of judgment, He speaks of the division between the blessed and the damned as dependent not on what they professed but on what they did. Those who neglected the hungry, and the stranger, the naked and the prisoner, had neglected Him ; those that sought to meet their needs had been serving Him although they knew Him not.[2]

After our Lord's death and resurrection, the remembrance of His teaching was cherished in the Church, and love gained a new meaning, for love now meant the love which Christ had shown. The first believers were conscious of the power and guidance of the Spirit, but neither they, nor the writers of the New Testament, were concerned with social theories. The Book of Acts speaks, indeed, of the Christians at Jerusalem having all things in common ; that was not communism in the modern sense, but the spontaneous generosity of those who felt themselves united in the close bonds of a common faith. As Christianity spread into the pagan world, new problems had to be faced. The small and obscure congregations could make no attempt to change social conditions. Christianity was not an authorized religion ; its adherents were regarded with a suspicion which led later to persecution. Lacking the discipline of the Jewish Law, many converts from paganism found the Christian ideal not only

[1] Luke x. 25–37.   [2] Cp. Matt. xxv. 31–46.

hard but unattractive, and the Church's main concern had to be not the Christianization of the world on which it had at first no influence, but the creation in its members of a Christian character corresponding to the Christian faith. We have seen how St. Paul, though he had to advise his converts in their perplexities and chide them for their moral failures, refused to lay down laws, but, instead, relied upon the appeal of the great Christian facts of Christ's death and resurrection and on the presence of the Spirit in the Church. The unity of Christians in Christ was strongly emphasized ; the suffering of any was the suffering of all ; it was by bearing each other's burdens that the law of Christ could be fulfilled. Yet religious enthusiasm was no excuse for idleness ; " If any man will not work, neither let him eat ".[1] Jew and Gentile, rich and poor, master and slave, were one in Christ, and the needs of each were to be the concern of all. It was useless to profess to love God whilst failing to be compassionate to those in distress. Christian love is not mere emotion ; it means caring for others, and we may not claim to love God whom we have not seen unless we are caring for the brother we have seen and so can help.[2]

The New Testament reflects a time when Christians not only had no responsibility for the social order but when many converts from paganism were slaves, and some of them slave-owners. This slavery was not the relatively humane domestic slavery of Palestine in which the slave retained some rights, but the slavery of the pagan world in which the slave was subject to his master's arbitrary will and cruelty. In Christ all were free, and yet St. Paul, the great apostle of Christian liberty, did not attack slavery as an institution. In his earlier years the expectation of the speedy end of the age had made social distinctions seem unimportant, and later, when this expectation had grown less, he had to be content to bid masters and slaves treat each other as those who knew that masters and slaves had the same Master in heaven. Within the Church there was the equality of love. Thus Tertius, who acted as Paul's amanuensis in the writing of the Epistle to the Romans, greets its readers

---

[1] 2 Thess. iii. 10. For St. Paul's teaching, see earlier, pp. 84 f.
[2] John iii. 17 ; iv. 20.

as one who, though a slave, was yet one whose salutation " in the Lord " they would be glad to receive. And St. Paul sent Onesimus back to Philemon, but bade Philemon treat his runaway slave as a " brother beloved ".[1]

It is unfortunate that our Authorized and Revised Versions speak not of " slaves " but of " servants ", for this mistranslation has led many to suppose that, from the first, Christian teachers taught an undue subservience of the employed to their employers. St. Paul's admonitions are not immediately applicable to our modern social problems. The relevance of the Epistles lies in the illustrations they afford of the possibility of living the Christian life even in an essentially wrong relationship. Character does not depend only upon circumstances and even in a wrong social system the Christian life can still in part be lived.

(4) THE " SOCIAL GOSPEL "

New Testament Ethics does not provide us with a blue-print for a just society. As Dr. William Temple wrote, " there is no such thing as a Christian social ideal, to which we should conform our actual society as closely as possible ".[2] Had our Lord provided such an ideal, His teaching would have been as limited to His age and place as Islam is to the Arabia of Muhammad's time. His teaching was primarily religious ; the ethics He proclaimed was the correlate of the Kingdom of God He preached, whilst the perfection He enjoined was the perfection of that Kingdom and not of an earthly society. That He, the Holy One, was rejected by men and crucified, is the most poignant reminder of our radical and racial sin, and that reminder should save us from a sentimental Utopianism which is irrelevant to the conditions in which we live. Yet our recognition of the redemptive nature of His mission ought not to be used as a pretext by those who, themselves profiting by the present industrial order, rationalize their condonation of unjust social conditions by saying that only when men are changed can the social framework of society be improved.

[1] See earlier, p. 84.   [2] *Christianity and Social Order*, p. 38.

T.C.W.

When lecturing in the United States a few months before the outbreak of the Second World War, in city after city, I was asked, " Do you believe in the Social Gospel ? " It was impossible to answer by a simple " Yes " or " No ", for either answer would have been inadequate. I could not answer, " Yes ", for, if I had, I should have been understood to hold that the Christian Ethic could be separated from Christian doctrine, and be used as a panacea for the troubles of a world as yet unchristianized. And, besides, is " Gospel " the right word here ? Is the Christian message in its social aspect Good News alone ? May it not be, instead, News not good, but bad, news of God's judgment on injustice ? But to answer the question in the negative would have been equally misleading, for that answer would have been understood to mean that, while condemning the inadequacy of the " Social Gospel " and affirming a closer approximation to Protestant orthodoxy, I was content to regard Christianity as relevant only to individual needs, and as having nothing to say, whether in judgment or in hope, on the social order in which men live.[1]

It is possible so to blame the social order for all evils as to benumb our sense of obligation. Thus Mr. Bernard Shaw told his " intelligent woman ", " Should you become a convert to Socialism, you will not be committed to any change in your private life, nor, indeed, will you find yourself able to make any change that would be of the smallest use in that direction ".[2] That is a comforting doctrine to the rich, for it makes it possible to combine the profession of advanced social doctrine with personal selfishness. Anyone in contact with undergraduate life in the inter-war period will have observed how sometimes those who denounced most vigorously the existing social order were not only self-indulgent, but were inconsiderate to those of the so-called lower classes with whom they had to do. They

[1] For a history of the Social Gospel in America in addition to W. Rauschenbusch's well-known books, *Christianizing the Social Order*, 1912, and *A Theology for the Social Gospel*, 1917, see C. H. Hopkins, *The Rise of the Social Gospel in American Protestantism*, 1940 ; F. E. Johnson, *The Social Gospel Re-examined*, 1940 ; and A. I. Abel, *The Urban Impact on American Protestantism*, 1943.

[2] *The Intelligent Woman's Guide to Socialism and Capitalism*, p. 99.

were devoted to the " proletariat ", but failed to treat with common human kindness those of its number with whom they were in contact. The New Testament reminds us, as we have seen, of the possibility, within a social order as evil as that of ancient slavery, of transcending in part hindrances to a right relationship. The social order was wrong, and yet in this wrong order it was still possible to respond to the Christian proclamation of God's grace. When Philemon received back his runaway slave as a brother-beloved, the difference of social status became far less important than the bond which united them in Christian faith and love. But, if the ancient and extreme case of slavery shows that men need not merely be the victims of a system, it also shows the moral perils which spring from a social order which is cruel and oppressive. Not all Christian slave-owners succeeded in acting in a Christian way in an unchristian relationship.[1] When the Church became dominant in the Empire, it encouraged the manumission of slaves and sought to mitigate the hardships of slavery, but it was very slow in securing the abolition of that wrong relationship. The slavery of more modern times, based on the African slave trade, provides many an illustration of the way those professing the Christian faith not only tolerated the evils of an unchristian system but succumbed to its temptations.

St. Paul's teaching on slavery is an imperishable witness to the possibility of living the Christian life in a social order which was fundamentally opposed to the Christian estimate of man, but we may not use that teaching as an excuse for acquiescing in an unjust social order. If we claim to be Christians, we may not fall below the insights of the Hebrew prophets with their stern insistence that God desires mercy more than sacrifice, and will not receive the worship of those who are conniving at oppression. Otherwise our guilt will be like the guilt of those our Lord condemned, who, professing to be religious, were yet

[1] Even as early as the Council of Elvira held at the end of the third century, a " Christian " mistress had to be condemned to many years of penance for beating a slave so cruelly that she died a few days later.

profiting by injustice.   The Cross of Christ is not only a reminder of our race's sin and stupidity, and so a warning against the facile optimism which supposes that the command of love has only to be taught to be obeyed ; it is also the supreme revelation of how God holds men dear.   We may not be indifferent to the needs of those for whom Christ died ; it is useless to proclaim the Fatherhood of God if we make no attempt to live as the brothers of men.

The obligations of family life are known to all.   Any father, who is worth the name, will regard the provision of the necessities of his children as the first claim on his income, and, if one of them be ill, will count no expense within his power too much to secure his restoration.   But justice in the family is not strictly equalitarian.   An idle son will be maintained by his father, but may not claim that he should have as much to spend as a brother who works.   One son may choose a vocation which is ill-paid ; another a profitable career.   Justice does not demand that brothers should equalize their incomes, and yet what brother will allow another to remain unhelped in time of special need ?   Members of a family have more immediate responsibility for each other's welfare than they have for that of others.   Mrs. Jellyby, who was so interested in the natives of Borrioboola-Gha that she neglected her own children, was not a pattern Christian mother.   " If any provideth not for his own, and specially for his own household, he hath denied the faith and is worse than an unbeliever ".[1]   We cannot bear the sorrows of the world as we bear the sorrows of those bound to us by the closest ties.   Only God is equal to such a burden ; that He bears it, is part of the significance of Christ's Cross, and that Cross rebukes us for our indifference to others' needs. The care we seek to give to our own children should remind us of those other children whose requirements are no less than those of ours.

In an earlier part of this chapter reference was made to the acquiescence of good men in the employment of young children in factories and mines, and to their opposition to state legislation to prevent these and other social evils.   Some of these evils

[1] 1 Tim. v. 8.

were mitigated by philanthropy. Our voluntary hospitals, orphanages and ragged-schools, gained much support and service from Christian people. Many an employer, though he opposed all interference with the industrial system, yet himself lived without luxury, and privately did far more for his employees than his contractual obligations required, and there were many churches in industrial areas where employers and employees shared the concerns of their Church in equal honour and held each other in mutual respect.

The false doctrine of *laissez-faire* has now fallen into the background, although its influence continues in " economic individualism ". It seems strange now to remember the opposition given to the measures passed by the Liberal Government after they came into power in 1906. Old Age Pensions, Unemployment and Sick Benefits are now regarded by all parties as necessities, and the Beveridge Report on Social Security, prepared at the request of the War Coalition Government, has, with certain modifications, been implemented by the Labour Government. The preparation of that Report was a task for an economist, not for Church leaders. Yet, as Lord Beveridge wrote in his *Full Employment in a Free Society*, " We should regard Want, Disease, Ignorance and Squalor as common enemies of us all, not as enemies with whom each individual may seek a separate peace, escaping himself to personal prosperity while leaving his fellows in their clutches. That is the meaning of social conscience ; that one should refuse to make a separate peace with social evil ".[1] It is now common ground with all political parties that the good of the community must come before sectional interests, and, in spite of two devastating wars, this century has seen an immense improvement in social conditions. Our nation can no longer be divided into the " dandies " and the " drudges ". Whereas taxation has made the rich poorer, there is less acute poverty than there was. Welcome as this is, there is no ground for complacency. As *Our Towns—A Close-up*, the Report on children evacuated through the War, reminded us, there is still not only poverty and bad housing, but almost incredible ignorance and squalor.

[1] *Summary*, p. 43.

Our country has still a long way to go before it can be claimed that proper conditions of life have been generally secured.

In a society as complex as ours now is, some measure of planning is inevitable, and on this all parties are agreed. The differences are in regard to the amount of planning that is desirable, and this is a problem more technical than ethical. When asked to secure the division of a family inheritance, our Lord replied, " Who made me a judge or a divider over you ? " and, by so speaking, as Brunner says, " Christ explicitly rejects the responsibility for answering questions which do not refer to the Kingdom of God, to the totality of human existence, but to matters of expert knowledge in which reason is competent to judge ".[1] Some Christians feel that Christian values will be best preserved by Conservatism or by Liberalism ; others, that as Christians they must be Socialists. No social programme can be fully Christian in a world where Christians are in a minority, and in which the Christianity of us all is fragmentary and imperfect and it is well that there are Christians in all parties. As a great sociologist has said, " It is better for the Christian faith itself if it is not identified with one party, but carries its spirit into all ".[2]

Of parties existing in our land, only the Communist is definitely anti-Christian. So long as the Communist International adheres to its Programme, adopted at its Congress in 1928, it is impossible for any Christian to give it his support, for that Programme declares that " one of the most important tasks of the cultural revolution affecting the wide masses is the task of systematically and unswervingly combating religion— the opium of the people ". " The proletariat State, while granting liberty of worship and abolishing the privileged position of the formerly dominant religion, carries on anti-religious propaganda with all the means at its command and reconstructs the whole of its educational work, on the basis of scientific materialism ".[3] This opposition to religion is explicable from Karl Marx's observation of the Industrial Revolution in England,

[1] *Revelation and Reason*, p. 381 (on Luke xii. 14).
[2] Karl Mannheim, *Diagnosis of Our Time*, p. 109.
[3] *Handbook of Marxism*, pp. 1009 f.

and from the identification in the minds of Russian workers of the Church with Czarist tyranny.   Yet, as a recent writer puts it, " There is nothing anti-Christian about collective farms, the control of factories by workers' councils, the collective ownership of the means of production, or the principle, ' From each according to his ability, to each according to his need ' ". Marxism began not only as anti-religious, but as anti-State.   It taught that the State was an instrument of oppression and that, when Communism had eliminated class-distinctions, the State would " wither away ".   Where Communism itself has gained control of the machinery of the State, its opposition to the State has ceased, " The anti-State features of Marxism then are an historical accident; it seems possible that the anti-religious features are an historical accident also ".[1]   There has been the communism of monasteries and convents ; there have been Perfectionist communities, none of them very successful or enduring, which have sought to practice a Christian Communism.[2] A communism which has abandoned its hatred of religion is not inconceivable.   In communist Russia, the idle are turned into the industrious by the Labour Camps in Siberia, and we may well feel that even a communist society, which had been purged of its anti-religious spirit, would still make personal freedom precarious, and would give its planners a power too great for sinful men to have.   Yet we cannot say that in such a society Christianity could have no place, although the tasks and trials of the Church would be very different from those which confront us now in the modern West.   Meanwhile, Communism in its present form is not only a menace but a challenge to Western Christendom, a reminder of those whose experience of life has been such as to fill them with bitterness and hatred and who feel that as " proletarians " they " have nothing to lose but their chains, they have the world to win ".[3]

In our country the choice is often stated as that between

---

[1] J. D. Mabbott, in his significant article, *Conflict of Ideologies*, *Philosophy*, July 1948.

[2] Cp. B. B. Warfield, *Studies in Perfectionism*, II. pp. 219–333, for an account of the " Bible Communists ".

[3] From the last paragraph of the *Communist Manifesto*.

capitalism and socialism, but the issue is obscured by the variety of meanings given to each of these two terms. Capitalism has come in for much condemnation and some condemn all taking of interest. To buy Government securities or Building Society Shares, or stocks issued to extend the range of a business, does not come under the Old Testament prohibition of taking interest from a brother; for receiving interest on such investments is not taking advantage of another's poverty in order to make a gain. The medieval argument that to take interest on a loan is " unnatural ", because money is a " barren thing ", is a relic of Aristotelianism unconvincing to the modern world, where new capital may mean new equipment and so increasing productivity. The gravest indictment of capitalism is of its irresponsibility. There have been, and are, employers who think of those they employ as persons, and of management and workmen as partners in a common concern.[1] But in Limited Liability Companies responsibility may be so divided that the shareholders may feel that the responsibility lies with the directors ; the directors that it lies with the managerial staff and the managerial staff that it lies with the directors. The making of larger profits may thus become the sole criterion of action, and the welfare of those engaged in the industry be ignored. There is a capitalism which merits Berdyaev's condemnation, " Capitalism is above all anti-personal, the power of anonymity over human life, capitalism uses men as goods for sale. . . . Man is a wolf to man. The life of the capitalist world is lupine ".[2] Any system which treats men as " goods for sale ", is obviously opposed to the personalism of Christianity. But there are capitalists against whom such a charge cannot be justly made, and the power of capitalism is to-day balanced by the immense power of the Trade Unions whose dominance of one of the great political parties of our time has given their members a large measure of protec-

---

[1] I have in mind a profit-sharing concern like that of Mr. Theodore Taylor of Batley, and I think of a great shoe-manufacturing firm, of which I happened to know the leading directors, and also some of the operatives, in which these directors, who were also large shareholders, knew all whom they employed, thought of them as persons, and without patronage helped them in any time of unexpected need.

[2] *The Fate of Man in the Modern World*, p. 15.

tion from any capitalist oppression. But the peril of "anti-personalism" still remains, and will not necessarily be removed by nationalization. Wherever relationships are impersonal, those who receive orders tend to be estranged from those who give them. Men will not find satisfaction in their work unless they feel that they count as persons, and are not regarded merely as tiny fragments of a vast machine.

Socialism is used in so many senses that it has often more an emotional than an intelligible meaning. If, with Proudhon, we define it as consisting of "every aspiration towards the amelioration of society", then, indeed, we are all socialists. But, as Dr. Gray has said, "One need not be a socialist to feel indignation against those who sow upon the furrows of un-righteousness, or who buy the poor for silver, and the needy for a pair of shoes. It requires more than indignation to make a socialist, and not all who are indignant are socialists ".[1] If by socialism is meant the extension of the control of the State in industry, then, although such control has the dangers described by Professor Hayek in his book with the sombre title, *The Road to Serfdom*, yet the extent to which industry should be nationalized is primarily a technical problem—the problem of how the needs of the community can best be met. Provided there be proper security and reward for those engaged in the industry, and proper compensation for shareholders, Christian Ethics has nothing to say on such a problem, though Christians as citizens have to decide whether or not to give such schemes their approval and support. No system is without defects, but, as Lord Lindsay has written, "The defects in the system will really only be cured by those who are inside the system. There is not the least likelihood of the Church thinking out a programme for industry of any value. It has not got the technical, economic or political knowledge ".[2] But it can inspire those of its members who have, and it can help to create a relationship in which difficulties can be faced and, in part, overcome.

The old assumption has long since been exposed that if each

---

[1] Alexander Gray, *The Socialist Tradition*, p. 491.
[2] *Christianity and Economics*, p. 140.

pursued his own self-interest, the good of all would be secured. Yet the myth of the " economic man " survives—that there are no goods except material goods, no motives except those of selfishness. If that myth were true, then there could be nothing before us but bitter strife, and in the contest for larger spoils, the material goods would themselves be lost. This chapter is written at a time when our country is dependent on American aid for the maintenance of its standard of life, and when it is not clear whether prosperity or poverty lies before us. Some lessons, it is hoped, we have as a country learned ; that the necessities of all must be met before the comforts of any, and that, if food be scarce, those who require it most should have the larger share. If scarcity comes, there will be the greater need for the hard work of all ; if prosperity, that will not suffice to bring contentment, for in material things it is always possible to desire more.

The material well-being of our land does not depend on external circumstances alone ; it could be hindered or even destroyed by economic strife. The legacy of the past is bitter, and part of the Christian task is to bring men, severed in other ways, to a better understanding of each other and of each other's needs. Our Lord's warning against the perils of riches and the peril of anxiety still stand. A society which heeded those warnings would seek to exclude the extremes of wealth and of poverty, and strive as eagerly to secure freedom from the ear of want as once men strove for freedom of speech and of religion. That in our complex industrial order involves planning, but, as Mr. C. R. Attlee said, in his speech to the Labour Conference on Purpose and Policy, " Whatever organizations are set up, the vital thing is that they should be energized by men and women ". Systems alone do not secure just dealing. The public employee who plays for safety, evades responsibility, and has no regard to the welfare of his subordinates or of the general public, can be as mischievous as any manager in a private firm who thus fails in his duty. In a *laissez-faire* society inefficiency or idleness brought its cruel punishment of unemployment and poverty ; in the totalitarian state it brings the more cruel punishment of the labour camps. In a planned democracy moral qualities are required that men may do their work without such harsh compulsion.

The Christian may neither acquiesce in the ideals of what Professor Tawney called the *Acquisitive Society*, nor may he ignore the complexities of the economic situation and the help the economist can give in dealing with them. It is futile to say that if only men would obey Christ's law of love, all our economic problems would be solved.[1] No one obeys perfectly that law of love, and most do not even recognize its authority. Sinners ourselves, we live in a sinful society ; the industrial problems of the modern world are technical as well as moral, and no amount of good-will would eliminate all the difficulties which confront us. Even were these difficulties removed, and freedom from want secured for all, work might still bring only boredom and frustration. We are taught to pray, Give us day by day the bread that we need, and to pray that prayer not for ourselves alone, but for others. And yet, as we are also taught, a man's life does not consist in the abundance of things which he possesses, and, if he thinks it does, his work ceases to have meaning. The relevance of Christian Ethics to social needs is indirect. It provides no detailed instructions for the structure of society, but it gives to work significance, for work may be interpreted as service to men, and so part of our service to God, a means by which God's gifts are made available to all His children. The true wealth of a nation lies not in possessions but in persons. However varied and complex modern industry must be, its purpose should be so to obtain and to share material resources as to remove hindrances to the development of the personal life of all.

The Christian knows that the provision of material needs is

---

[1] Those who do thus speak, and they are many, would do well to heed Mr. Christopher Dawson's warning ; " A century ago there was the tendency to treat Christianity as a kind of social sedative that kept the lower classes obedient and industrious, and the consequence of this was the Marxist denunciation of religion as the opium of the poor. And if to-day we treat Christianity as a social tonic that will cure economic depression and social unrest and make everybody happy, we shall only ensure future disillusionment and reaction ". *Religion and the Modern State*, pp. 121 f.

not enough ; that a man's life is incomplete unless it be lived in humble dependence upon God.   But that knowledge should make him the more eager to secure that the material needs of all are met, and that none be deprived of things necessary to a healthy life through the greed or indolence of any.

CHAPTER X

THE COMMUNITY OF THE STATE

(1) THE ENIGMA OF THE STATE

Suffered under Pontius Pilate : these words of the Apostles' Creed may serve to remind us of the enigma of the State.[1] God is " the Father Almighty, Maker of heaven and earth ". Yet on earth the State has power ; the Christian faith in " Jesus Christ His only Son our Lord " includes the recognition that He suffered at the orders of the Roman State, and goes on to affirm that He who thus suffered will be the final judge of all. " God the Father Almighty ", and yet His Son suffered under Pontius Pilate. Those who secured the crucifixion of Jesus have their counterpart in the modern world and should be remembered by them. Ecclesiastics should think often of Caiaphas the High priest, religious teachers of the Scribes and Pharisees ; since politicians have less time to give to the reading of the Bible than the professed exponents of religion, it is well that every time they hear the Creed recited, they should be reminded of Pontius Pilate, the representative of the State's authority. Governors are sent " for vengeance on evil-doers and for praise to them that do well ".[2] Pontius Pilate released Barabbas who had been arrested for insurrection and for murder, and Jesus, whom he knew to be innocent, he ordered to be crucified. Yet we read that Jesus recognized his power to have been given him " from above ".[3]

These words, *Suffered under Pontius Pilate*, epitomize the gravest problem of Christian Ethics. Christians are called to live a life of love in the fellowship of the Church, and yet they

---

[1] For a suggestive comment on this clause of the Creed, see Karl Barth, *Dogmatik im Grundriss*, pp. 127–33.

[2] 1 Pet. ii. 14.　　　　　　　　　[3] John xix. 11.

have to recognize the authority of the State. A State should be the sphere of justice; yet it is constituted not by justice but by power, and power, which in itself is morally neutral, may be used, as Pontius Pilate used it, not justly but unjustly.

(2) THE NEW TESTAMENT AND THE STATE

Our Lord lived at a time when His countrymen were subject to Roman rule. Judaea was under a Roman procurator; Galilee under a tetrarch subservient to Rome. There were many who looked for a deliverer from the power of pagan Rome and, had Jesus been a political Messiah, they would have rallied to His support. As the initial success of Bar Cochba a century later shows, Jesus could, had He wished, have led a great movement of revolt. But He refused to seek the kind of success that might thus have been His; He would not tempt the Lord His God, nor seek to win the kingdoms of the world by the way in which worldly success might be obtained. Instead, He proclaimed the Good News of God, and called men to receive the Kingdom of God, to enter into the redemptive rule of the God who was their King and Father.

Our Lord ignored the political issues of His time.[1] When the Pharisees came with their clever question, Is it lawful to give tribute to Caesar? He asked for a silver *denarius* on which were inscribed Caesar's name and image, and bade them " Render unto Caesar the things that are Caesar's, and unto God the things that are God's ". Lord Acton said that these words " spoken on the last visit to the Temple, three days before His death, gave to the civil power, under the protection of conscience, a sacredness it had never enjoyed, and bounds it had never acknowledged; and they were the repudiation of absolutism and the inauguration of freedom ".[2] The Jews, as

---

[1] Dr. C. J. Cadoux in his long and learned book, *The Historic Mission of Jesus*, denied this, and sought to show that *e.g.* our Lord's commands in the Sermon on the Mount that His hearers should be as the salt of the earth, the light of the world, a lamp set on a stand (Matt. v. 13–16) were addressed not " to some little group of faithful disciples Jesus had gathered around Him ", but " to Israel as a people " (p. 156). I find this quite unconvincing.

[2] *The History of Freedom and Other Essays*, p. 29.

the coin showed, were subject to Rome's demands, and those demands they should fulfil. Yet they, and all men, were under obligation to obey God. The legitimate claim of civil government was recognized, but in such a way as not to conflict with what was owed to God.

We, who live in an age in which totalitarian governments have demanded the unconditional obedience of their subjects, note at once the limits which our Lord's words impose on the authority of the State. His hearers resented, instead, the recognition of the obligations they owed to the hated Roman Government. As Dr. Klausner, a Jewish scholar, points out, " the people supported him when he entered Jerusalem as the Messiah and purified the Temple ", and yet they " did nothing to save him three days later when he was crucified ". " His answer about the tribute money proved that not from this Galilean Messiah could they hope for national freedom and political redemption ".[1] Our Lord's method of rule was not that of earthly kings. They lord it over their subjects, and are called Benefactors. He was in the midst of His disciples as one who served, and service, not lordship, should be the mark of His followers.[2] St. John records that, when asked by Pilate if He was the King of the Jews, He replied " My kingdom is not of this world ". Had His kingdom been of the world, His servants would have fought for Him as men fight for earthly kingdoms.[3]

Easter and Pentecost brought to the first believers so vivid an experience of the powers of the Kingdom, the Reign of God, that they were more conscious of being citizens of that Kingdom than of being citizens of any earthly state. Jesus, the Master whom they had loved and partly trusted, they now knew to be their risen Lord, and the presence of the Spirit brought to them both joy and guidance. They rendered unto God the things that were God's and, when ordered by the high priest to cease to teach in the name of Jesus, the apostles replied, " We must obey God rather than man ".[4] These words express an essential

---

[1] *Jesus of Nazareth*, p. 318.
[2] Luke xxii. 24–7.
[3] John xviii. 33, 36.
[4] Acts v. 29.

aspect of the teaching of the New Testament on the State. God must be obeyed, even though that means disobeying the official leaders of Church or State.

Yet there is another aspect of that teaching. As Christianity spread in the pagan world, it owed much to that order of justice which Roman rule secured. However harsh and defective that order might be, it was better far than anarchy. Some of St. Paul's converts at Corinth, as we have seen, interpreted Christian liberty as licence, and the Christian proclamation of spiritual freedom might have led to a premature proclamation of social and political liberty, and the submergence of the Christian movement in the horrors of a slave revolt. Not law but love was the principle of the Christian life, but that did not free believers from their obligations to the State, unless these were in direct contradiction to their fidelity to God. Christians were an enclave in a world ruled by Law and " Wrath " ; their citizenship, their real commonwealth was in heaven.[1] Although they belonged to the City of God, they were subjects of the earthly State whose function, given it of God, was to maintain the course of justice. The ruler was " the minister of God, an avenger for wrath to him that doeth evil ".

These celebrated words in Romans xiii can be understood only in the wider context of St. Paul's thought. As we have seen, St. Paul, like others of his age, thought concretely, not abstractly, and conceived of " Wrath " as an almost personal power which, though it emanated from God, yet acted on in partial isolation from Him. In the opening chapters of the Epistles, St. Paul had depicted human history as a great drama in which the sin of man is followed always by punishment. The Wrath of God is revealed " against all ungodliness and unrighteousness of man ". That " Wrath " denoted for St. Paul not a passion, like the anger of man, but the retributive order in which we live. Punishment was not so much the direct act of God as the inevitable consequence of " the Wrath " which, although it represented the divine judgment upon sin, yet worked in a certain detachment from God, much in the way

---

[1] Phil. iii. 20, where Moffatt translates, " we are a colony of heaven ".

that many modern men believe that " laws of nature ", though framed by God, do not express His full purposes, but operate in partial independence of His control.[1] Retribution works on ; actions go on to their effects, and what we sow, we reap. Christians must give place to the " Wrath ", not seeking to avenge themselves, but instead showing their enemy kindness, not being overcome of evil but overcoming evil with good. It is in this context that St. Paul bids his readers be in subjection to the higher powers, " The powers that be are ordained of God ". The ruler is " a minister of God ", the embodiment of the " Wrath ", that principle of retribution by which the world is governed. Christians must therefore be in subjection to the ruler, not only because of the " Wrath ", the retribution which would befall the disobedient, but for conscience' sake. After this digression on the State, St. Paul resumes his appeal to Christians to show that love which is the fulfilment of the law. He thus conceived of two spheres, two kingdoms, the one the sphere of earthly rule, whose highest word is the justice which punishes the evil and so protects the innocent ; the other, the sphere where love has sway.

When St. Paul wrote his Epistle to the Romans, the Roman Empire had not yet declared war upon the Christian cause. Christians were soon to find that the ruler could be a terror to the good as well as to the evil, and that " the sword " could be used not only as an instrument of justice but to destroy those who, in fidelity to God, refused to join in that Caesar-worship which was the symbol of loyalty to the State. The Book of Revelation is the reminder of that great conflict, when it seemed that all Christians might be killed. Against the massed cruelty of the Empire, Christians opposed not force of arms but only their patient endurance of suffering. In 1 Peter, Christians, liable to suffer at any time for their faith in Christ, were bidden not only to love the brotherhood, but to fear God and honour the king. Let them take care not to suffer as wrong-doers, and, if they suffer because they are Christians, let them glorify God

---

[1] Cp. the writer's *The Gospel of St. Paul*, pp. 136–9. The lexicographical evidence for this view will be found in *Der Vergeltungsgedanke bei Paulus*, by G. P. Wetter.

for they are partakers of the sufferings of Christ.[1] In an Epistle attributed to St. Paul, but probably compiled after his time, the command is given to pray " for kings and all that are in high place ; that we may lead a tranquil and quiet life in all godliness and gravity ".[2]

(3) THE TWO KINGDOMS

So long as the State was pagan and persecuting, the relation of Church to State was clear. Christians prayed for the Emperor, but they would not call him " god and lord ", nor burn incense before his effigy. The situation was completely changed when Christianity became, in A.D. 313, a " licensed cult " (religio licita), with the Emperor Constantine as first its patron, and then its proselyte. What should be the relation of Church to State when the State itself was nominally Christian ? It is impossible to understand the history of Europe, or the present predicament of the Church, without some reference to the solutions adopted by the Church of the East, by the Latin Church, by Lutherans and by Calvinists, and by the Church of England at the Elizabethan Settlement.

Constantine's conversion made the profession of Christianity not only safe but profitable. Under Christian influence, laws were passed making marriage more stable, and the treatment of dependents, whether wives, children or slaves, more humane. But the Church paid a heavy price for imperial favour and became subservient to the Emperor whom it recognized as God's vicegerent, prince and sovereign by divine appointment. Constantine himself, in A.D. 325, convened the Council of Nicaea and enforced its decisions, although he did not claim to define the Church's Creed. Eusebius of Caesarea, writing of the banquet Constantine gave to the bishops at Nicaea, tells us that " detachments of the body-guard and other troops surrounded the entrance of the palace with drawn swords, and through the midst of these the men of God proceeded without fear into the innermost of the imperial apartments, in which some were the emperor's own companions at table, while others reclined on

[1] 1 Pet. ii. 17 ; iv. 12–16. [2] 1 Tim. ii. 1, 2.

couches arranged on either side ". He adds, " One might have thought that a picture of Christ's kingdom was thus showed forth and a dream rather than a reality ".[1]

But Christ's kingdom is not of this world. Constantine's son claimed authority even to modify the Church's Creed, and those who, under Athanasius, abode by the decision of Nicaea, were treated as the Emperor's enemies. The long conflict about the Creed of Nicaea, continued under successive emperors, was embittered by the interference of the imperial power. When at last that controversy ended through the accession to power of Theodosius, all within the Empire were ordered to accept the tenets of orthodoxy, and not pagans alone but heretics were threatened by the Emperor with " the vengeance of that power which we, by celestial authority, have assumed ". Orthodoxy thus became the principle of cohesion of the Empire.[2] We have here a further stage towards the Byzantinism of the East in which the State protected orthodoxy and enforced it on its citizens. And Russia illustrates the disastrous effect on religion of this subservience of the Church to the State.

The Church of the West did not share in the " Byzantine " subservience of the Church to the State ; the Emperor was far away at Constantinople, and, in the chaos caused by the barbarian invasions of the West, the Roman See gained increased prestige and power, until at last it could claim that the Latin Church was the City of God on earth, and so superior to all earthly states.

This claim was based on St. Augustine's treatise *On the City of God*. Begun three years after the sack of Rome by the Goths in 410, this great defence of Christianity was not finished till thirteen years after, and its teaching is far less decisive than the use of it later by the supporters of the Papacy would suggest. In it Augustine illustrates from the history of the race the development of the two cities, the earthly city (*civitas terrena*) and the city of God (*civitas dei*). The earthly city has been

---

[1] *The Life of Constantine*, I. 24. E.T. from *Nicene and Post-Nicene Library*, Series II, vol. I.

[2] For this edict promulgated in 380, and for its consequences, see C. N. Cochrane, *Christianity and Classical Culture*, pp. 327 ff.

formed " by the love of self, even to the contempt of God, the
heavenly, by the love of God, even to the contempt of self ".[1]
The relation of the two cities cannot be equated with the relation
of State to Church. Without justice, kingdoms are, indeed,
nothing but " great brigand bands ", and not even a brigand
band can hold together without some kind of justice.[2] Yet, by
obedience to natural law, the earthly community may win an
earthly peace, and this the heavenly city, while in its state of
pilgrimage, uses in the interest of that " peace of heaven "
which consists " in the perfectly ordered and harmonious enjoyment of God and of one another in God ".[3] And, in his famous
Mirror of Princes, Augustine depicts the happiness of Christian
Emperors who rule with justice and with mercy " through love
of eternal felicity ", " offering up the sacrifices of humility,
contrition and prayer ".[4] St. Augustine's teaching on the City
of God is as ambiguous as his teaching on the earthly City.
The City of God is the community of the elect, of which each
citizen is " predestinated by grace, elected by grace, by grace
a stranger below, and by grace a citizen above ".[5] But
Augustine thought of grace not only as grace freely given to the
elect but as grace infused through the sacraments of the Church
and, at times, he identified the City of God with the visible
Church. " The Church even now is the kingdom of Christ and
the kingdom of heaven ".[6]

In the controversy on the relation of Church and State, St.
Augustine's authority could be claimed for very different
solutions of this problem. The State and the Church might be
conceived as two powers, each ordained by God, and given
separate functions, or pre-eminence might be claimed either for
the authority of the Christian Emperor, or of the Pope.[7] It
was this last view which came to dominate the Middle Ages in
the West. It found its most dramatic expression in the excom-

---

[1] XIV. 28.   Quotations from Marcus Dods' translation.

[2] IV. 4.   [3] XIX. 17.   [4] V. 24.

[5] XV. 1.

[6] XX. 9. Even here he is careful to point out that tares grow in the
Church with the wheat.

[7] The Gelasian, the Imperial (Ghibelline), or the Papal (Guelph),
view respectively.

munication of Henry IV, the Western Emperor, by Gregory VII (Hildebrand), and in the humiliation inflicted on him at Canossa in 1077 where, for three days, he stood in the snow, waiting till the Pope would receive him and give him absolution. A little more than a century later, Innocent III declared that the Pope is as the sun, the King as the moon, so that the authority of the King is not only less than that of the Pope but derived from it. Later, Boniface VIII claimed that both swords, the temporal as well as spiritual, belonged to Peter and so to Peter's successors. " The temporal sword is to be used by kings and knights, but at the bidding and by the forbearance of the priests ".[1]

In the moral chaos of our time it is not strange that many should be attracted by the conception of the Church through its official head claiming lordship over all secular powers and thus securing peace and order. As an Anglican scholar has said, " There was, undoubtedly, a certain impressive magnificence in the theory of a Christendom united under one visible personal Head, or in the relation of Pope and Emperor as the two great luminaries, the twin rulers of the world, the lieutenants of God upon earth. Undoubtedly, also, there were many popes of high aims and noble character, such as Gregory I, or Gregory VII ". " Yet ", as he adds, " neither the splendour of a theory nor the veneration for great names, nor the advantages of outward unity, must blind us to the facts. And the facts are (1) that the system of the medieval Papacy tended to secularize the Church more than it spiritualized the world, and (2) that the principle which underlay it is not one which can be reconciled with the New Testament and with the teaching and method of Christ ".[2]

A few months after the death of Boniface VIII, the Papacy went into its " Babylonian Exile " at Avignon, and these seventy years of exile were followed by thirty years of Papal Schism when there were rival popes at Rome and at Avignon, each claiming to be the Vicar of Christ. The claim of Boniface VIII that the Pope was supreme over the Emperor thus became harder to believe. The intellectual ferment caused by the

[1] In the Bull *Unam Sanctam* of 1302.
[2] Walter Hobhouse, *The Church and the World*, pp. 208 f.

Renaissance, the wide-spread corruption of the clergy, and the rapacity of some of the Popes, damaged the Church's influence, and prepared the way for the breakdown of the unity of Western Christendom, and when, at length, Luther, as a loyal doctor of the Church, made his protest against the sale of indulgences, his protest shook the Western world.

In 1520 Luther was excommunicated, and in that year of crisis wrote his three *Primary Works*. We have seen with what power and fervour he proclaimed *The Liberty of the Christian Man*,[1] but the liberty he sought was not civil but religious, and it is significant that the first of these " *Primary Works* " was addressed *To the Christian Nobility of the German Nation concerning the Christian Estate*. In it he summoned the temporal authorities to suppress not only secular abuses, like those connected with monopolies and money lending, but to take their part in removing abuses from the Church. The temporal power is " a member of the body of Christendom and is of the spiritual estate though its work is of a temporal nature ". " It is a pure invention that pope, bishops, priests and monks are to be called the ' spiritual estate ' ; princes, lords, artisans and farmers the ' temporal estate '. . . . All Christians are truly of the ' spiritual estate ', and there is among them no difference at all but that of office ".[2] Luther spoke here for many in an age when it seemed as necessary to prevent the subservience of the State to the Church as in other ages it has been to prevent the subservience of the Church to the State. Men despaired of gaining from the Papacy any reform ; instead they put their hope in a " godly prince ". The history of our own land at this time illustrates how ready most were to follow the dictates of the sovereign in matters of religion. The Elizabethan Settlement brought a measure of religious peace, based on uniformity of religious observance, so that to be an Englishman was to be a member of the Established Church. This conception of the visible Church in England as identical with the nation received a magnificent defence in Hooker's *Of the Laws of Ecclesiastical Polity*. But

[1] See earlier, pp. 139 f.
[2] *The Works of Martin Luther*, E.T. edited by H. E. Jacobs, II. pp. 71, 66.

for him, as Dr. John Oman said, " The Church and the State are merely two aspects of the same society, which has as much right to determine how men shall worship as how they shall pay taxes. The authority of the Church, which it is mere insolence in the individual to question, is in the last issue the authority of the Queen ".[1]

In appealing to the German Princes, Luther wrote as a man of his age. More distinctive was his teaching on the two kingdoms in which he revived one aspect of Augustine's thought. There is the kingdom of God, to which belong all true believers in Christ, and were all such there would be no need of secular sword or law; there is the kingdom of the world in which restraint is needed in order that the unchristian may " keep the peace outwardly even against their will ". To attempt to govern a whole country with the Gospel would be as foolish as for a shepherd " to place in one fold wolves, lions, eagles and sheep ", and expect them to live in harmony. A Christian must be ready to suffer injustice, and thus " resist not evil ", but, if he be an officer of state, he must do his duty, and, in doing so, can still be Christian and in a state of salvation. But the secular power has its limits; it must not interfere in matters of faith, and, if it seeks to do so, must be disobeyed. " In matters which concern the salvation of souls nothing but God's Word shall be taught and accepted ".[2]

Luther's teaching on the two Kingdoms found its most famous expression in his *Open Letter concerning the Hard Book against the Peasants*. " God's Kingdom is a Kingdom of grace and mercy, not of wrath and punishment. In it there is only forgiveness, consideration for one another, love, service, the doing of good, peace, joy, etc. But the kingdom of the world is a kingdom of wrath and severity. In it there is only punishment, repression, judgment and condemnation, for the suppressing of the wicked and the protection of the good. For this

---

[1] *The Church and the Divine Order*, p. 265. In the recent report on *Catholicity* presented to the Archbishop of Canterbury, p. 19, we read : " The West has never allowed Caesar to make law in the things of God ". I do not understand this statement.

[2] *On Secular Authority. To What Extent it should be obeyed, op. cit.* III. pp. 234, 237, 249, 251 ff.

reason it has the sword, and a prince or lord is called in Scripture
God's wrath or God's rod (Isa. xiv) ".   " Now he who would
confuse these two kingdoms—as our false fanatics do—would
put wrath into God's kingdom, and mercy into the world's
kingdom ; and that is the same as putting the devil in heaven
and God in hell ".[1] His " Hard Book " had preached the
perfectionism of love to the peasants, whilst to the princes it
had spoken only of the need for violent action.   It was written
by one who not only regarded rebellion as " intolerable ", but
who believed " that the destruction of the world is to be expected
every hour ".[2] In this *Open Letter*, he explains that he had
written only " for rulers who might wish to deal in a Christian
or otherwise honest way " with the rebels and who, after victory,
would be merciful, and he denounces as " bloody dogs " " the
furious, raving senseless tyrants who even after the battle
cannot get their fill of blood ".[3] But the violence of his words
illustrates the danger of speaking of the two kingdoms without
at the same time emphasizing that both are subject to the God
whose love is justice and whose justice is love.

It was from Calvinism that there came a clearer realization
of the sovereignty of God in every sphere of life.   The universal
recognition of the need of laws and the general agreement on
" ideas of equity " is a sign that God has given to all the light
of reason.[4] The civil government is distinct from " the spiritual
and internal kingdom of Christ ", and yet, whilst " we are
pilgrims upon the earth ", we need " the peace and tranquillity "
which it secures.   Magistrates are ministers of God, called to
execute judgment and righteousness by defending the innocent
and repressing the violence of the wicked.[5] Even the injustice
of princes is to be endured, though if there be magistrates
" appointed to curb the tyranny of kings ", these would fail
in their duty did they not check their " undue licence ".[6] Later
Calvinists learnt not only to suffer but to check the injustice
of despotism.   If God's will is the supreme arbiter of duty, then
that will must be obeyed in every sphere.

---

[1] *Op cit.* IV. pp. 265 f.   [2] *Op. cit.* p. 254.
[3] *Op. cit.* p. 280.   [4] *Institutes*, II. ii. 130.
[5] *Op. cit.* IV. xx. 2 and 9.   [6] *Op. cit.* IV. xx. 31.

The varying conceptions of the relation of Church or State, which have emerged in history, still exist.   There are those who hold the " secessionist " view common in the early and persecuted Church.   Where Christians live under a totalitarian government, dominated as in Nazi Germany by a false religion or, as in modern Russia, by atheism, it may still have to be " secessionist ", praying for the State, and giving it obedience in so far as obedience is not disloyalty to God, but not attempting to influence the course of public affairs.   The complete subservience of the Church to a nominally Christian Emperor led in the Eastern Church to that identification of the Church with autocracy which made it appear as the accomplice of oppression.

The claim of the Church of the West that the Church should be supreme over all temporal rule still lingers on in the Roman Church, but, since the Reformation, has had little relation to historic realities, and has given rise to that anti-clericalism found in some Roman Catholic lands.   The Elizabethan Settlement, which made the Established Church co-terminous with the nation, failed through the rise of the Separatists and the strength of later Dissent, and has become an anachronism now that Christians not only exist in separate communions but are a minority in the nation.[1]   There remain the Lutheran and Calvinist traditions.   Luther's drastic separation of the " Two Kingdoms " can be so interpreted as to imply the restriction of morality to the sphere of individual life, and this has been the interpretation of many German Lutherans.   Luther, like many another popular preacher, emphasized one aspect of his message at a time and did not qualify his words.   Bishop Berggrav tells us [2] that, next to the Bible, he and other Norwegian Churchmen gained most encouragement in their resistance to Nazi oppression from those words of Luther in which he denounced the tyranny of Princes, and bade men " never to remain silent and assent

---

[1] The nomination by the Prime Minister of Bishops for appointment by the Crown might be not only an anachronism but a deadly peril to the Established Church should there be an anti-Christian Prime Minister of a totalitarian government.

[2] In his Foreword to *Luther Speaks*.

to injustice whatever the cost ".   It is absurd to speak of *Martin Luther : Hitler's Spiritual Ancestor*.[1]   Lutheranism in Germany has been influenced not only by Luther but by German Nationalism, by the exaltation of the State in Hegelian philosophy, by the temporary success of Bismarck, by the patronage of the Hohenzollerns, and by the abandonment by many later Lutherans of the conception of Natural Law.   Over-emphasizing Luther's distinction between the two kingdoms, some Lutheran theologians have spoken as if the State was not subject to the moral law, and have denounced as " cant " what they call " Anglo-Saxon Calvinism "—the attempt to bring both kingdoms under the law of God.[2]

That self-deception is always the peril of the Christian moralist who, in his eagerness to claim God's approval, may identify the interest of his class or nation with the purposes of God, and claim to be doing God's will when he is merely doing his own.   We may neither forget the sins of society, in which our own sins are writ large, nor, rightly recognizing the strains and sins of our social life, use that recognition to evade responsibility for seeking to make the State the sphere of justice.

(4) THE JUSTICE OF THE STATE

Justice may seem a cold and forbidding word.   Why not speak instead of love ?   The quest for justice is for the Christian a response to the divine Love, but love is concerned with personal relationships, and the State has as its distinctive task the maintenance of justice.   As Dr. R. W. Dale wrote long ago, " The State is primarily the visible representative and defender of the Divine justice in the temporal order ; the Church is primarily the visible representative of the Divine mercy and the Divine redemption in the eternal order.   The State has

[1] On Mr. Wiener's book with that title see Gordon Rupp, *Martin Luther, Hitler's Cause or Cure*.

[2] Instead of " Anglo-Saxon Calvinism " some speak of *Amerikanismus*, which was much attacked at the Stockholm Conference by German theologians.

other functions; the Church has other functions; but there is that deep distinction between them ".[1]

The State is dependent on power for its existence. An unjust State is still a State; a State without power would be a contradiction in terms. And the State has coercive power. In this some have seen its condemnation. Certainly the State, as we know it, manifests clearly the signs of human sinfulness. The formidable title of one of Dr. Reinhold Niebuhr's books, *Moral Man and Immoral Society*, expresses in exaggerated form a truth which should not be ignored. As Esdras complained to the most High, " Thou shalt find that men who may be reckoned by name have kept thy precepts; but nations thou shalt not find ".[2] " In the State ", as Brunner puts it, " we human beings see our own sin magnified a thousand times ". Yet the State is not merely, as he claims, " the product of collective sin ". Nor does it seem right to say that " compulsion is contrary to love; it is sinful ", for, as he admits, " without this power of compulsion the State cannot fulfil its divinely appointed purpose in and for society ".[3] It was of the cruel and violent period of the Judges that we read, " In those days there was no king in Israel; every man did that which was right in his own eyes ". Even the simplest community needs some form of civil government and a civil government cannot be effective unless it has coercive power. The State cannot fulfil the tasks of love, nor make men good, but it can, and ought to, provide an order of peace and justice in which personal relationships are protected and preserved. There are what Lord Lindsay calls " The Two Moralities ", " the morality of my station and its duties ", and " the morality of grace ", that morality which in gratitude to God seeks to show something of that love which, as the Christian believes, exists perfectly in God alone. It is with the first of these moralities that the State is concerned.

---

[1] *Fellowship with Christ*, p. 204. The work of the Church, as the " visible representative of the divine mercy ", is dealt with in the next chapter.

[2] 2 Esdras (= 4 Ezra) iii. 36.

[3] *The Divine Imperative*, p. 445.

In a previous section of this book the attempt was made to explain the meaning and significance of the Law of Nature as binding on all alike.[1] Difficult as that conception is, and remote as it may appear from the harsh realities of modern politics, it is yet of paramount importance for the consideration of the Justice of the State. If there be no law but positive laws ; if justice, that is, be merely of man's creation, then man may destroy what he has made. But if there be what St. Paul calls a law written in man's heart, then justice does not depend on the dictates of the State, but is the expression of the justice of the Creator and, in spite of its obscuration by sin, has an authority to which all men owe obedience. It is this justice of which the Hebrew prophets spoke—a justice which demands consideration for others' needs, and without which no nation is secure. Our Lord, as we have seen, had no need to emphasize that righteousness of God of which earthly justice is the imperfect counterpart, for He proclaimed God's love to those who already knew of His righteousness, and, whereas the message of the Prophets was primarily social, His message was, for the most part, addressed to individuals, and dealt with their personal relationship to God and to their neighbours. Yet, when He spoke of the nation, as in the Parable of the Husbandmen,[2] He, too, spoke of God's stern justice, and His greatest interpreter, St. Paul, proclaimed, as we have seen, the Good News of God's grace against the background of a world ruled by Law and that principle of retribution which he called " the Wrath ".

Before the rise of totalitarianism, it seemed that the supremacy of legal justice was secure in large parts of Christendom. The processes of law might be too expensive ; its punishments unduly harsh ; but civil liberty was secured by the independence of the Judiciary from the executive powers of the State. The Nazi substitution of People's Courts for Courts of Justice, and the claim that whatever the *Führer* willed was right, meant the abandonment of this conception of legal justice.

---

[1] See earlier, pp. 107–17.
[2] Matt. xxi. 33–46. Cp. His sorrow over the ruin which would befall Jerusalem because it knew not the time of its visitation. Luke xix. 41–6.

The same abandonment is found where justice is subordinated to the supposed interests of the " proletariat ", and the actual interests of those who, in the name of the proletariat, have made themselves the masters of the State. The " Police-State " in which, without judicial process, any man may be deprived of life or liberty, is the acme of injustice.

Yet justice cannot be secured merely by the impartial administration of laws, unless the laws themselves be just. Thus it was not just but unjust to forbid workmen the right to combine, for only by combination could poor employees secure their just rights against rich employers. Nor is justice done if punishments be disproportionate in their incidence, so that e.g. offences against property are judged more severely than offences against persons. And if punishments be harsh, justice falls into disrepute, for criminal justice then appears not protective but oppressive. The task of justice is not exhausted in the protection of the innocent by the punishment of the guilty. Even the guilty are still potential sons of God, and should be given opportunities which make possible their reform ; it is part of the justice of the State to seek to remove conditions which make dishonesty and violence seem attractive.

(5) THE FOUR FREEDOMS

In his famous speech delivered early in 1941, President Roosevelt spoke of the Four Essential Freedoms not as the " basis of a distant millenium " but as " a definite basis for a kind of world attainable in our own time and generation ". " Freedom of speech and expression, freedom for every person to worship God in his own way, freedom from want, and freedom from fear ". These Four Essential Freedoms well express what should be the aim and task of the Justice of the State, though, even if they were all secured, they would not suffice to meet men's needs for there would still remain, to use the title of Erich Fromm's book, The Fear of Freedom itself. In our land the first two Freedoms, Freedom of Speech and Worship, were long ago secured ; there have been many who were free from want and, in the years immediately after the First World War, most felt free from the fear of another world war. Yet some of those who believed that these Four Freedoms were theirs, were still not free. They were free from political and ecclesia.-tical tyranny, from economic insecurity, and from fear of war, and yet they were not free from inner tyranny—from that sense of frustration and futility which no outward circumstances can remove. We are made for God, and our hearts are restless till they find their rest in Him. But this deepest need is not one the State can meet. It is not its business to be a Church ; it has as its sufficient task the securing of these Four Essential Freedoms which would form the basis of a just society.

The elimination of the first two Freedoms in many lands in recent years is a reminder that these Freedoms, secured only after long struggle, still need to be defended. The Reformation in England did not bring with it freedom of worship, but only freedom to worship as the sovereign enjoined. At the time of the Elizabethan Settlement, Episcopalians and Presbyterians differed much in their views on the necessary structure of the Church, but were at one in their desire to use the civil power to secure religious uniformity. It was an obscure man, Robert Browne, who insisted that the Church is a voluntary society ; religion and the Church of Christ cannot be forced on men, nor " the inheritance of Christ given to magistrates ".[1] The Independents (or Congregationalists), not only claimed for themselves liberty of worship ; in the intimate life of their small fellowships the government lay not with ecclesiastical or civil authority but with ordinary Christians, who yet were recognized as belonging to the universal priesthood of believers. As Dr. Woodhouse has said, " the consciences of common men were a new phenomenon in politics, and one that has never since disappeared ".[2] The attainment of religious liberty has been due to this recognition of " the consciences of common men ". Those who refused to acknowledge the authority of the State

[1] Full quotations from Robert Browne will be found in W. K. Jordan, *The Development of Religious Toleration in England*, Vol. I (To the Death of Queen Elizabeth), pp. 268 ff.

[2] *Puritanism and Liberty*, p. 53 of his Introduction to the Army Debates (1647–9) at Putney, which are of great importance for the study of democracy and religious liberty.

in matters of religion did so not on account of a political theory but in obedience, as they believed, to God. Such obedience was a limitation of the sovereignty of the State and, by making the State no longer unitary, secured in principle civil as well as religious liberty. Freedom of speech has been a consequence of Freedom of worship. Where there is full religious liberty, there cannot be a totalitarian state, for full religious liberty means the recognition by the State that it is not supreme over the consciences of men. Where the State claims that supremacy, civil liberty is at an end.

Even in our country we have a long way to go before Freedom from Want is secured—the want consequent on unemployment, on illness, or old age. We can rejoice that the energies of the State are now directed, as never before, to the achievement of a greater measure of Social Security for all, and to this there was reference in the last chapter. It is the fourth Freedom—freedom from fear of war—which still eludes our grasp. Our hope of a time when none shall lack the necessities for a healthy life is mocked by the menace of a war more horrible even than the last grim conflicts. And to the Christian war is not merely, as it is for everyone, a terrible calamity; it presents him with the gravest of all problems. In no other regard is the tension between the Two Moralities so acute, for, in time of war, justice and love seem to be not merely different in their reference but to be in sheer opposition to each other.

It is needless to speak of the glorification of war by a Nietzsche or a Treitschke, or of the position of some German theologians, before and after the First World War, that the State is an ethical absolute, and that war is the legitimate means of testing the strength of nations and securing to the stronger territorial gains. No reader of this book is likely to hold such views. Who is there of us who does not think of war with loathing ? War is not only a monstrous absurdity, involving appalling loss of life, and destroying the accumulated resources of the nations ; it is the product and the occasion of sin and, as such, an immeasurable evil. As the Oxford Conference of 1937 on *Church, Community and State* declared : " Wars, the occasion of war, and all situations which conceal the fact of

conflict under the guise of outward peace, are marks of a world
to which the Church is charged to proclaim the Gospel of redemption.   War involves compulsory enmity, diabolical outrage
against human personality, and a wanton distortion of the truth.
War is a particular demonstration of the power of sin in the
world, and a defiance of the righteousness of God as revealed
in Jesus Christ and Him crucified.   No justification of war must
be allowed to conceal or minimize this fact ".[1]   Every Christian
must seek to be a peacemaker, ought he also to be a " pacifist " ?
To that the Oxford Conference could give no consentient answer.
It is part of the tragedy of the situation that the question on
which the leaders of the Churches have found themselves in
disagreement is a question which for lads of eighteen is not
merely a problem to be discussed but something on which they
have to make a definite decision.   Those of us who, as Principals
of Theological Colleges, have much to do with devout and earnest
young men, feel deep sympathy with them and concern for their
painful perplexities.   In youth it is natural to think that every
choice is between black and white; and this choice is not of
such a nature.

An issue so complex cannot be solved merely by quoting
texts without reference to their context.   Thus the commandment, " Thou shalt not kill ", is not a prohibition of war, and
in the Revised Version is translated " Thou shalt do no murder ".
The Old Testament contains visions of a Messianic kingdom in
which war shall be no more, but it contains also commands to
engage in war which, it was believed, were given by God to
His people.   It is not the Old Testament but the New which
is the supreme challenge to war, and especially the Sermon on
the Mount, with its presentation of the perfect love of God
which, as God's children, we are bidden to imitate.   That love
is the condemnation of all our sin, and so the condemnation of
the hatred and suspicion from which war springs, and which
war engenders.   Christians are called in all the relationships of
life to seek to imitate the perfect love of God and, if Christians
are persecuted, they must not defend themselves by violence.
This new and better righteousness which the Sermon describes

[1] *Reports*, Vol. VIII, *The Churches Survey their Task*, p. 178.

is the righteousness of the Kingdom of God, and does not deal directly with the duty of the earthly State. The command to love not only friends but enemies is hard to obey, and yet is obeyed even in time of war. We think not only of British sailors off the coast of Norway, diving into the icy sea to rescue Germans who had tried to torpedo their ship, but of German surgeons using their best skill in operations on British airmen who had had to bale out when raiding Germany. The old law, " an eye for an eye, a tooth for a tooth ", was, in its time, a necessary restriction of indiscriminate revenge. Our Lord bade us, instead, Resist not evil and, when struck on one cheek, to turn the other. In St. Matthew's version, the passage goes on, " If any man will sue thee at the law and take away thy coat, let him have thy cloak also." The word here translated " coat " would be better translated as " shirt ", whilst " cloak " denotes " the outer garment ", a sort of blanket or plaid which served as clothing by day and bedding by night. And this plaid, by the humane Jewish law, the plaintiff could not claim. In St. Luke's version, the picture is that of " the footpad who snatches the outer garment and is to be presented with the shirt as well ". " In either case ", as Dr. T. W. Manson adds, " the issue would be nudism, a sufficient indication that it is a certain spirit that is being commended to our notice—not a regulation to be slavishly carried out ".[1] If this passage on non-resistance is given " a direct political reference ", then it " rules out not only war but also all civil government ".[2] That was Tolstoi's conclusion. " Christ said ' Resist not evil ' ; the sole aim of tribunals is to resist evil. Jesus exhorted us to return good for evil ; tribunals return evil for evil. Jesus said that we were to make no distinction between those who do good and those who do evil ; tribunals do nothing else ". " In saying ' Judge not ' Jesus did actually speak of judicial institutions ".[3] Tolstoi's teaching was a salutary rebuke to the harshness of

[1] *The Mission and Message of Jesus*, p. 343.

[2] As Dr. J. Lowe pointed out in his review of Dr. C. J. Cadoux's *The Historic Mission of Jesus*, *Journal of Theological Studies*, Jan.–April 1943.

[3] *My Religion*, chap. iii.

the judicial system of his time and land, but shows little understanding of the true function of the State. The reference to
the coat and cloak, the shirt and plaid, is, as Lord Lindsay says,
" a vivid, dramatic way of saying that we are not always to
stand on our legal rights, that we are to be ready to rise above
the world of claims and counter-claims, and be prepared to be
better than can be reasonably demanded of us ". " But ", as
he adds, " if we love our neighbours or, for that matter, our
enemies, we must desire that there should be rules, and we must
desire that those rules should be maintained, and be prepared
to do our part in maintaining them. . . . If when we are told,
' resist not evil ', we are being told to have nothing to do with
that maintenance of rules which resists evil, then we are told
something which is incompatible with loving our neighbours.
That is the real point at issue between those who do, and those
who do not accept these particular verses literally ".[1] On the
other hand, as Dr. Raven points out, the pacifist position is not
disproved by such words from the Gospel as " let him sell his
cloak and buy a sword ", " render unto Caesar the things that
are Caesar's ", " the strong man armed ", or the " scourge of
small cords ".[2]

The attempt is sometimes made to solve the grave problem
of the use of force by a reference to the example of Christ. We
cannot, indeed, conceive of Christ as a soldier. But nor can
we think of Him as a husband. His vocation was to be the
world's Redeemer and He could not be anything incompatible
with that vocation. He recognized the authority of earthly
rulers, and yet gave no guidance as to earthly government.
Thus the Parable of the Good Samaritan condemns the priest
and Levite who, seeing the robbed and wounded man, passed
by on the other side, and praises the Samaritan who bound
up his wounds and made provision for his needs. But, as we
have seen,[3] the parable says nothing about the duty of the
official responsible for keeping order on the road from Jericho
to Jerusalem. Would his duty have been adequately fulfilled

---

[1] *The Two Moralities*, pp. 64 f.
[2] *Church, Community and State*, Vol. VII, p. 292.
[3] See earlier, p. 64.

had he provided those who, like the Good Samaritan, would have mercy on the wounded, or ought he not, as a representative of Government, to have cleared the road of robbers, that harmless travellers might puruse their way unhurt ? To this problem the parable gives us no answer.

An early Christian tract declares " Love those that hate you and you will have no enemy ".[1] So many a worker in mission field or city slum has found. But love does not always overcome enmity, even in personal relationships. Preachers who declare, as so many did in the inter-war period, that love will melt the hardest heart, show a strange forgetfulness of the incidents of the Gospel story. What of Judas who lived with Jesus and betrayed Him ? What of Annas and Caiaphas who became His malignant enemies ? Some martyrs by their radiant courage have won to Christianity their persecutors. But there would have been no martyrdoms had Christian love secured immunity from suffering. Before the last war, we were told that'no unarmed nation would be attacked and that Denmark thus was safe. It did not prove so. Lack of defences saved the Danes some suffering, but only at the cost of their land being used more quickly as a base against a friendly nation. It has seemed worth while to discuss these familiar arguments because of the perplexity they have caused in recent years. There are many who have abandoned Christianity not on intellectual but on moral grounds ; accepting the view that Christianity means non-resistance, they conclude that they cannot, without hypocrisy, remain Christians and yet take their part in the world's affairs.

The pacifist position need not be based on an interpretation of a few texts which would condemn not only war but civil government, nor do the wiser advocates of pacifism hold out illusory promises that, if a nation disarms, it will be safe. Instead, they base their refusal to participate in war on the incompatibility of the Christian gospel with warfare.[2] On that

[1] *The Teaching of the Twelve Apostles*, 1. 3.
[2] Cp. the powerful Essays in *Church, Community and State*, in Vol. VII by C. E. Raven, *The Religious Basis of Pacifism* ; in Vol. IV by H. H. Farmer, *The Revelation in Christ and the Christian's Vocation.*

incompatibility, Pacifist and non-Pacifist Christians agree. Thus Dr. P. T. Forsyth, whose book, *The Christian Ethic of War*, is a pungent attack on the Pacifist position, wrote, " War is the greatest of all the awful and complex moral situations of the world—second only to the final judgment day. It is a moral monstrosity if only because it is purely destructive. It is moral pestilence. It is a wrong on both sides ". And yet, he added, " It may be the less of two immoralities, and in so far at least, a negative contribution to righteousness. . . . For peace at any price can be the abnegation of morality entirely, the refusal of even a negative contribution to righteousness ".[1]

No relief can be found in the conception of just wars (*iusta bella*) in the Latin version of the thirty-seventh of the Thirty-Nine Articles for, as the anonymous author of the Crockford Prefaces puts it, the adjective *iustus* merely means " regular, authorized or legal ",[2] and, in this sense, even Mussolini's attack on Abyssinia could be so described. If war involved the destruction only of the guilty men who plot it, it might be regarded merely as an act of judgment. Instead, it involves the destruction of the innocent, of those who, as Jonah was reminded, " cannot discern between their right hand and their left hand ". When the bombs fell on us in London, it was to some of us no comfort but only added sorrow to know that bombs were falling also on Berlin. Obliteration-bombing, and the atomic bomb, have made war race-suicide and Hiroshima is the awful warning to our generation of what war may become.

Yet the problem of defence cannot be dealt with in isolation. War is the product of hatred and distrust. As we cross from the U.S.A. into Canada, we find no armed men at the frontier, and between our country and the U.S.A. there is no dispute which cannot be settled by negotiation or arbitration. War is, to use the title of Sir Norman Angell's book, *The Great Illusion* ; from it both victors and vanquished lose. But men are not swayed only by hope of material gain or fear of material loss, and the policy of appeasement before 1939 failed partly because of this myth of the " economic man ". What did Hitler care for the economic advantages that were offered to him ? It was

[1] p. 32.   [2] *The Editor Looks Back*, p. 250.

the domination of the world that he sought, and that domination would have meant the extinction of freedom and of civil justice. But peace might have been maintained had those who desired peace been strong, and had the League of Nations not been made futile by peaceful powers who, in the name of peace, echoed the words of Cain, " Am I my brother's keeper ? " Those who seek peace need to have power till all seek peace. And meanwhile infinite patience is required, and readiness to co-operate with all who recognize the authority of justice. If the world is to be saved from war, it will not be because all are wise and good, but because the general will has secured protection for all, and thus made possible a reign of law instead of anarchy.

To secure that reign of law should be part of the function of the State. No war can be a " holy war ", no war a " crusade ". The Pacifist protest is a salutary reminder of war's enormity, and pacifists who so undertake alternate work that their convictions bring them no evasion of toil or danger, can make that protest with a good conscience. Those who refuse to do any form of service, and base their refusal on the Sermon on the Mount, would do well to remember those words of Matt. v. 41, " Whosoever shall compel thee to go one mile, go with him twain ",—if the State conscripts you into its service, do double what is asked.[1] The New Testament, as we have seen, recognizes the function of the State, and, as citizens, we have our duty to it. Many in the armed Services felt acutely the tension between their military duty and their Christian faith, and that tension must have been still more acute for those in the resistance movements in Europe. We remember what a French Protestant wrote as he left his family of six children to join the resistance movement, from which he did not return. " I pray God to grant each one of you the peace of His pardon and the power of His faith, at this hour when our hearts are heavy with the weight of our own sins and the sins of the world ; at this hour when we are weary of suffering and of seeing others suffer, and when we sometimes fear death and seeing those we love die.

[1] The word translated " compel " is of Persian origin and is used of the forced labour demanded by the State.

I ask God, too, that He now forgive me my sins, and the decision which I voluntarily take this day (for I know that recourse to violence has need of pardon).   But I am leaving without hate and fully convinced that we Christians have not the right to leave it to non-Christians alone to offer their lives in the name of a mere political ideal, in a struggle in which the fate of the community and that of the Church and the spiritual destiny of our children are at stake ".[1]

The immediate issue before us is not the legitimacy of war ; it is how war may be prevented, and men saved from suffering of body and strain of spirit.   War is now so monstrous an evil that only one worse evil can befall a State—the extinction of its liberty by some alien totalitarian rule which seeks the domination of the world.   Those who have the grave responsibility of government at this time have to take account of means as well as ends, and not only to aim at peace but to consider how peace may be maintained.   Defence of its citizens from war is part of the justice of the State ;   peace may be secured as all peace loving nations combine to establish and defend a reign of Law under which war would become as remote a possibility as is in our land armed civil strife, and The Fourth Freedom—freedom from the fear of war—be thus at last secured.[2]

We return again to the enigma of the State.   A State without power cannot fulfil its function of justice, and yet power can

[1] Jacques Monod from a letter published in *The Student Movement* and reprinted in *The Christian News Letter* No. 238.

[2] I have not discussed the new and terrible possibilities of atomic warfare, as I have nothing useful to add to the Report of the Commission appointed by the British Council of Churches, *The Era of Atomic Power*, 1946.   (There is also the more elaborate Report of the Commission appointed by the Archbishop, *The Church and the Atom*, 1948).   This culminating horror of total warfare seems to me to differ in degree but not in kind from the use of rocket bombs by the Germans and of obliteration-bombing by the Allies.   It does not create a new problem but reveals with dreadful clarity the cruelty and folly of modern warfare and makes more urgent the need for the patient and persistent quest for peace by all peace-loving peoples.

be used unjustly. Lord Acton's often quoted words, " All power corrupts and absolute power corrupts absolutely ", are only partly true. " Absolute power corrupts absolutely " ; no man, and no organization of men, is good enough to be trusted with absolute power. But power need not corrupt, although it always tends to do so, for power tends to arrogance, and arrogance is incompatible with internal or external peace. Poor fools that we are, even as we pray for God's mercy on " frantic boast and foolish word " and for deliverance from " such boasting as the Gentiles use ", we may still be thinking of others as " lesser breeds without the Law ". The power of the State should be power reinforcing justice, but, without humility and understanding, even what men think to be justice may be unjust. To do justly we need to love mercy and walk humbly before our God.

> All true democracy begins
> With free confession of our sins.[1]

The justice of the State, whether at home or abroad, will not endure, except it be based on the fear of God in whom justice and love are one. The Church needs the justice of the State to provide the framework of an ordered society. But the State needs the Church, that its justice may be kept free from pride, and from pride's cruelty. As Professor Reinhold Niebuhr has said, " Nothing short of the knowledge of the true God will save " men " from the impiety of making themselves God and the cruelty of seeing their fellow-men as devils because they are involved in the same pretension ".[2]

---

[1] W. H. Auden, *A New Year's Letter.*
[2] *An Interpretation of Christian Ethics*, p. 247.

EPILOGUE

CHAPTER XI

THE CHURCH'S TASK

(1) THE CHRISTIAN FELLOWSHIP

WE have spoken of the Ethical Teaching of the New Testament, of The Motives and Sanctions of the Christian Life and of the Communities of Marriage, Industry and the State. But this book would be incomplete without some reference to the Church's Task. God does not ask from us the impossible. He has called us to serve Him not in solitariness but in fellowship with others. The Church brings us to the knowledge of God in Christ ; it speaks to us of God's forgiveness, and summons us to that faith from which love springs. By its preaching and its sacraments, the Church bears witness to God's grace ; through its worship our flagging zeal may be revived, and our faith strengthened through others' faith, and, as we face the problems which beset men in the modern world in regard to the Communities of Marriage, Industry and the State, we may do so not in isolation but in association with those who also have experienced God's mercy and are seeking to do His will. The Christian task is too great for any of us to fulfil alone. Instead, we belong to the Family of God, the Church in which the Spirit works, continuing Christ's work for men, and giving us not only tasks to be accomplished but help in their fulfilment. As Calvin wrote, " By the faith of the Gospel Christ becomes ours, and we are made partakers of the salvation and eternal blessedness procured by Him ". But we " have not yet attained to the rank of angels ". " As our ignorance and sloth (I may add, the vanity of our mind), stand in need of external helps, by which faith may be begotten in us and may increase and make progress until its consummation, God, in accommodation to our infirmity, has added such helps and secured the effectual preaching of the Gospel by depositing this treasure with the Church. He has appointed pastors and teachers by whose lips He might edify His people, He has invested them with authority, and, in short, omitted nothing that might conduce to holy consent in the faith and to right order.   In particular, He has instituted sacraments, which we feel by experience to be most useful helps in fostering and confirming our faith ".   And so Calvin claimed that to whom God is a Father, the Church is also a " mother ".[1]   We are called to live the Christian life, not alone, but in co-operation with all who belong to the one family of God.

And the Church's task is not only to nourish and inspire those who share its life.   It has a duty to those who do not share its faith.   It has by loving service to reveal the power of love ; it is under obligation to combat evil in any form, and to seek to secure that the Orders of Creation should be conformed to the will of the Creator.

To state the Church's task is to confess the Church's failure. The words of the pagan which Tertullian quoted, " See how these Christians love one another ", have been more often spoken since in mockery than in admiration.   The Church which claims so high a task and so rich a heritage impresses men more by its spiritual poverty than by its spiritual wealth, whilst its demand for love and justice goes unheeded because of its failure to show in its own life the qualities which it demands from others.   It speaks of the need of international co-operation, and is itself divided.   To many its love seems but cold " charity ", its justice a pretext for maintaining the privileges of the prosperous. In our brief survey we have had to record many Christian failures which seem to support this condemnation.   The Church's history has been marred by intolerance and strife, and, as we face to-day the problems of Marriage, Industry and the State, we do so as those who know that suggestions from the Christian side are suspected because of the errors of the past.   The Christian ideal of marriage has been distorted by prudery and false asceticism ; the Christian approach to the social problem is discredited because of those who, in the past, acquiesced in social injustices, whilst the Christian estimate of the State is obscured through the support given by Churchmen in the past

[1] *Institutes*, IV. 1.

to tyranny and aggression, and through the sentimentalism of those who in recent years have, like the false prophets of old, sought "to heal the hurt" of the people, "lightly, saying, Peace, peace and there is no peace". The Church, which exists to manifest Christ to men, has sometimes seemed to hide Him from their sight. By many in the modern world, the Church is regarded as effete and futile, and yet this Church, of whose "Failure" we hear so much is, in spite of its divisions, the *Una Sancta*, the only holy Church, whose essential ministry is the ministry of Christ, in and through His people.

(2) THE "FAILURE" OF THE CHURCHES

There are many who speak of Christ with reverence and profess to admire His teaching, who yet despise the Church. We remember Swinburne's words, "I could worship the Crucified if He came to me without his leprous bride the Church". But we remember also that, when Jesus walked in Galilee, when there was no Church to repel men by the failures of its members, no dogmas to obscure the supposed simplicity of His teaching, He was popular only so long as He was misunderstood, and in the end He was rejected and crucified. We whose lives have been given to the service of the Church, know better than those outside its defects and weakness, but we know that the Church is the Church of God, and that Christ uses it still in the continuance of His ministry to men.

It has become a commonplace to speak of the "Failure" of the Churches, as if this was something too obvious even to be discussed. There is a fashion in churchgoing, as in other matters. Thus in the latter half of the nineteenth century the Church was held in conventional esteem, and churchgoing was a requirement of middle-class respectability. All that has changed, and the change is not only loss. In his great allegory, Bunyan, with true Christian insight, includes among those who reach the Celestial City, not only Great-heart, Valiant-for-truth, Honest, and Standfast, but also Feeble-minded, Ready-to-halt, and Despondency with his daughter Much-afraid. The Churches still number among their members the counterparts of these genuine, though in some cases, feeble Christians. But they no longer contain, as once they did, the followers of those whom Bunyan calls Mr. and Mrs. By-ends, who " differ in religion from those of the stricter sort yet but in two small points : First we never strive against wind and tide. Secondly, we are always most zealous when Religion goes in his silver slippers ; we love much to walk with him in the street, if the sun shines and the people applaud him ". Religion has to-day no " silver slippers ", and gets no applause ; those who " never strive against wind and tide " are no longer in the Churches.

The customary talk about the " Failure " of the Church makes the judgment of the great historian, Dr. Latourette, all the more significant. The three decades since 1914 he tells us have been not years of failure but " ages of advance, but of advances through storm. There were what appeared to be startling losses. Yet in the main, in 1944, Christianity found itself in a stronger position than in 1914. Indeed, if one views, as one must, the world-wide story as a whole, it becomes clear that the thirty years which followed 1914 constituted one of the greatest eras in the history of the Church ". " Measured by the criteria of geographic extent, vigour as evinced by new movements and effects upon mankind as a whole, Christianity had not lost but gained ". " If mankind was surveyed as a whole, Christianity was clearly a growing factor in human affairs ". " Here in an age of storm was a power which, usually unnoticed and unappreciated by those whose self-function it was to interpret the day by day passage of events, was quietly at work, transforming individuals and societies, and more widely potent than ever before ".[1]

That judgment gives ground for encouragement but not complacency, In our own land churchgoing is less common than it was ; in our great cities many never go to Church, and many others belong to the Church only in the sense that they have a church from which to stay away. A recent Mass Observation Report, *Puzzled People*, concludes that in a London Borough only one in ten goes to Church " fairly regularly ", and suggests

---

[1] *A History of the Expansion of Christianity*, by K. S. Latourette, vol. VII, pp. 3, 410, 414, 415.

that even this figure may be an over-estimate. That conclusion comes as no surprise, but if, even in London, one-tenth the population was convincedly Christian, the Church would be far stronger than it is. That many should reject the Church's Gospel and its Fellowship is to be expected. What is disappointing is that, as this Report confirms and all experience suggests, what they reject is often not the Gospel, and of the Fellowship of the Church they have no understanding, whilst some who are churchgoers have little conception of the greatness of the Gospel which the Church proclaims, or of the possibilities of a life lived in communion with God.

If the significance of the Christian message was realized, it might arouse more opposition than it at present does, but it could not be treated as a trivial thing, no more to be attacked than the pretty myth of Santa Claus, and, like that myth, irrelevant to the serious choices of adult life. It is not opposition but indifference which is the most serious obstacle to the reception of the Christian message, and that indifference is not restricted to the sphere of religion. Many are disillusioned, allergic to all serious discussion, and leaving enthusiasm to those who think to save the world by slogans and the gestures of the uplifted arm or the clenched fist. So far, these false religions, Fascism and Communism, with their bitter hatred of Christian values, have had little influence in our land. The danger here is nihilism—the belief that nothing matters very much. There are many, especially of the younger generation who, as the Nazi leader Ernst Juenger boasted of German youth, are not anti-Christian but post-Christian.[1] They belong to a generation for which Christianity is not of sufficient interest to be attacked. Where God is banished, the half-gods return and, as Nazi Germany showed, the vacuum of irreligion is filled with a false religion. As Blake said long ago, " Man must and will have some religion ; if he has not the religion of Jesus he will have the religion of Satan and will erect a synagogue of Satan ".

Christians know that men need not live without hope or guidance, that in the Gospel is given not, indeed, the solution of every problem, but the answer to men's deepest need : the

[1] See Erich Kahler, *Man the Measure*, p. 596.

experience of God's forgiveness and a communion with Him which takes from life its futility and frustration. But they know also that the Church, in whose Fellowship they have discovered God in Christ, has not only revealed Christ to men, but has also hidden Him from them. In every Christian age there have been those who have shown in their lives something of the strength of Christian faith, and the radiancy of Christian love. Yet there is the other side, and the folly and failure of the Church should prevent our speaking as if the relation of the Church to the world was merely that of good to evil.

The Church is the representative of Christ to the world, but the temptation He withstood is a temptation into which the Church has often fallen ; it has seen " the kingdoms of the world and the glory of them ", and, instead of serving God alone, has fallen down and worshipped their master. Who, that has read it, can forget Dostoievsky's Myth of the Grand Inquisitor ? Jesus appears in Seville in His human form at the time of an *auto-da-fé*, when many heretics were burnt. The crowd recognizes Him. " It is He ; it must be He, it can be no other but Him ! " The Grand Inquisitor, who had presided at the burning, orders His arrest. At night-time he comes to visit Him in His cell and tells Him He has been mistaken. The tempter knew better than He did how to win the allegiance of men. Men cannot bear to be free. " We have corrected Thy work ". " Why hast Thou come now to hinder us ? " " We have taken the sword of Caesar and in taking it have rejected Thee and followed *him* ". " If anyone have ever deserved our fires it is Thou. To-morrow I shall burn Thee. *Dixi* ". The Prisoner waited for a while, and then softly kissed the aged Cardinal on the lips. " The old man shuddered. His lips moved. He went to the door, opened it and said to Him, ' Go and come no more . . . come not at all, never, never ' ". " The Prisoner went away ".[1] The Church has neglected our Saviour's warning, " They which are accounted to rule over the Gentiles lord it over them ; and their great ones exercise authority over them. But it is not so among you ; but whosoever would become great among you, shall be your minister ".[2]

[1] *The Brothers Karamazov*, Book V, chap. v.   [2] Mark x. 42 f.

The truth of God is many-sided. Our " unhappy divisions "
are not only unhappy. What some call " schisms " were usually
due to the discovery of some aspect of Christian experience
which had been contradicted or obscured, and Christ's presence
and power are not restricted to any one communion. Yet
divisions may lead to sectarian pride. Like St. Paul's converts
at Corinth, some say, " I am of Paul ; and I of Apollos ; and I
of Cephas ", and others, with still greater arrogance, say, " I
am of Christ ", mine and mine alone is the true Church. The
Church which claims to be the " Catholic " Church, unchurches
all other Christians ; some Anglo-Catholics speak as if only
those ordained by Bishops in the Apostolic Succession are true
ministers of Christ,[1] whilst some who belong to " gathered "
Churches have been tempted at times to think of themselves as
better Christians than their brethren.[2] And Christ ignores all
such distinctions and is present wherever His people gather.
Since His presence is known and realized in every section of the
Church, sectarian pride is an absurdity. One is our Master, and
there are many " folds " but there is only one flock for there is
only one Shepherd, Jesus Christ who is the Lord of us all.[3]

[1] The comments of two modern historians are of interest. R. C. K.
Ensor, *England, 1870–1914*, p. 141, writing of about 1870, says that
" the anglo-catholic movement met a peculiar professional need of the
anglican clergy of this time ".   " During the later eighteenth and early
nineteenth century there had been little or no doctrinal difference between
most of them and most of the dissenting ministers. The vantage-ground
which they enjoyed over these rival practitioners was legal, since the
state inflicted heavy civil and educational disabilities on the latter and
their flocks. But between 1828 and 1871 all these disabilities were
repealed and in the latter year even the ancient universities were thrown
open. Unless anglicanism redeveloped some convincing doctrinal
difference, its clergy would have difficulty in maintaining any exclusive
professional position. Here the new movement . . . supplied exactly
what the profession needed ". Dr. Trevelyan in his *English Social
History*, p. 564, makes a similar comment.

[2] And inclined to agree with the two yokels in Thomas Hardy's
Far From the Madding Crowd. " ' Chapel-folk be more hand-in-glove
with them above than we ', said Joseph thoughtfully. ' Yes ', said
Coggan, ' we know very well that if anybody do go to heaven they will.
They've worked hard for it, and they deserve to have it, such as 'tis ' ".

[3] In John x. 16, for " there shall be one fold and one shepherd ",
of the A.V. the R.V. rightly translates " they shall become one *flock*
and one shepherd ".

T.C.W.

(3) THE *UNA SANCTA*

The Church exists that in it Christ may do His work for men. When it is concerned first with its own prestige and power, it is failing in its task, for a Church which thinks first of its own greatness is ill-fitted to represent to men the Christ who on earth was rejected and crucified. Yet that is always the temptation of the Church. Like St. Peter, the " rock " on which the Church was built, the first stone in the Church built of believing men, we think the thoughts of men and not of God, and would have Christ do His work by some other way than the way He chose. The Church had its beginnings in that confession of St. Peter that Jesus was the Messiah. But the Church of the New Testament is a continuation of the " Remnant " of Old Testament times. The earlier hope had been that all the children of Israel would be God's people. Instead, as we have seen, the " people of God " was limited to that part of the nation faithful to Him, the " Remnant " of which Isaiah spoke. This conception of the Remnant gained new significance in the Servant-Songs found in the later half of the Book of Isaiah, in which is depicted the Servant of God, who, by suffering and obedience, should be the agent of God's saving works ; in the book of Daniel the purified Israel is depicted as a Son of Man in contrast to those pagan empires symbolized as beasts. Jesus united in His mission these two conceptions. He, the Son of Man, was the suffering Servant of the Lord. And He associated His " little flock " with His vocation. It was to them that He would give the Kingdom, and they too were called not to be ministered unto but to minister.[1]

Our Lord lived on earth in lowliness and neither sought nor won the recognition of the powerful. He was content to bring to men the Good News of God's Kingdom and to serve them in any way He could. His work seemed a failure for the people turned from Him and their leaders sought His death. Yet, although the world knew it not, the hope of the future lay not in the impressive power of imperial Rome, nor in the Temple with the splendour of its worship, but in an upper room, not

[1] See earlier, pp. 40 f.

consecrated for religious use, in which Jesus ate his farewell meal with His twelve disciples of whom one had already arranged for His betrayal.

At Pentecost the first believers felt the power of the risen Lord in the presence with them of the Spirit. The Church knew itself to be the people of God, the " Remnant ". But although Christians felt the power of the risen Christ, their task was that of humble service. The Church on earth is militant but not triumphant, and St. Paul bitterly rebuked those who acted as if they already " reigned ", as if the time of conflict was past, and the Kingdom already perfected. Instead, Christians were called to fill up that which remained of the afflictions of Christ, to continue the work of the incarnate Christ by the way He chose—the way of service. The Church is one, for God is one ; its Communion Table does not belong to any section of the Church but is the Table of the Lord. The Church is " holy ", not because its members are saints in the modern sense, but because it is the Church of God, and consists of those who, in spite of their imperfection, have been brought into communion with Him. The Church is " Catholic ", *i.e.* universal, because in Christ distinctions of race, privilege or status, have become unimportant ; the unity of the Church was so strongly realized that the persecution of any part of it was the persecution of the whole Church of God, whilst the sin of any was the shame of all.

Amid all the disappointments of these last years, we have reason to rejoice at the rediscovery of this conception of the One Holy Church—the *Una Sancta*, as it has become customary to call it. Christians are still divided on questions of Order and the Sacraments, and yet there is a more general recognition that the Church is one because it is the Church of Christ. That Church is not the monopoly of any nation. It is a world-wide Society, international as is nothing else. Christians, persecuted under Nazi rule, have discovered anew the Kingship of Christ. " *Regem habemus*, we have a King ! " has become the watchword of a revived Christian faith, and to have Christ as King is to be one in Him. Christians belonging to the warring nations found it easy to understand each other when peace came and were the first to renew their fellowship. *Christian Reconstruction in Europe* has been not an expression of patronage but of our unity in Christ. It is a deeply moving experience to be with theological students brought over to this country by *Christian Reconstruction in Europe* : students of Eastern Europe exiled from their homes because of communist rule ; students from the lands which were in German occupation, and students from Germany itself. They belong to different ecclesiastical traditions and from nations but lately bitterly estranged, but all have the same King and all are one in Him. This new realization of unity finds expression in the World Council of Churches to which the British Council is related. " The one holy Catholic Church " has become in our age a new reality.

This Church exists that it may be used by Christ in His ministry to men, and for the continuance of this ministry, the service of the whole Church is required. The ministry of Christ to men is not the work of the official ministry alone, nor is it restricted to the Preaching of the Word and the Administration of the Sacraments. Modern missionary experience is instructive here, for in the mission field the New Testament conception of the Church's task has been more clearly realized than in nominally Christian lands.

It has long been a commonplace of missionary experience that no man, or class of men, is adequate for the continuance of the Ministry of Christ. The modern missionary enterprise sprang from an overwhelming desire to " save souls ", to bring to men who knew Him not, the Christ who is the Saviour of the world. Thus William Carey, that " consecrated cobbler " of Sydney Smith's sneer, taught as well as preached, and there stands to-day at Serampore the great College which he founded. No part of the continuance of Christ's ministry has been more influential than that of the medical missionary, healing the sick even as the Saviour did. Even before the means of checking leprosy was discovered, there were leper settlements near mission hospitals where lepers, regarded by others as unclean, could be cared for and tended. Though I have realized the continuance of Christ's ministry in great congregations addressed by gifted preachers, yet my most vivid impression of that ministry has been in a leper village in the immediate care of an

Indian medical evangelist, where it was often my privilege to baptize those there who, through the influence of Christian love in action, had become Christians, and to give communion to those whose rotted hands could not take the bread or hold the cup.   Where those outside the caste system, whose very presence was regarded as a pollution, were received into the Church, they could not be left in their utter poverty ;   education and new industries have helped to meet their economic needs.   In such work men learn to revise their scale of virtues ;   to realize how hard for some are truthfulness and honesty, and, learning this, have learned to be very patient and not to give up hope for any. In the mass-movement areas from those who were always despised and often degraded, a Church has been created which, in spite of weakness, can be the representative of Christ.   Its task of proclaiming Him is the task not of some within the Church but of the Church itself, and in the work of making Him known, while educated speak to the educated, ignorant men and women may be effective evangelists to the ignorant ;   they know one thing, and one thing only, more than those to whom they speak : the power of Christ to rid them of their fear of demons and to inspire them with the desire to do His will.   The Church seeks to continue every aspect of the ministry of Christ to men, and, like its Lord in His earthly life, it does not seek to rule.   Without prestige or temporal power, it has its sufficient task in being among men as one that serves.

(4) THE ESSENTIAL MINISTRY

Since the publication of *The Apostolic Ministry*, by the Bishop of Oxford, Dr. Kirk, and his associates, we have heard much of " the essential ministry ", which they take to be that of the Apostles, represented later in the Church by the episcopate which, Dom Gregory Dix tells us, " is the only means by which our Lord's own commission to stand in His Person before God and man is given afresh to each new minister of His Church ".[1] " Our Lord ", says Dr. Kirk, " endowed the Church with two great gifts : the means of grace (the word and the sacra-

[1] p. 303.

ments) and the ministry of grace (the apostles and their fellow labourers) ".[1] But, as Dr. T. W. Manson says, " Our Lord did better than that ; He gave the Church Himself. His real and abiding presence in the Church is the supreme ' means of grace ' and the supreme ' ministry of grace ' ". " There is one ' essential ' ministry, the only ministry which is unchallengeably essential. That is the ministry which the Lord Jesus Christ opened in Galilee after John the Baptist had been put in prison, the ministry which He continues to this day in and through the Church which is His body ".[2] That " essential ministry " is exercised wherever there are those who have felt the power of Christ and have put themselves at His disposal. He ignores our distinctions, and meets with men in the splendour of High Mass, in the Divine Liturgy of the Eastern Church, in Anglican Cathedral and in village Church, in the simple solemnity of the Reformed tradition, in Quaker silence, and in the noisier worship of revivalist sects.

To describe the Church's task would be to rewrite what we have already written on the Mission and Teaching of Jesus, on the New Testament Interpretations of Christian Ethics, on Law and Grace, on Faith and Works, on Evangelical Asceticism, the Relevance of the Eternal, and on Life in the Communities of Marriage, Industry and the State.

This book has been concerned with Christian Ethics. But the prime task of the Church is not to present the Christian Ideal. Ideals alone lead only to illusion or despair.[3] If we think that of ourselves we can meet the demands of Christ, then we know neither ourselves nor those demands. As a recent writer has said, " A Christian does not live by practising any ethic or moulding himself on any ideal, but by a faith in God which finally ascribes all good to Him. To detach the ethic from the whole context of the Christian secret is to make it irrelevant because it is impossible. The main function of the impossible ethic is to drive us away from ourselves to God, and

[1] p. 8.

[2] *The Church's Ministry*, p. 11. For Dr. Manson's criticism of the interpretation of the Hebrew term *Shaliach* as equivalent to *apostolos*, see pp. 30–52.

[3] On *The Mischief of Ideals*, see Canon V. A. Demant's article with that title, *Theology of Society*, pp. 148–63.

then there grows that peculiar type of goodness which can never be achieved by mere moral endeavour, the Christian kind, which is all unconscious of itself and gives all the glory to God ".[1]

The greatest service that the Church can render to Christian Ethics is not in the first instance the formulation of an ethical demand ; it lies in its proclamation of the Gospel, its presentation of Christ to man. Worship is thus central to the Church's task for, as the Bishop of Oxford has said, it is worship that " lifts the soul out of its preoccupation with itself, and centres its aspirations entirely on God ".[2] Public praise and prayer, the Preaching of the Word, the Administration of the Sacraments—these are not substitutes for action, they are the source from which Christian action springs, for in them God's grace is manifested, and from grace comes gratitude. The Christian is not a benefactor but a debtor ; when he has done all he is still an " unprofitable servant ". He lives by God's forgiveness ; he has nothing to boast of, unless it be the greatness of that love which he has seen and experienced in God's gift to the world of Christ, and in Christ's acceptance of the Cross.

In the preceding chapters of this book, tentative suggestions were made in regard to the perplexing problems which confront us from our life in those Orders which, ordained as we believe of God, are known to us only as perverted by human sin : Marriage, Industry and the State. Long and patient discussion will be needed before Christians reach, if reach they do, a consentient judgment on such problems as Divorce, the right Industrial Order and the Justice of the State. But all these problems look different to those who have experienced God's forgiveness. The forgiven can forgive, and Christian marriage thus be stable ; differences of opinion may remain, and yet the old antagonisms which menace industrial peace may be overcome ; and, although the State is primarily the sphere of justice, Christians can find a way to show that love which the love of God inspires. We rejoice that the representatives of many different traditions now confer together in mutual confidence. But the Church's task cannot be left to the Church's

[1] D. M. Baillie, *God was in Christ*, p. 116.
[2] *The Vision of God*, p. xiii.

leaders. Our task in this country also is that of a Church in a predominantly pagan land, and that means that the Church itself, through all its members, must be ready to be used of Christ to do its work. It is not World Councils, nor great Assemblies, nor even the ordained ministry, that can fulfil the Christian task ; the local congregation has here a supreme part to play, and the more intimate its fellowship the better it can do its task. There are the young to be trained, the weak to be strengthened, the proud to be made humble, and the sinful to be restored. Where Christ is known, and the power of His Spirit experienced, men and women, separated by class or calling, can learn to understand each other's difficulties, and help each other to be the better servants of Christ. As we have seen, it has long been a commonplace in the mission field that to represent Christ to men, preaching and teaching are not enough. The Church is called not only to proclaim the love of Christ, but to manifest it in the lives of all its members. There is a spurious sanctity which isolates men from the struggles of their age. Like the Priests and Pharisees, who " went not into the judgment hall lest they should be defiled ", and so unable to eat the Passover, some have allowed their worship to isolate them from the needs of men, and so were not found where decisions have to be taken and injustices opposed. A Church absorbed in itself and its solemnities is not rightly representing to men the Christ who, when on earth, walked life's common ways. Yet without worship faith loses its energy and zeal grows cold. The Ethics of the New Testament is not a code of morals or a set of rules. It derives its impulses and its content from the Christian Gospel, the Good News of what God has done in Christ. We know only in part and are perplexed by many a problem. Yet we know enough for our pilgrim way, and, as members of Christ's Church, are called so to live that in our various callings Christ may be able to use us in His ministry to men. It is through Him that Christian character is created and we may discover the relation to present problems of the Ethics of the New Testament as we seek to follow the Christian Way made known to us in Him who is not our Teacher only but our Saviour and our risen Lord.

INDEX

ABEL, A. I., 222
Abrahams, I., 47, 49, 63
Acton, Lord, 234, 259
Agricola, 122, 128
Ambrose, St., 103, 183
Angell, Sir Norman, 107, 256
Antinomianism, 90, 122, 124, 128
Aquinas, St. Thomas, 103 f., 108 f.,
    119 f., 130 f., 136, 210
Aristotle, 103, 108
Arnold, Matthew, 154
Asceticism, 81, 91, 102, 145–57,
    182–8
Athanasius, St., 183
Atomic Warfare, 165, 258
Attlee, C. R., 230
Auden, W. H., 259
Augustine, St., 103, 130 ff., 184 f.,
    195, 239 f.

BAILLIE, D. M., 274 f.
Barry, F. R., 97, 102, 198
Barth, Karl, 60, 106, 113, 172 f.,
    188 f., 233
Basil, St., 148
Baxter, R., 128, 157
Berdyaev, N., 228
Berggrav, Bishop, 245
Beveridge, Lord, 179 f., 225
Binyon, G. C., 215, 223 f.
Blake, W., 193, 267
Böhlig, H., 70
Bonaventura, St., 101
Bowman, J. W., 34
Bradley, F. H., 153
Browne, Robert, 250
Browning, R., 165
Brunner, E., 61, 106 f., 115 ff.,
    120 f., 156, 172 f., 199, 226, 247
Bunyan, 56, 265 f.
Burke, Edmund, 208

Burnaby, J., 185
Butler, J., 105

CADOUX, A. T., 89
Cadoux, C. J., 234, 253
Calvin, 111, 119, 131, 151 f., 191,
    211 f., 244, 263 f.
Capitalism, 211–17, 224–8
Carlyle, A. J., 107
Cassian, 55
Casuistry, 50 f., 118 f., 123
Christian Socialist Movement, 213
Church, R. W., 174 f.
Clapham, J. H., 212
Clement of Rome, St., 129
Cochrane, C. N., 239
Communism, 69 f., 226 f., 249
C.O.P.E.C., 196 f.
Counsels and Precepts, 149
Coward, Noel, 20
Cyril of Alexandria, St., 55

DALE, R. W., 156, 246 f.
Darwin, C., 16 f.
Davies, J. L., 17
Davis, H., 118, 202
Dawson, C., 107, 231
Declaration of Independence, 112
Deissmann, A., 73
Demant, V. A., 274
Denifle, H., 128, 186
Dewar, L., 107, 149
Divorce, 62 f., 181, 200–5
Dix, G., 278
Dodd, C. H., 39, 75, 107, 114
Doddridge, P., 216
Dostoievsky, F., 268
Dryden, J., 142
Duty and Love, 156 f.

ELIOT, George, 14 f., 209
Elliott, Ebenezer, 217